From Testing to Assessment:
English as an International Language

APPLIED LINGUISTICS AND LANGUAGE STUDY

General Editor
Professor Christopher N. Candlin, Macquarie University

Error Analysis
Perspectives on second
language acquisition
JACK C. RICHARDS (ED.)

Stylistics and the Teaching of
Literature
HENRY WIDDOWSON

Language Tests at School
A pragmatic approach
JOHN W. OLLER JNR

Contrastive Analysis
CARL JAMES

Language and Communication
JACK R. RICHARDS AND
RICHARD W. SCHMIDT (EDS)

Learning to Write: First Language/
Second Language
AVIVA FREDMAN, IAN PRINGLE
AND JANIC YALDEN (EDS)

Strategies in Interlanguage
Communication
CLAUS FAERCH AND
GABRIELE KASPER (EDS)

Reading in a Foreign Language
J. CHARLES ALDERSON AND
A.H. URQUHART (EDS)

An Introduction to Discourse
Analysis
New edition
MALCOLM COULTHARD

Computers in English Language
Teaching and Research
GEOFFREY LEECH AND
CHRISTOPHER N. CANDLIN (EDS)

Language Awareness in the
Classroom
CARL JAMES AND
PETER GARRET

Bilingualism in Education
Aspects of theory, research and
practice
JIM CUMMINS AND
MERRILL SWAIN

Second Language Grammar:
Learning and Teaching
WILLIAM E. RUTHERFORD

The Classroom and the Language
Learner
Ethnography and second-language
classroom research
LEO VAN LIER

Vocabulary and Language Teaching
RONALD CARTER AND MICHAEL
McCARTHY (EDS)

Observation in the Language
Classroom
DICK ALLWRIGHT

Listening to Spoken English
Second Edition
GILLIAN BROWN

Listening in Language Learning
MICHAEL ROST

An Introduction to Second Language
Acquisition Research
DIANE LARSEN-FREEMAN AND
MICHAEL H. LONG

Language and Discrimination
A study of communication in
multi-ethnic workplaces
CELIA ROBERTS, TOM JUPP AND
EVELYN DAVIES

Translation and Translating:
Theory and Practice
ROGER T. BELL

Process and Experience in the
Language Classroom
MICHAEL LEGUTKE AND HOWARD
THOMAS

Rediscovering Interlanguage
LARRY SELINKER

Language as Discourse:
Perspectives for Language Teaching
MICHAEL McCARTHY AND
RONALD CARTER

Analysing Genre – Language Use in
Professional Settings
V.K. BHATIA

From Testing to Assessment:
English as an International
Language
CLIFFORD HILL AND KATE PARRY
(EDS)

From Testing to Assessment: English as an International Language

Edited by
Clifford Hill and Kate Parry

LONGMAN

London and
New York

Longman Group UK Limited
Longman House, Burnt Mill,
Harlow, Essex CM20 2JE, England
and Associated Companies throughout the world.

*Published in the United States of America
by Longman Publishing, New York.*

First published 1994

ISBN 0-582 218853 PPR

British Library Cataloguing-in-Publication Data
A catalogue record for this book is
available from the British Library

Library of Congress Cataloging-in-Publication Data
From testing to assessment: English as an international language/
edited by Clifford Hill and Kate Parry.
    p. cm. -- (Applied linguistics and language study.)
    Includes bibliographical references and index.
    ISBN 0-582-21885-3 (pbk.)
    1. English language--Study and teaching--Foreign speakers.
    2. English language--Foreign countries. 3. Communication,
International.   I. Hill, Clifford.   II. Parry, Kate.   III. Series.
PE1128.A2F778 1994
428'.0071--dc20
                                                                93-38002
                                                                CIP

Set in 10/12pt Ehrhardt Regular
Produced by 8
Printed in Malaysia

Contents

List of Contributors

Kate Allen Lecturer, Department of Foreign Languages and Literature, Nanjing University, Nanjing, People's Republic of China

Laurie Anderson Lecturer, Department of English, Siena University, Siena, Italy

Andrew Cohen Professor, Program in English as a Second Language, University of Minnesota, Minneapolis, Minnesota, USA

Patrick Cummins Literacy consultant, Ottawa, Canada; Lecturer, College English Teacher Training Program, Department of Applied Foreign Language Studies, Nanjing University, People's Republic of China

Clifford Hill Arthur I. Gates Professor of Language & Education, Program in Applied Linguistics, Teachers College, Columbia University, New York, USA

Deryn Holland Educational Personnel Officer, Buckingham County Council, Aylesbury, Bucks, UK

John E. Ingulsrud Lecturer, College English Teacher Training Program, Department of Applied Foreign Language Studies, Nanjing University, People's Republic of China

Stan Jones Professor, Department of Linguistics, Carleton University, Ottawa, Canada

Kate Parry Associate professor, Department of English, Hunter College, City University of New York, USA

Bonny Norton Peirce SSHRC Postdoctoral Fellow, Modern Language Centre, Ontario Institute for Studies in Education, Toronto, Canada

Brian Street Senior Lecturer in Social Anthropology, School of Social Sciences, University of Sussex, UK

Editors' Acknowledgements

We would like to thank Eric Larsen and Joye Smith for their help in preparing this volume – their intellectual and practical contributions were rich and varied throughout the course of our work. Special thanks to Joye for copyediting the manuscript and preparing the references.

We thank the many students at Teachers College, Columbia University, who have read various parts of the book in draft form. As always, graduate students in the Program in Applied Linguistics have been generous and astute in their support. We acknowledge the important contributions of a personal friend and alumnus of the program, Thomas Adeyanju, who arranged for us to offer an international seminar on testing and assessment at Ahmadu Bello University in Zaria, Nigeria. It was on our return to Nigeria, the place where we have had such enriching experiences as teachers, that we struggled most intensely with policy issues of English language testing and assessment. We thank the British Council and the United States Information Service for their generous sponsorship of the seminar.

We thank the individual contributors to this volume for many helpful suggestions. They were kind and forbearing as they waited for us to bring the work to completion. We are grateful for their having welcomed us into their homes as we worked on the book in different parts of the world. We here acknowledge the warm hospitality of Kate Allen and John Ingulsrud in Nanjing, China; Laurie Anderson and Massimo Brandigi in Florence, Italy; Patrick and Vivian Cummins in Ottawa, Canada; Deryn Holland and her family in High Wycombe, England; Bonny and Anthony Peirce in Toronto, Canada; and Brian Street and his family in Brighton, England. We particularly acknowledge the editorial help of Vivian Cummins as well as the hospitality and work facilities offered by the Department of Linguistics at Carleton University in Ottawa, Canada.

A final word of thanks to Kathleen Hill who has personally embraced our work, whether in New York or abroad, as she struggled to complete her own. Her book and our own were conceived in 1987 and completed in 1993. As the Hausas like to say, *Karatu: da farko, 'daci; amma da k'arshe, zuma ke nan* ('Working with words: it begins bitter yet ends sweet').

Publisher's Acknowledgements

We are grateful to the following for permission to reproduce copyright material:

CTB Macmillan/McGraw-Hill for an extract from *Test of Adult Basic Education* (1976) and an extract from *Test of Adult Basic Education* (1987), copyright © 1976, 1987 by McGraw-Hill, Inc. All rights reserved; Educational Testing Service for TOEFL test questions and a pre-test passage, copyright © Educational Testing Service; National Center for University Entrance Examination for extracts from *Joint First-Stage Achievement Test*, English (1986); New Scientist, IPC Magazines Ltd, for the article 'Computing pyramids' from *New Scientist* magazine, 16.2.84 and the article 'Pocket video cameras' from *New Scientist* magazine, 27.10.83; Newsweek, Inc for the article 'Murder of the Gorilla Scientist: A New Suspect' from *Newsweek* magazine, 1.9.86, © 1986 Newsweek, Inc. All rights reserved; University of Michigan, English Language Institute, for an extract and questions from *Examination for the Certificate of Proficiency in English*, Preliminary test 2, (1990-1991), copyright 1990 by the Testing and Certification Division, English Language Institute, University of Michigan; West African Examinations Council for a question from *School Certificate and GCSE*, English Language 1 (June 1982), copyright © 1982 by the West African Examinations Council; Zimbabwe Newspapers (1980) Ltd for the article 'Mbanje Smoking Boys Expelled' from *Sunday Mail* 22.9.85; The Adult Literacy and Basic Skills Unit (ALBSU) for Figures 9.1, 9.2 and 9.3; *The Economist* for the article 'The Exclusive People' (Figure 7.2) © *The Economist*, March 1985.

We have been unable to trace the copyright holder in the article 'Ask the Specialist: Managing Migraines' by Donald J Dalessio from *McCall's* magazine, September 1986 and would appreciate any information that would enable us to do so; also for figures 8.2, 8.3, 8.4 and 8.5.

Introduction

It is increasingly acknowledged that English is the nearest to an international language that the world has ever had. In many countries it is widely used in commerce, and corporations often specify English language skills as a condition of employment. English is also widely used in mass media: for example, radio and television networks such as the BBC and CNN broadcast international news in English on a daily basis. It is thus not surprising that English has become prominent in education; students throughout the world spend an increasing amount of time learning the language. This increased attention to English has been accompanied by a concern about how non-native learners' knowledge and skills might be best assessed.

It is our conviction that appropriate assessment of English depends crucially upon how the language is used within a particular society. This conviction is evidenced throughout this volume as we discuss relations between assessment practices and the way English is used within an individual country. Although the use of English varies considerably from one country to another, certain patterns can be usefully established at the outset of this volume. We here present three dominant patterns that should be understood cumulatively; that is to say, the first and second are entailed in the third, just as the first is entailed in the second:

1. English functions as an ancillary language in countries where non-native speakers learn it so that they can participate in international communication (e.g. France and Germany in Europe, Brazil and Chile in Latin America, and China and Japan in Asia);
2. English functions as an official language in multilingual countries where non-native speakers learn it so that they communicate with each other and participate in national institutions of education and government (e.g. India, Nigeria, Singapore and other countries where Britain was once a colonial power);
3. English functions as the dominant language in countries where non-native speakers learn it so that they can participate broadly in the larger society (e.g. Australia, Canada, the United Kingdom, and the United States).

The first pattern is the most widespread, since virtually every country now uses English, at least to some degree, for purposes of international communication. These purposes are more readily discerned in economically prosperous countries such as Japan, where people frequently travel abroad for commerce or tourism. But even in less prosperous countries, individuals who remain at home are still expected to use written English for international communication as they advance within the educational system: for example, university libraries often maintain considerable resources in English and students are expected to use the language to build their knowledge in specialised areas.

As English has taken on an international character, it has developed new varieties in different parts of the world (Bailey and Görlach 1982; Platt, et al. 1984). This diversification complicates the task of educators who must assess the knowledge and skills of non-native learners. One question that they continually face is the degree to which non-native learners in a particular country should be tested on local as opposed to metropolitan varieties of English. Their response to this question tends to be conservative (Fairman 1988), which constrains the kind of English used for testing purposes.

This constraint is paralleled by a number of other constraints that increase even further the gap between the English used in a society and the English encountered on its tests. We here describe four such constraints that contribute to this gap. First, an English test makes greater use of written as opposed to oral language. This reliance on written language is dictated by practical concerns, for it is difficult in any large-scale testing to evaluate responses to oral language. Even when such responses are elicited, they are generally not themselves oral. Consider, for example, the listening comprehension component of the Test of English as a Foreign Language (TOEFL), where students listen to recorded samples of speech and then respond to written multiple-choice tasks.

Second, reading tests are used more frequently than writing tests, with the consequence that greater weight is placed on non-native learners comprehending written English rather than producing it. On certain reading tests, non-native learners do provide short written answers to questions, but even this form of writing is excluded by the increasing use of multiple-choice tasks. The reliance on reading tests can, once again, be viewed as a practical matter: it is quite difficult to evaluate the extended samples of prose that are elicited in any large-scale use of a writing test.

Third, a reading test is based on a relatively narrow range of the texts used in the larger society. Although test makers attempt to include different kinds of text, they usually end up with a fairly restricted sample – short bits of descriptive or expository prose written in rather formal English. The different kinds of texts that non-native learners read outside of school – for example, newspaper and magazine articles – are usually not well represented. One consequence of this restricted sampling is that non-native learners do not have much opportunity to respond to local varieties of written English.

Fourth, the way in which non-native learners must respond to these texts is highly constrained. They are forced to limit themselves to surface information and avoid the natural extensions of such information that take place in ordinary reading: for example, when non-native learners read in order to acquire new knowledge, they actively assimilate what the text contains to what they already know. If they are to perform successfully in a testing situation, they must resist such assimilation for it leads them to make responses that go beyond what the text, strictly speaking, can support.

To sum up, non-native learners in a testing situation confront not only a restricted sample of written English but respond to it in an artificial way. They do little or no writing and even the reading they do is highly constrained; they must avoid any critical engagement with the text so that they can concentrate on the surface information it contains. As a result, their experience of English in a testing situation can become so impoverished that it bears little resemblance to what they experience in many real-world situations.

We would be willing to tolerate, though reluctantly, such impoverishment if it did not have such profound effects on English language teaching around the world. There is increasing awareness that how English is tested crucially determines how it is taught (Hill and Parry 1992b). Such influence is not surprising when we consider that the manner in which students perform on an English test can severely restrict their access to further educational opportunities and ultimately to important resources within the larger society. Even in countries where English functions only as an ancillary language, performance on an English test can determine whether students gain admission into national universities: Asian countries such as Japan and Taiwan provide vivid examples of such practice. Certainly if students from these countries wish to study in colleges or universities within North America, they must perform well on the TOEFL. As a consequence, commercial coaching schools have been established whose sole purpose is to prepare students for this test. Even within regular schools, the pressure on teachers to prepare students for important English tests is enormous, with the result that the impoverished English found on tests actively spreads to the classroom. A tension is thus set up between what we might call test English and the real-world English that non-native speakers need to learn. It is this tension that we seek to address in this volume, and in advocating an approach to assessment that goes well beyond testing, we suggest ways in which this tension may be reduced.

This volume is divided into four parts. Part I provides a theoretical orientation: it first presents a dominant model of literacy and shows how it has been reflected in traditional testing; it then develops an alternative model that is used to examine such testing and to develop other methods of assessment. Part II examines reading tests, first from the perspective of test makers and then from that of test takers. It uses these dual perspectives to uncover the gaps in communication that often occur as non-native learners interact with tests. Part III then draws on the model of literacy developed in Part I to present alternative kinds of testing as well as broader approaches to assessment. Part IV examines assessment from a policy perspective and suggests practical ways in which it can reflect more faithfully real-world uses of English and thus encourage a pedagogy that is more responsive to what non-native learners need.

PART I

THEORETICAL CONSIDERATIONS

A central theme of this volume is that a reading test, like any other text, is embedded in a social and ideological context. Accordingly, we begin Chapter 1 by examining the historical development of reading tests in both Britain and the United States. We show the social and ideological origins of the two traditions as well as the intellectual and pedagogical concerns that have informed test development within each. We then illustrate the differences by presenting and analysing a sample of test discourse from each tradition.

The differences are, however, largely superficial, since both traditions are premised on similar assumptions about text and how it works. We characterise these assumptions collectively as an *autonomous model of literacy* and we examine this model with reference to text, of readers and writers, and the skill of literacy itself. We claim that this model is misleading for it underplays the social dimensions of written communication.

We then develop an alternative model, which we characterise as a *pragmatic model of literacy*. We present this model with reference to the same three parameters, demonstrating that communication is necessarily social in character, whether it is achieved by spoken or written language. We present this model both as a tool for critically examining reading tests and as a guide for developing alternative methods of assessment. It thus serves as a theoretical basis for the remaining parts of this book.

1 Models of literacy: the nature of reading tests

Clifford Hill and Kate Parry

Those who have taught or studied English in different parts of the world may well have come across two distinct kinds of reading test. One consists of a relatively small number of passages with tasks that require students to write their own responses. It is generally included in a larger English Language paper, and is found in the school certificate exams of many countries where English is an official language; it will be familiar, too, to anyone educated in Britain before the mid-1980s. The other consists of a larger number of shorter passages, with tasks that require students to select a response from a given set. This kind of test is often administered on its own, and it is a basic educational tool in the United States and in countries that have come under American influence. These two kinds of test represent distinct traditions of assessing literacy skills in English, the British and American, and they have quite different social and ideological origins.

Let us first examine the British tradition, which is the older of the two.[1] It originated in the late 1850s with the foundation of the first public examination boards – the Oxford Delegacy of Local Examinations and the Cambridge Local Examinations Syndicate – and in the opening of London University's matriculation exams to the general public. At this point the three universities were working with a somewhat élitist model of education: all three were attempting to provide support for 'schools for the middle classes' (Bruce 1969, p. 78) and were focusing on the end-point of students' school careers, the exams being intended to demonstrate that a student had acquired knowledge of a range of subjects. For the population that took these exams, the ability to read was hardly in question: where concern was expressed about language, it centred on the ability of students to write about what they had read. In 1858, for example, the Oxford Delegacy's examiners reported:

> There was often a tolerably wide range of information, and sometimes no small amount of original thought: but candidates who showed both these, frequently showed little power of putting their information together, and still less power of expressing it in clear language. (Bruce 1969, p. 77)

In 1917, these university exams, together with those of various professional bodies, were incorporated into a single set of School Certificate exams, the regulations for which required that students should pass in a range of subject areas. While there was a certain amount of latitude within this range, all candidates were required to pass in English Language, an exam designed to address the problem noted by the first Oxford examiners. This exam did include reading components – a comprehension section and an exercise in summary – but the emphasis, again, was not on students' ability to read as such, but rather on their ability to express their understanding of what they had read. Thus, the British tradition examined reading and writing together, and this feature distinguishes it most sharply from the testing tradition that developed in the United States.

Since 1917 many changes have been made in the British examination system, reflecting an increased concern with a wider spectrum of the population. In 1947 the School Certificate was superceded by the General Certificate of Education (GCE), which allowed both teachers and students more latitude. But although its proponents had liberal intentions, the GCE retained the élitist character of its antecedents: it was meant to be taken only by those who were likely to pass, and since such candidates were overwhelmingly middle-class, working-class students often got no certificate at all. Later, an alternative Certificate of Secondary Education (CSE) was introduced to address the needs of less academically inclined, and more often working-class, students; but this led to a two-tiered system in which the GCE unquestionably represented the upper tier. In recent years both these certificates have been superceded by the General Certificate of Secondary Education (GCSE), a qualification which presents a more radical departure from tradition: it is open to students of a wider range of abilities, and it depends less on exams and more on the assessment of projects completed over an extended period.

These changes did not affect those countries that were British colonies or protectorates at the time when the School Certificate was developed. As early as 1862, the Cambridge Local Examinations Syndicate received appeals to make its exams available in the colonies, and the first Cambridge overseas exams were held in Trinidad in 1864. With the introduction of the School Certificate, the Cambridge Syndicate instituted School Certificate exams in the colonies, and then, as independence approached, it fostered the development of regional examination boards to take over its responsibilities. The West African Examinations Council, described in Chapter 4, is one such board. These regional boards have revised their syllabi to reflect local conditions and interests, but the basic examination model has remained much the same, especially with respect to English Language. In some countries this model has been extended to other levels of the education system: in Chapter 6, Allen describes its use at the junior secondary level in Zimbabwe, and we have observed its influence on exams for primary teacher-training institutions and universities in Nigeria. Thus, despite recent changes in Britain, this older tradition flourishes in many parts of the world; and it has continued not only to examine reading and writing in one paper but to require candidates to write their own responses to reading comprehension tasks. We present material from the British tradition in Figure 1.1; it is taken from the West African School Certificate and is quite typical of what are called comprehension tests throughout the British Commonwealth.

The American tradition of testing springs from a more egalitarian conception of education: however inconsistently applied in practice, the American ideal has always, since the time of Jefferson, been of a public education system that would make literacy available to all (Graff 1987). In the late nineteenth century, however, as changing patterns of immigration produced a larger and more diverse school population, politicians and educators became increasingly aware of the system's inadequacies. The problem was diagnosed as one of efficiency. Edward L. Thorndike, in a government-commissioned report, complained in 1907 that

> many pupils are held back unduly. ... The work which they are given to do but fail to do is unsuited to them. (Quoted in Jonçich 1968, p. 301)

He suggested that the solution lay in

> special classes, careful regulation of promotion, the substitution of industrial and trade schools or courses for the regular school, and the like. (Quoted in Jonçich 1968, p. 302)

But how could such differences in education be reconciled with the egalitarian ideal? The answer lay in making the necessary distinctions independent of wealth and social status – and also of teachers' individual prejudices – by basing them instead on intrinsic ability; and this ability should be judged on 'indices of merit that [were] fair and objective, standardized, competitive – and quantified' (Jonçich 1968, p. 295).

The initial inspiration for developing such indices came from the tests developed by Alfred Binet, whose aim was to assess 'a beautiful native intelligence [freed] from the trammels of the school' (1908, quoted in Gould 1981, p. 151). His American followers seized upon the notion that intelligence was a separate faculty, independent of schooling and cultural background, that could be measured by a simple test. Unlike Binet, who used these tests only for diagnosing individual difficulties, psychologists such as Robert Yerkes and Lewis Terman developed tests to be used on a massive scale. During the First World War, intelligence tests were used in assigning nearly two million army recruits to specialised units. Similarly, after the war, the Stanford–Binet tests were developed and widely used to place elementary and high school students in what were considered to be homogeneous groups (Resnick 1982).

At about the same time, reading tests were developed along similar lines. Indeed, Thorndike, who was their leading proponent, claimed that reading and intelligence tests measured much the same thing, since, as he put it, 'reading is reasoning' (Johnston 1984, p. 148). Like Binet, he sought to develop instruments that would assess reading as an independent variable, and when he published his scaled tests of reading comprehension, he pointed out that not only were they easily scored, producing numerical results independently of individual judgements, but they minimised demands on test takers' powers of expression (Thorndike 1915). Thorndike did not himself use a multiple-choice format but it was being developed at that time for use on intelligence tests by Arthur Otis who worked with Terman (Chauncy and Dobbin 1969); and it was not long before this format was extended to reading tests.

In the 1930s the arrival of machine scoring assured the triumph of the multiple-choice format. The consequence has been that in American tests reading and writing have been kept firmly separate. Tests of the two skills are independently developed and administered, and test takers, in demonstrating the one skill, do not, in principle, need to demonstrate the other (of course a writing test requires at least some reading, though it is common practice for given topics to be read aloud). Reading tests are much easier to administer and score and so have come to be viewed in public discourse as the primary indices of literacy. The basic format of these tests is illustrated in Figure 1.2. This material is taken from the University of Michigan's Examination for the Certificate of Proficiency in English, a test used with non-native speakers throughout the world.

When test materials from the two traditions are placed together like this, the differences are readily discernible, and they often arouse hostile reactions. Those trained in the American tradition are likely to see the British tradition of test as élitist and irrelevant, while those trained in the British style may view the American form as reductionist and arbitrary; and students often experience difficulty in moving from one tradition to the other. For example, when well-educated Jamaicans enter an

American university, they are sometimes misplaced in a remedial English course on the basis of exam performance; they complain that they are unable to decide among all the choices provided on a multiple-choice task. Similarly, students trained in the American tradition initially have considerable difficulty in composing responses to the British type of task. We have observed, however, that individuals who do reasonably well on one style of test ordinarily adapt rather quickly to the other. The reason, we suggest, is that beyond differences of format are basic similarities, both in the kind of text used and in what test takers are required to do with it.

If we consider the two sample passages apart from the tasks, we cannot readily tell which is American and which is British. while they deal with different subject matter – one with botany, the other with medical technology – the way the subject-matter is handled is strikingly similar. Both passages present information in a deliberately neutral way: while evaluative responses are described, there is no indication that they are shared by the writer. Nor is there any orienting material that explains matters such as where the passage came from, who wrote it, or why it was written. When such material is present within a text used on a test, test makers tend to excise it or simply ignore it (Hill and Parry 1988).

Yet another similarity can be seen in the structure of the two passages: each begins with a general definition and then moves rapidly into a mass of detail. This kind of text is no accident: it has been expressly chosen, adapted, or constructed because it provides test makers with material around which they can build what they conceive to be valid tasks. Central to their notion of validity is that tasks be built around the odd bits of fact that readers cannot be expected to carry around in their heads. Consider, for example, the tasks that follow the *Radial K* passage: they require readers to recycle details such as the meaning of *radial keratotomy* and the expected use of this surgical technique. Following the *Orchids* passage, four of the five tasks call for a similar recycling – the definition of *hybrid*, the reason why orchids are expensive, the nature of orchids' roots. If there is a difference in the kind of processing required, it is in the more obviously metalinguistic tasks in the British-style test: in task (d), for example, candidates are required to 'explain the grammatical function' of a clause. But in either test the essential approach to the passage is the same: in working through the tasks, test takers must first determine what information is called for, locate it in the passage, and then decide on an appropriate response by comparing the exact wording of the passage and the task.

Moreover, readers who work through the tasks on either test will notice that they are not moving through the text in sequence. In *Radial*

Read the following passage carefully and answer the questions on it.

Orchids are flowers that are highly regarded and very expensive in some parts of the world, whereas they grow wild and are barely noticed in other places. They are found in their greatest variety and abundance in tropical climates.

There are two main categories of orchid: ground orchids, which are the common type in temperate regions; and epiphytic orchids, which grow on trees and are usually found in the tropics. Although these epiphytes grow on trees they do not <u>derive</u> nourishment from them. The plants often have large solid swellings of the stem in which water and nutritive materials are stored. They derive this moisture from the air by aerial roots.

More than 300 species are in cultivation but there are many thousands of <u>hybrids</u> which have been developed by cross-fertilization by horticulturalists all over the world. The orchid has developed a prestige of its own, which is not only due to its fragile beauty, but also to its scarcity value, and to the fact that its cultivation is somewhat specialized.

(a) Explain the word *hybrid* in one sentence.

(b) Give an alternative word that would fit in the place of *derive*.

(c) Why are orchids expensive in some parts of the world?

(d) Explain the grammatical function of the clause 'Although these epiphytes grow on trees'.

(e) What word in the passage tells you that the roots of epiphytic orchids do not reach the ground?

Figure 1.1 Comprehension passage and tasks in the British tradition. (From the School Certificate and GCE (English Language 1, Question 8), June 1982, Lagos, Nigeria: West African Examinations Council. Copyright 1982 by the West African Examinations Council.)

K, for example, the third task moves them into paragraph 3, but the fourth task returns them to paragraph 2. In *Orchids,* readers are forced to move around even more. They must begin with paragraph 3 and then go back to paragraph 1. For the third task, they return to paragraph 3; for the fourth and fifth tasks, they go back to paragraph 2. Such movement forces readers to operate at a local level rather than a global one.

We would claim that these similarities between the American and British approaches to reading assessment are not accidental. Rather they reflect a common set of assumptions about what text is and how individuals should read it. These assumptions are so deeply embedded in the western tradition of formal education that they have long remained unexamined. In recent debate about the nature of literacy, however, they have been made explicit. We here present this debate by drawing on various fields – history, anthropology, psychology, linguistics – and showing how dominant practices of testing are related to a certain conception of literacy. We then present a contrasting model of literacy that can serve as a basis for the emerging practices of alternative assessment.

Until recently only glasses or contact lenses were available for the correction of myopia, a vision defect in which objects can be seen distinctly only when very close to the eyes. In 1978, a surgical technique known as radial keratotomy, also termed radial K, was touted as a possible "cure" for nearsightedness. Since its introduction, however, radial K has been the subject of controversy and intense scrutiny.

In this procedure a diamond blade is used to make 8 to 16 cuts that radiate out from the center of the cornea of the eye like the spokes of a wheel. The resulting flattened curvature of the cornea decreases myopia. While close to 50% of patients achieve 20/40 vision on standard eye charts without glasses, the later side effects aren't fully known. The surgery itself involves certain risks, such as corneal perforations, which occur in about one in 600 eyes and which require stitches. Errant incisions can cause blindness and the need for corneal transplants; even tiny holes invite infection. Radial K patients' most common disappointment is that their vision isn't perfect. Some vision is overcorrected, some is undercorrected and sometimes the outcome is one eye each way.

The risks of radial K are real and considerable but at the same time many patients are satisfied will the results. Some experts predict that as more operations are performed surgeons with improve their technique and complications will be reduced; furthermore, they say that future radial K will be automated using a computer attached to a robotic arm with the diamond blade being replaced by a laser. Other experts counter that improving technique won't help much because the concept itself of cutting the cornea is a bad one, fraught with inherent problems. Though it may become more widespread and routine in the future, at present radial K is not the method of choice for correcting nearsightedness.

26. The term radial keratotomy refers to...
    a. a new type of contact lens.
    b. a type of corrective surgery.
    c. a diamond blade used in eye surgery.
    d. a technique used in corneal transplants.

27. The passage states that half the radial K patients...
    a. have partially corrected vision.
    b. have perfect vision.
    c. lose vision in one eye.
    d. require corneal transplants.

28. According to the passage, some experts predict that in the future radial K will...
    a. not require the cutting of the cornea.
    b. produce perfect vision.
    c. use computer and laser technology.
    d. become obsolete.

29. The chief disappointment of radial K patients is that...
    a. their vision isn't the same in both eyes.
    b. they must undergo surgery.
    c. their vision isn't overcorrected.
    d. they do not achieve perfect vision.

30. The author's attitude towards the use of radial K in the future is...
    a. very worried.
    b. enthusiastic.
    c. suspicious.
    d. neutral.

Figure 1.2 Comprehension passage and tasks in the American tradition. (From the Examination for the Certificate of Proficiency in English (Preliminary Test 2), 1990-1991, Ann Arbor, MI: Testing and Certification Division, English Language Institute, The University of Michigan. Copyright 1990 by the Testing and Certification Division, English Language Institute, The University of Michigan.)

Fundamental assumptions: the autonomous model of literacy

The phrase *autonomous model of literacy* has been used by Brian Street (1984) to describe a set of assumptions that, he claims, underlie western educational practice. He identifies these assumptions by examining critically the work of various researchers: Goody (1968, 1977), Goody and Watt (1968), Greenfield (1972), Hildyard and Olson (1978), Lyons (1981), and Olson (1977). Street shows how these researchers associate literacy with such qualities as logic, objectivity, and rationality – qualities that are highly valued in western societies and that are explicitly promoted in formal education. He claims that these associations add up to a model of literacy which, despite its attractions, is dangerously misleading. To support this claim, he draws on the work of anthropologists, historians, and linguists and uses this evidence together with his own fieldwork to construct an alternative model of literacy that he characterises as *ideological*.

Street's approach has been controversial, for he groups researchers who do not necessarily regard themselves as associated; and in discussing their work, he represents them as adopting positions that they are not always willing to acknowledge. He offers, however, a convincing justification for this approach:

> The writers I am discussing do not necessarily couch their argument in the terms that I am adopting. But, nevertheless, I maintain that the use of the term 'model' to describe their perspective is helpful since it draws attention to the underlying coherence and relationship of ideas which, on the surface, might appear unconnected and haphazard. No one practitioner necessarily adopts all of the characteristics of any one model, but the use of the concept helps us to see what is entailed by adopting particular positions, to fill in gaps left by untheorised statements about literacy, and to adopt a broader perspective than is apparent in any one writer. (1984, p. 3)

We have found the autonomous model to be a valuable heuristic in our consideration of reading tests. This is an area that is particularly rich in 'untheorised statements about literacy'; test makers, for example, often provide detailed reports of their findings, but rarely, if ever, spell out their assumptions about what they take reading to be. Those assumptions can be elucidated if we consider how the notion of autonomy is applied in characterising text, literate individuals and institutions, and the skill of literacy itself. In doing so, we will extend the discussion to material that Street does not consider.

Autonomy of text

As Street points out, the writers he discusses do not use the phrase *autonomous model of literacy.* The word *autonomous*, however, does appear frequently, usually with reference to writing. Jack Goody and Ian Watt, for example, maintain that writing is distinctive because it is, at least potentially, 'an autonomous mode of communication' (1968, p. 40); and Walter Ong explicates this idea more fully:

> By isolating thought on a written surface, detached from any interlocutor, making utterance in this sense autonomous and indifferent to attack, writing presents utterance and thought as uninvolved in all else, somehow self-contained, complete. (1982, p. 132)

But it is David Olson who gives clearest expression to the idea that writing is autonomous. This position is set up as fundamental in what is probably his best-known article, 'From utterance to text: the bias in language in speech and writing':

> My argument will be that there is a transition from utterance to text both culturally and developmentally and that this transition can be described as one of increasing explicitness, with language increasingly able to stand as an unambiguous and autonomous representation of meaning. (1977, p. 258)

Olson does not assert that this quality of autonomy is characteristic of all texts, but only that it can be seen most clearly in expository prose of the English essayist tradition. Nevertheless, he does suggest that it is the ideal for texts used in schooling:

> Ideally the printed reader [i.e. a book used to teach reading] depends on no cues other than linguistic cues; it represents no intentions other than those represented in the text; it is addressed to no one in particular; its author is essentially anonymous; and its meaning is precisely that represented by the sentence meaning. (1977, p. 276)

This view of text is clearly operative in the construction of reading tests. Each passage in such tests, like the printed reader that Olson describes, 'depends on no cues other than linguistic cues', as the passages discussed earlier exemplify. Similarly, a passage in a reading test 'represents no intentions other than those represented in the text', or, at least, test takers are required to view it in this way. When tasks call for a statement of 'the author's purpose' (a common formulation, especially in an American-style test), the target response is either a recycled version of an explicit statement of intent or a summary of the passage's content. Again, the test passage, like Olson's printed reader, 'is addressed to no one in particular' and 'the author is essentially anonymous'. Both *Orchids* and *Radial K* are cases in point, and even where a passage, as in the case of recent tests, takes the form of a letter, the accompanying tasks are so constructed that test takers who treat it as real communication between people with defined social identities often select a distractor (Hill and Parry 1989). Finally, the meaning of each passage is presumed to be, in Olson's words, 'precisely that represented by the sentence meaning'; students must attend carefully to what Olson and Hildyard (1980) have characterised as 'the very words', and even where figures of speech are used, their expected interpretation is not merely conventional but extraordinarily literal. Taken as a whole, Olson's description of 'autonomous text' corresponds closely to text as it is presented in reading tests.

Autonomy of institutions and individuals

That text is, ideally, autonomous is the basic premise of this model of literacy, but we have found the word *autonomous* used in other ways as well. Goody (1986), for example, claims that the autonomy of text has much to do with the creation of autonomous institutions within a society such as the Church in medieval Europe; and he suggests that literacy can confer autonomy on individuals as well. In discussing the relationship between literacy and economic development, he remarks:

> If we take recent moves to expand the economies of countries of the Third World, a certain rate of literacy is often seen as necessary to radical change, partly from the limited standpoint of being able to read the instructions on the seed packet, partly because of the increased autonomy (even with regard to the seed packet) of the autodidact. (1986, p. 46)

At a more advanced level, Goody suggests that writing enables individuals to integrate and develop their thinking far beyond what would be possible in speech. His earlier book, *The domestication of the savage mind* (1977), is devoted almost entirely to considering how the mind of what he calls *homo legens* (a reading sub-species of *homo sapiens*) is 'domesticated' by the ability, through writing, to rearrange words in a physical space and thus to see new ways of connecting ideas.

Ong (1982) makes even stronger claims about the radical changes in an individual brought about by literacy:

> Primary orality fosters personality structures that in certain ways are more communal and externalized, and less introspective than those common among literates. Oral communication unites people in groups. Writing and reading are solitary activities that throw the psyche back on itself. (p. 69)

Thus both Goody and Ong present *homo legens* as a species whose members, through the solitary activity of reading, not only gain access to more information, but are enabled to analyse their own assumptions, develop new insights, and perceive themselves as separate from the social groups to which they belong.

This aspect of the autonomous model of literacy – that is, the assumption that literacy confers autonomy on institutions and individuals – again is fundamental to traditional uses of reading tests. As far as institutions are concerned, the major producer of tests within the United States – the Educational Testing Service (ETS) – insists on its status as a private, non-governmental organisation. Outside the United States, examining bodies are often set up by governmental legislation, but the whole point is that they should operate, in theory at least, as independent institutions, unaffected by the vagaries of political life. This image of such bodies as self-contained and autonomous is, in fact, essential to the testing enterprise. The purpose of using an exam rather than, say, interviews or personal recommendations is that it can be seen as an independent arbiter of knowledge or ability, one that is unaffected by social interests or political preferences. The idea that test-making institutions, like religious ones, are not 'homologous with other aspects of the social system . . . [or] ordered . . . by the infrastructure of the political economy' (Goody 1986, p. 20) is crucial to their authority.

At the individual level, too, the autonomy of the reader is a basic premise of testing. However many candidates are in an exam room, each is considered to be alone with the text. This isolation is reinforced by the exam procedures: desks must be a certain distance apart, separate materials are handed to each student, no talking is allowed, and questions addressed to the proctor are to be only about practical and administrative matters. The candidates work alone, writing their responses on answer sheets that are identified by their own individual numbers. When the allotted time expires, all must stop writing; the papers are handed in, and only then is any social exchange permitted. In short, readers, when taking a test, must adopt the solitary habits of *homo legens*, for to be social in this context is to cheat.

Autonomy of skill

That institutions and individuals become autonomous through literacy implies another aspect of the autonomous model, one that we have characterised elsewhere as 'autonomy of skill' (Hill and Parry 1989). This idea is that literacy – the ability to read and write – can be considered separately from other factors as a necessary, if not sufficient, cause for certain kinds of social and cognitive development. It is characterised as a 'technology' (Goody 1968, p. 1; Olson 1977, p. 262), the use of which may be 'restricted' because of limitations in other technologies (such as the manufacture of paper) or because of particular social attitudes, but which is in itself socially neutral. Goody (1968) demonstrates this point by suggesting an analogy between writing and the wheel: the relationship between literacy and the development of philosophical and scientific thinking parallels the relationship between understanding rotary motion and the development of wheeled transport. The potential of the technology in question may not always be realised. In Tibet, for example, both texts and wheels exist, but they are so closely associated with religion (the wheels are prayer-wheels) that the use of either for secular purposes is inhibited. Thus Goody concedes that social factors are important in determining the uses to which literacy may be put, but he does not consider reading and writing as social processes in themselves.

The presumed autonomy of the skill of literacy is closely linked to the presumed autonomy of text. If text is considered as object rather than action, it can then be understood as the sum of its elements ('the very words') rather than as a means of human communication. Reading is therefore a technical rather than a social skill – a difficult one, however, for it involves learning not simply the writing system, but a new way of approaching language. Olson (1977), for example, points out that children come to school already competent in speech, a form of language that

> relies for its comprehension on a wide range of information beyond that explicitly marked ... [including] a shared knowledge of events and a preferred way of interpreting them; a shared perceptual context; and agreed-upon prosodic features and paralinguistic conventions. (p. 272)

Children must then learn to interpret written language in which this 'wide range of information' is not available, but in which there is, by way of compensation, 'an enlarged set of explicit linguistic conventions' (p. 272). Someone who is learning to read has to master this enlarged set and also develop the ability to discount certain elements used in oral comprehension such as 'a shared perceptual context'. Readers, unlike listeners, must focus exclusively on 'the sentence meaning, the meaning in the text' and apply interpretive procedures to the text alone (p. 273). The ability to do this is acquired through experience with text, so 'children familiar with the use of textlike language through hearing printed stories' have an obvious advantage (p. 276); but once the ability has been acquired, it should not, in principle, be affected by the social identity of the reader, the origin of the text, or the purposes for which the text is being read.

The belief that literacy skills can be isolated from the personal and social characteristics of readers is basic to reading tests. The purpose of such tests is to assess reading as an autonomous skill: other qualities, such as individuals' factual knowledge, their ability to use it in obtaining new information from text, or their capacity for remembering and using such information for purposes other than immediate interpretation are all considered irrelevant. Thus test makers deliberately use a wide range of passages that candidates are unlikely to know much about, and they try to construct tasks that cannot be answered without reference to the text, even by someone well informed about its content. Indeed, the use of specialised knowledge can be a disadvantage, for it often leads to the choice of a distractor in a multiple-choice task or the inclusion of too much information in an open-ended one. Moreover, test makers make no attempt to assess readers' ability to remember information from a text and apply it in other situations. The skill that they test, and thereby propagate, is a circumscribed kind of reading: it consists solely of perceiving 'the very words' of the text and drawing logical inferences from the propositions that they convey.

A corollary to the assumption that a reading test assesses only reading ability – and no other knowledge or skill – is the assumption that the results are representative of how well individuals read in other contexts. The test takes a sample of each person's reading and the resulting score is used as a measure of a more general ability. In the pyschometric tradition the scores are not used directly; they are correlated with those of a norming population and then commonly expressed in terms of a construct such as grade level. These levels, once established, are widely used as a basis not only for pedagogy but also for research. Many empirical studies, for example, use test scores to place subjects into groups defined by grade level; and once the groups are established they are then identified by terms such as *high skill* and *low skill,* or even *good* and *poor* readers. Such studies generally focus on what attributes of the individuals in question might account for the difference in their levels: they do not question what the basic division of the population means. If researchers subscribe to such reification of grade levels, it is hardly surprising that teachers and, even more, students accept grade levels as authoritative indicators of where individuals stand with respect to an essential and highly valued skill – even where, as in the case of adult ESL students, the implied comparison with children seems quite inappropriate.

To sum up, the autonomous model of literacy suggests not only that text is autonomous, but that it confers autonomy on both institutions and individuals. It also treats reading as an autonomous skill that is independent of other factors and transferable across all kinds of texts. We find such assumptions consistently reflected in the practice of reading assessment; yet, like Street, we find many objections to the model not only from our own experience as teachers, but from recent theoretical work, in various disciplines, on literacy in general and reading in particular. In the following section, we summarise Street's position and then outline our own, adding to the anthropological and historical material as he draws on evidence from the field of linguistics, particularly as it deals with social and psychological processes.

An alternative perspective: the pragmatic model of literacy

Before we present what we call the *pragmatic model* of literacy, we would like to summarise Street's own ideological model in relation to the three aspects of the autonomous model that we distinguished above. First, Street denies the autonomy of text: he cites his own work and that of J. Parry (1989) in India to show, on the one hand, how text often depends on oral mediation, and, on the other, how variable its interpretation may be. Second, Street asserts that literacy is far from being a universal means to autonomy for its practitioners, whether in the social or cognitive sense: he concedes that particular literacy practices may bring economic advantages – as in the use of Arabic script for commercial purposes in Iran – but he also cites historical research (Clanchy 1979; Graff 1979) that counters the commonly held notion that literacy skills necessarily bring social and economic benefits; he further points out that if being able to read and write has any cognitive effects, it is only in specific operations and as a function of particular practices in particular scripts (Cole and Scribner 1981). Third, Street insists that literacy cannot be considered a neutral or independent technology: he cites Heath's work with different communities in South Carolina (1983) to show the extent to which it is embedded in ideology and social practice. He concludes that it is such embedding that determines the nature and therefore the consequences of literacy.

As linguists rather than anthropologists, our perspective differs somewhat from Street's. Whereas he is interested in literacy in general and how it is used in different societies, we are more concerned with particular texts – those used on reading tests – and how they are interpreted by particular readers from various language backgrounds. This perspective leads us to conclusions that, in some respects, differ from his, and so we distinguish our own model of literacy by describing it as pragmatic rather than ideological. The choice of the word is deliberate: pragmatics is that area of linguistics concerned with 'the use of language in communication' (Richards *et al.* 1985, p. 225). Hitherto it has largely dealt with oral interaction, but obviously our concern is with how communication takes place through text.

Text as communication

We would first like to establish our own view of text. We have seen that those who subscribe to the autonomous model tend to view text as object, emphasising certain physical properties of writing: (1) given its means of production (e.g. making marks on paper), it can be easily separated from its producer; (2) given appropriate technology (e.g. printing on a durable substance), it can be relatively permanent; and (3) given its visual form (as opposed to auditory), it can be easily retrieved. In effect, as language becomes, in a purely physical sense, more separable, durable, and retrievable, it acquires a greater independence from the context in which it is produced. To paraphrase Olson (1977), the meaning comes to reside in the text itself.

From our vantage point, however, this focus on physical properties has obscured the essentially social character of text, a point that becomes apparent when we consider the various activities involved in its production, storage, and retrieval. First, in producing text, even the most solitary writer, by the very fact of using words, draws on communal property, the system of communication that de Saussure has described as *'langue'*. This system, as de Saussure points out, is inherently social:

> It [langue] is the social side of speech, outside the individual who can never create nor modify it by himself; it exists only by virtue of a sort of contract signed by the members of a community. (1966, p. 14)

Thus, in selecting words, writers do not simply refer to the world they are writing about; they associate themselves with particular communities of language users. Our own selection, in writing this particular text, is a case in point: we had to decide, for example, whether to use 'ideological' or 'pragmatic' in describing an alternative model of literacy, and are well aware that the former links us with an anthropological perspective, the latter with a linguistics one; and, of course, we are locating ourselves in relation to current debates about literacy by using such expressions as 'autonomous model'. The very act of producing text involves continuous evocation of other text makers, and so text itself can best be understood as social gesture.

Second, the act of preserving text necessarily involves social judgement. Right from the beginning, when individual writers save what they have written instead of tossing it in the wastepaper basket, they are deciding that it has some worth. They are envisioning it as a vehicle of communication, even if its only readers are to be the selves that they eventually become. When text is not simply preserved but reproduced, this ascription of communicative potential – and hence social value – is even more apparent. Within the manuscript tradition of medieval Europe, a text would be copied only when it was viewed as having intrinsic worth for future generations; in the case of present-day publication, a book is printed only when publishers anticipate sufficient response to justify their effort and expenditure.

Third, when a text is retrieved, it can only be understood in a social context, one that necessarily differs from the one in which it originated. It still draws on social property, language, but then that property will have changed, however slightly, as will the world, especially the social world, to which it refers (in fact, change within language and the world are mutually reinforcing). Further, the understanding of any text is affected by the literacy practices within the particular community to which the reader belongs. Clanchy (1979) shows how these practices change over time; Besnier (1986), Conklin (1949), J. Parry (1989), and Street (1984) document widely differing uses of writing in cultural settings around the world; and Heath (1983) shows how three communities, living within the same geographical area and drawing on the same language, vary in their attitudes towards text. Finally, a particular reader approaching a particular text must have some reason for doing so, even though it may remain unconscious and unarticulated; and this, too, affects how the text is understood. We have all experienced how much a text can change as our approach to it varies: *Jane Eyre* when read on holiday is hardly the same as when studied in school.

What is the significance of all this in relation to reading tests? From the vantage point of production, a reading test is particularly complex because of its declared intention of representing many different kinds of text. There are thus several passages, each of which is embedded in a textual world of its own. Test makers often extract these passages from larger texts, editing them in minor ways to ensure that they function independently. But as Hill and Larsen (1983) illustrate in their analysis of a passage taken from Lewis Carroll's *Through the Looking Glass*, these efforts are seldom successful. The skilled writer has woven text so carefully that any effort to take out a piece inevitably results in a number of loose threads – and it is just these threads that the reader may use to weave a larger story. Other passages, intended to represent particular genres such as children's stories, are written specifically for test purposes. In these instances, however, the role of the writer is not what it seems to be, for close examination of the passages often reveals a discrepancy between the ostensible intention – to tell a story or convey information – and the actual one – to present a text that will discriminate between readers.

A further level of complexity derives from the new context into which the passages are put. Each passage is necessarily accompanied by tasks whose presence often has a distorting effect. This effect is particularly evident in the case of specifically written passages in which certain peculiarities of text structure seem to result from the very process of constructing tasks. Such distortion can also be present in the case of excerpted text where a particular word or phrase may be altered in the light of the tasks to be constructed. Moreover, various passages, each filtered through its own set of tasks, are then grouped together to form a larger whole; and within this whole the various passage-task configurations inevitably – though they are not supposed to – influence each other. Beyond the individual test, there is a further context – the larger world of reading tests itself comprising a textual tradition closely associated with formal schooling. Within this tradition text is viewed as autonomous, and so a passage, no matter how brief it may be, must be approached as if it were an independent vehicle of meaning.

The manner in which reading tests are preserved and reproduced has a particularly marked effect on their status. In order to maintain face validity, the physical form of a particular test varies little: the same typeface is used from year to year and the layout of headers, passages, and items is relatively stable. Moreover, the printing of tests is managed in great secrecy, and the distribution of the finished product is carefully controlled. In many countries, the tests are sent out in sealed envelopes to be opened only in the presence of the candidates; at times, tests are even kept at the police station until the day of the exam.

Thus, when test takers come to retrieve a text included in a test, they are doing so at several removes from the original. Moreover, the context in which they approach it can be quite powerful. In many instances, students' future careers depend on their responses, and we have noted how the solemnity of the occasion is reinforced by exam procedures. Indeed, it is our claim that reading tests, as commonly used around the world, demonstrate not so much that text is autonomous as that its significance, like that of any other social gesture, depends largely on context.

Communication between readers and writers

The autonomous model of literacy does not simply emphasise the isolation of text but the isolation of those who use it. Goody (1986) claims that various institutions develop a separate identity by virtue of writing, and he, along with others, suggests that individuals do so as well. The claims for institutional autonomy have been cogently addressed by Street, so we shall restrict ourselves to the claims made for individuals. In examining these claims, we can begin with a familiar picture of the solitary writer:

> Writing is a solipsistic operation. I am writing a book which I hope will be read by hundreds of thousands of people, so I must be isolated from everyone. While writing the present book, I have left word that I am 'out' for hours and days – so that no one, including persons who will presumably read the book, can interrupt my solitude. (Ong 1982, p. 101)

As a writer, however, Ong is hardly alone, for other people are intruding on his thoughts all the time. To begin with, the room in which he works is undoubtedly lined with books, and the book on which he is working is full of references to them. In a real sense, he is keeping company with the many people whose work he cites (and, for that matter, many others whose talk has influenced his thinking). Moreover, Ong is keenly aware of his readers, as indicated by his own reference to 'hundreds of thousands of people'. Of course they are not physically present, and so the writer must imagine them. As Ong himself puts it,

> The writer must set up a role in which absent and often unknown readers can cast themselves. Even in writing to a close friend I have to fictionalize a mood for him, to which he is expected to conform. (1982, p. 102)

From our perspective, the fact that the writer is addressing people who are not in a position to interject words or gestures does not make writing any less social. The audience may be invented but it still plays a powerful role in determining what words the writer actually puts on the page; and it is, of course, these words that allow us to infer what kind of audience the writer is constructing. The same can be said of oral interaction: speakers, too, must socially construct their listeners, even though they may be physically present; and by virtue of what speakers say, we are able to ascertain what kinds of social identities they ascribe to those they are talking to.

These identities are often at odds with externally observable ones; but then listeners – and, of course, readers, too – are able to reject an ascribed identity. As readers, we are all familiar with refusing to play the role that the writer has set up for us, much as in conversation we let others know that we do not agree with what they have said. Indeed, the interactive dimensions that we associate with talk are much more present in reading than is commonly recognised (Bakhtin 1981). The fact that writers cannot immediately talk back does not prevent our challenging what they have put on the page. We may be even more prone to challenge their words simply because they have been granted the power to control the discourse. It is much like the resistance we feel when someone monopolises conversation.

In characterising this fundamental reciprocity of oral and written communication, we draw on the model that Henry Widdowson presents in *Teaching language as communication* (1978). In this work he rejects the traditional dichotomies between, on the one hand, speaking and listening and, on the other, reading and writing. As he points out, such dichotomies do not take account of the interdependence of productive and receptive activities. With regard to oral communication he writes:

> What is said ... is dependent on an understanding of what else has been said in the interaction.... Speaking ... is part of a reciprocal exchange in which both reception and production play a part. (pp. 58–9)

Widdowson's model of oral communication is displayed in Figure 1.3. He introduces *talking* as a generic term for this reciprocal exchange, distinguishing it from its productive and receptive aspects, *saying* and *listening*, and from their external manifestations, *speaking* and *hearing*. He uses the term *interpreting* in parentheses at the top of the display to

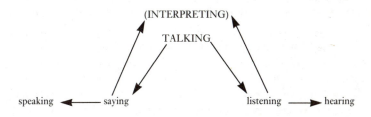

Figure 1.3 Widdowson's model of oral communication

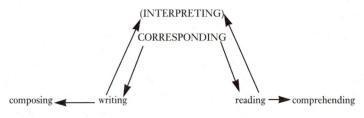

Figure 1.4 Widdowson's model of written communication

indicate 'a psychological process, which, unlike talking, is not realized as actual social activity' (1978, p. 64). This notion of reciprocal exchange is an important corrective to models of communication based on discrete skills, for it is clear that to engage in talk is to listen as well as to speak.

Widdowson sets up a parallel diagram for written communication, which is shown in Figure 1.4. As can be seen, he uses the terms *composing* and *comprehending* to parallel *speaking* and *hearing*, the terms *writing* and *reading* to parallel *saying* and *listening*, and the term *corresponding* to parallel *talking*. Widdowson justifies his use of a more specific term such as *corresponding* on the following grounds:

> Whereas it is reasonable to think of saying and listening as reciprocal aspects of the one basic activity of talking, reading and writing cannot so readily be considered as reciprocal activities in quite the same sense.... It is true that we do have written as well as spoken interactions, as in the case of an exchange of correspondence, and indeed correspondence might be considered as the larger-scale version of talking in the written mode. But there is a vast amount of written discourse that does not take the form of an exchange. Usually, what is written does not directly depend on a previous reading activity and a particular act of writing is not necessarily prompted by a particular act of reading. (p. 61)

From a strictly empirical point of view, Widdowson's focus on correspondence can be justified, for he is concerned only with what might be called *external reciprocity* (i.e. that which takes place between externally identifiable participants in written communication). He could also have presented oral communication in a more restricted way, for there are different kinds of talk that do not involve an empirically verifiable exchange (e.g. someone talking on a radio show where the listeners do not call in). To capture this restriction, he could have perhaps chosen a term such as *conversing* rather than *talking*.

Given our own view of communication, we are interested in moving beyond the strictly empirical and expanding Widdowson's model to include what may be called *internal reciprocity*, which we posit as fundamental to all communication. In explaining this notion, we would like to return to a point made above. In externally observable interaction – whether conversation or correspondence – language users can be viewed not simply as addressing externally identifiable language receivers, but rather as ascribing an identity to these receivers by virtue of the discourse they construct: the choice of particular vocabulary and syntactic patterns, the amount of background knowledge assumed, and so on. By the same token, it is by means of this discourse that language users take on an identity for themselves. We can refer to these linguistically constituted identities as an *ascribed identity* and an *assumed identity*, respectively.

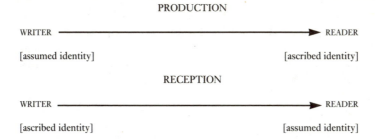

Figure1.5 Production and reception in written communication. (In both production and reception, the arrow runs from the writer to the reader simply to indicate temporal sequence: a writer must write before a reader can read.)

In characterising internal reciprocity, we can shift our perspective from the productive aspect to the receptive, in which case we can describe individual readers as assuming an identity and ascribing one to the writer. This contrast between production and reception is displayed in Figure 1.5. Indeed, it is only as readers actively assume an identity that they are able to ascribe an appropriate identity to the writer. This shifting of assumed and ascribed identities is not, however, the whole story on internal reciprocity: there is a further displacement that takes place within both the writer and the reader, for each engages in socially patterned behavior modelled on talk in the external world; namely, taking on the role of the other in order to negotiate meaning. Indeed, such displacement may be viewed as potentially more radical in literate as opposed to oral activity: a writer, in principle, has ample time in which to anticipate, even rehearse, the reader's response.

By the same token, we can view readers as involved in a similar displacement. By exploring the role that the writer assumes, they gain a sense of whom the text was written for: hence they continuously pose questions, whether consciously or not, about the writer's choice of words (why *code* rather than *style?*) or decision to include particular material (why is Bernstein brought in here?), and it is by means of this probing that they ultimately establish how reliable the writer is. As we suggested earlier, such exploration may lead readers to modify, even reject, the role that the writer has ascribed to them. Their negotiation of the writer's communicative stance is, in principle, continuous and thus can be paralleled to what the writer does in revision. In effect, reading, like writing, is an active negotiation of socially constituted meaning, which can be represented as in Figure 1.6.

Viewed in this way, the larger communication between writer and

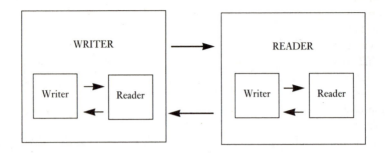

Figure 1.6 Internal reciprocity in written communication

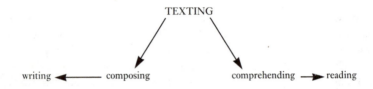

Figure 1.7 A revision of Widdowson's model of written communication

reader takes place only as each internalises the social reciprocity with which they communicate in the external world. Such internalisation is facilitated by the social character of language, the means by which both oral and written communication are achieved: the very structure of language calls forth social reciprocity.

Given this richer notion of reciprocal exchange, we would revise Widdowson's model of written communication as shown in Figure 1.7, where we have made a number of changes in the model. To begin with, we have reversed the position of the terms in the bottom line to reflect our sense of how they are ordinarily understood: *writing* and *reading* now describe externally observable activities (parallel to *speaking* and *hearing* in the model of oral communication), *composing* and *comprehending* describe the internal aspects of reciprocity (parallel to *saying* and *listening*). More importantly, we have coined the term *texting* to take the place of *corresponding:* this term parallels *talking*, thereby signalling that social reciprocity is fundamental to both written and oral communication.

There is one further change that we have made in the model. We have removed (*INTERPRETING*) from the top of the display, since we prefer not to separate the psychological from the social (as indicated by our characterisation of internal reciprocity as inherently social). Widdowson distinguishes interpreting from the social processes of talking or corresponding, because it is for him a 'non-reciprocal skill ... the psychological process of understanding' (1978, pp. 65-6). For us, interpreting cannot be separated from talking or texting. As Vygotsky (1962) observed, interpretation, when viewed developmentally, is best understood as incorporating social exchange into individual thought. It is the social character of all individual thought that underlies our own approach to written communication. Any literate activity, no matter how solitary it may be, necessarily embodies reciprocity: to write is to be a reader and to read is to be a writer.

What is the application of this revised model to reading tests? We should first observe that within a testing situation the reciprocity can be viewed as both external and internal. Test takers do, after all, produce externally observable responses to the writing presented by test makers. In Widdowson's terms, they are involved in corresponding. Their response is, of course, limited. On a machine-scored multiple-choice test it consists only of bubbles shaded in on an answer sheet, and even on a test with more open-ended questions, the answers are necessarily brief. Nevertheless, these responses constitute an important act of communication, one that revolves around the question of whether the test takers, from the test makers' perspective, know how to read.

As to internal reciprocity, the question naturally arises as to the linguistically constituted identities represented in the test material. As we have pointed out, this material ordinarily represents many writers, for test makers include samples of different kinds of writing in the interests of validity; their notion is that a test should represent the various kinds of text to which the target population is exposed. Hence in a test that includes many passages, the writers may be quite diverse. On the other hand, they are not ordinarily named, and few readers can recognise who they are simply reading from the passage. This anonymity is deliberate; for test makers, in the interests of fair play, seek out passages that are likely to be unfamiliar to those taking the test. Further, the passages come as a set, printed in the same format and framed by the same kinds of tasks, so that they look like the product of a single hand. In effect, the work of the various writers, and the manifold identities that they assume in writing, is mediated through the more encompassing identity of the test maker; and it is with the latter that test takers must engage in reciprocity if they are to be successful. In our own research we have discovered that inexperienced test takers are often led astray by focusing unduly on the individual writers themselves.

But then who are the test makers and what kind of identity do they assume in constructing a test? In many parts of the world, their actual identity cannot be known, since it is, for reasons of security, shrouded in secrecy. Test takers cannot thus resort to external clues in ascribing an identity; they must rather attend closely to what constitutes test discourse – the various passage-task configurations that the test makers have constructed; and from these they must infer the presence of *homo legens*, a figure that draws only on knowledge normatively associated with the words on the page. It is not easy, however, for inexperienced test takers to make this inference, since their own views of what constitutes normative knowledge do not necessarily correspond with those of the test makers; and such lack of correspondence is particularly likely to occur when the test takers are reading in a foreign language.

Homo legens, as represented by the test, can be quite an intimidating figure, for test takers know that they must produce responses that have already been designated as correct. Since these responses have little to do with the way that many test takers ordinarily read, they often become unsure about how to respond. In our own research, we have discovered that many become fearful that the questions have been set up for the express purpose of tricking them. As one of them put it, 'I can understand what I read, but not the questions; it's like they're there to trip me up'. Hence the test maker comes to embody an alien authority: he – and we feel *homo legens* is best described as a 'he' – is one who possesses peculiar powers with respect to how text is to be comprehended. In short, he is the kind of institutionalised figure identified by Foucault (1977) in his provocative essay 'What is an author?'.

It is not simply that test makers assume the identity of *homo legens;* they ascribe this same identity to anyone who can negotiate tests successfully. Test makers do acknowledge various sociocultural identities insofar as they avoid using passages that are obviously offensive to particular groups. They do not, however, use any means of evaluating how sociocultural norms of language, thought, and experience are reflected in how test takers respond; they do not, for example, draw on the process-oriented interviews or think-aloud protocols that are now common in reader-response research. Rather they assume that anyone who selects the target response, whether shading a bubble or writing the appropriate word or phrase, has responded as *homo legens*. In short, the test makers use a highly attenuated external exchange as evidence that a particular kind of internal reciprocity has taken place.

Literacy skills and communication

Our representation of text, and of those who use it, obviously entails a view of reading that differs radically from that implied by the autonomous model of literacy. As already indicated, this model presents literacy as a technology and reading as a technical skill. It is a complex skill, as everyone acknowledges. It involves familiarity, obviously, with the language of the text as well as with the writing system so that the reader can reconstruct words, phrases, and sentences from a series of discrete symbols. Moreover, it requires knowledge of a particular set of conventions for making meaning explicit. According to Olson, not only is a wider range of vocabulary typically used in text than in speech, but words are used in more precise ways; similarly, the syntactic resources of the language are exploited more fully for the purposes of rhetorical emphasis, especially given the substantial loss of paralinguistic cues in writing.

This view of reading as a technical, albeit complex, skill does not account for a rather obvious fact. Even the most proficient readers are incapable of interpreting certain texts – even though those texts are in their own language. We ourselves, for instance, as linguists, can identify and characterise in some detail all the constituent elements in an English text on, say, elementary particle theory in physics, but we have little confidence in our ability to learn much from such a text. We simply do not have enough knowledge of the relevant theory to make sense of the words on the page, even if we look them up in a dictionary. In short, much of the meaning that is said to be present 'in' such a text is there only by virtue of the highly specialised bodies of knowledge it assumes – and the skill of reading becomes largely a matter of having that knowledge and being able to apply it.

In addition, when we view reading as an act of communication, it becomes clear that more is involved than decoding the words of the text and applying appropriate background knowledge. Readers must also draw on the communicative skills that we have described under the notion of internal reciprocity. As they work with a text, they must not only ascribe an identity to the writer but assume one for themselves; and they must then work with these identities – revising them and reconstituting them in new ways – as they continuously negotiate meaning. As we have claimed, such social reciprocity is modelled on what we do as we negotiate meaning orally. In all our interactions, we are concerned, whether consciously or not, with such matters as how trustworthy our interactant is, why he or she is making this point, and what we should do in response. These interactive concerns are fundamental to negotiating text as well as talk; and the answers to the questions they raise vary considerably from one culture to another.

We have thus distinguished three kinds of skill that are necessary to reading. First is knowing a writing system and understanding the linguistic forms used in a text; second is possessing appropriate background knowledge and knowing how to apply it; and third is being able to engage in a reciprocal exchange that is appropriate to the text being read. Reading tests, as they exist at present, are designed to assess primarily the first of these three skills. Readers who do well on these tests can decode accurately. Moreover, they can perceive formal relationships between words, especially between those in the passage and those in the tasks; test takers are often asked to recognise or supply a word or phrase that parallels – or opposes – one used in the passage; consider, for example, tasks (*b*) and (*e*) in *Orchids*, Figure 1.1. Successful test takers can also manipulate the syntax; they can, for example, express the relations between subject and object in alternate ways; task 29 in *Radial K*, Figure 1.2, calls on just this ability.

As to the second kind of skill, reading tests are not designed to assess whether individuals possess appropriate background knowledge. On the contrary, test makers claim, following the tenets of the autonomous model, that the information given in any passage is sufficient for handling all the tasks. From our vantage point, such a claim is misleading, for no text can be altogether clear about everything. Test makers attempt to combat textual indeterminacy by using passages in which only commonplace knowledge is assumed. The problem is that the test maker's view of what is commonplace can diverge quite sharply from the test taker's view; and such divergence is exacerbated when a test is administered to people from a wide range of ethnocultural backgrounds who are dealing with a second or foreign language. Consider, once again, the *Orchids* passage, which assumes various pieces of information that would be useful in responding to task (*c*): 'Why are orchids expensive in some parts of the world?' Among potentially useful pieces of information are that (1) the expensive kinds of orchids grow in the tropics, (2) temperate regions are where orchids are expensive, and (3) in these regions people often pay high prices for a scarce entity, even though it lacks practical use or longevity. To students raised in the tropics where orchids are so abundant, and where plants are valued primarily for their practical use, these assumptions are far from obvious and many are unable to respond appropriately to this task (see Parry (1986), for a study of Nigerian students responding to this test material).

As for the third kind of skill, the traditional tests that we have described make no attempt to assess the ability to engage in different kinds of reciprocal exchange. Given the character of the passages used and the particular focus of the tasks, only one kind of exchange is called for, namely, the response of *homo legens* to 'the very words' of the text. The implicit message is that this is all that reading is; variation in literacy practices is ignored not only in different cultures but even in dominant forms of anglophone culture, where readers and writers engage in a much greater variety of reciprocal exchanges. More recently developed tests, it is true, do attempt to be more communicative, in that they include material, such as letters and advertisements, in which social reciprocity is overtly signalled – the 1987 edition of the Test of Adult Basic Education (TABE) is an example. In analysing the tasks based on such passages, however, we have found that they call for the same kind of limited response as do those in the older style of tests. The effect is unfortunate, for when such pragmatically oriented material is coupled with autonomously oriented tasks, the resulting discourse can be quite misleading, and the tests can engender even greater confusion than the ones they are replacing (Hill and Parry 1989).

Conclusions

Throughout our discussion of the pragmatic model, we have emphasised the social character of literacy: text viewed as social instrument, readers and writers as embodying social identities, and literacy skills as involving social interaction. When traditional tests of reading comprehension are considered in this framework, their limitations become immediately apparent. Based on a strictly autonomous model of literacy, they ignore the social dimension of written communication. For individuals who have developed literacy skills outside formal education, these effects are not necessarily serious: they can learn to treat testing as a distinctive genre that has little or no influence on their experience of text more generally. But when individuals depend on formal education for the development of literacy, particularly their English-based literacy, the tests can have a pernicious influence if they are allowed to play a dominant role, as they often do, in the classroom. Reading, and particularly reading in English, comes to be viewed as a narrowly circumscribed activity in which personal knowledge must be continually suppressed for fear of making an inappropriate response. Readers are encouraged to monitor closely what they know about textually mediated worlds and to hold such knowledge apart from that strictly assumed by the texts themselves; as we have pointed out, this assumed knowledge is often alien to their own sociocultural norms of language, thought, and experience. It is ironic that they are encouraged to hold separate the very knowledge which is crucial to their effective engagement with text, for there is clear evidence that readers learn best when integrating what they already know with what they are reading (Bransford *et al.* 1989).

It is because of these problems that the current development of alternative approaches to assessing literacy skills has taken on such importance. In Part III of this book we examine these approaches, first by discussing more pragmatically oriented tests and then by describing assessment that is increasingly independent of testing. In the final part, we use the pragmatic model of literacy to develop a policy-oriented framework for evaluating the various approaches to alternative assessment that are emerging.

Acknowledgements

We thank Sandra Silberstein, who, as editor of the *TESOL Quarterly*, contributed richly to an earlier version of this chapter. We also thank graduate students in Applied Linguistics, especially Patrizia Magni and Joye Smith, for their contributions.

Note

1. A shorter version of this chapter was published in *TESOL Quarterly*, 1992, 23 (3), pp. 433-61, under the title 'The test at the gate: models of literacy in reading assessment'. We would like to thank *TESOL Quarterly* for permission to reprint the article.

PART II

READING TESTS

This part falls into two sections, of which the first – Chapters 2 and 3 – considers reading tests from the test makers' perspective, and the second – Chapters 4 and 5 – from the test takers'. In that sense, the part embodies, to use a familiar phrase, an 'ethnography of communication' (Hymes 1964) between individuals who often reflect radically different social worlds.

In Chapter 2, 'The Test of English as a Foreign Language: developing items for reading comprehension', Bonny Peirce, writing from her own experience, tells the story of the development of an item set for the well-known Test of English as a Foreign Language. She shows how she, as a test developer, worked from the passage and items produced by an item writer, through a series of exchanges with colleagues, to prepare an item set to be piloted in a TOEFL administration. She then reports the statistical results of the piloting, showing how they reflect earlier concerns and suggest further revisions.

Peirce's story raises a number of interesting issues. First it demonstrates the professionalism of this particular group of test makers; they take great care to be accurate and to be fair to the test takers. A second point, however, is that the test makers refer only to each other, and the tone of their interaction suggests a closely integrated group. They share certain basic assumptions, which they have only recently begun to question (Peirce 1991, 1992), and these assumptions are clearly derived from the autonomous model of literacy described in Chapter 1. Finally, from the viewpoint of those who have conducted research on reader responses, the method of obtaining feedback from test takers is strikingly limited. The statistical analysis of responses, though sophisticated and, indeed, illuminating, can only confirm the test makers' assumptions since new items are judged successful insofar as they divide the population in the same way as older items have done.

In Chapter 3, 'An entrance test to Japanese universities: social and historical context', John Ingulsrud takes a broader perspective on the test-making process. He shows how it can be viewed as embodying long-established sociocultural practices that go well beyond the immediate purpose of the test. He begins by describing how the practice of testing, in Europe and America as well as in China and Japan, derives from the imperial examinations initiated in China some two thousand years ago. He describes how, in Japan, this practice was adapted in the nineteenth and twentieth centuries in response to social and political needs. He then examines the reading-assessment component in English of a particular test, the Joint First Stage Achievement Test (JFSAT), which governs entrance into the most prestigious Japanese universities. He explains how this test came to be established, based on the American format of a short passage followed by multiple-choice tasks, even though it differs, in certain important respects, from American standardised tests.

Ingulsrud then turns his attention to the test-making process itself. He describes the various committees that construct and evaluate test material, and he explains the procedures by which teachers and other education officials are able to publish their criticisms of the material used in any given year. The test makers then publish their own responses to this criticism, thereby achieving a kind of public dialogue around the test – in marked contrast to the more private world in which the TOEFL is produced.

The second section of this part shifts the focus to test takers' responses. In Chapter 4, 'The test and the text: readers in a Nigerian secondary school', Kate Parry considers material from the West African School Certificate (WASC) exam in the English Language, which is an example of the British tradition of testing. She bases her discussion on two item sets from this exam, one designed to test comprehension skills and the other summary skills. The passages are of particular interest since they both have to do with literacy; one deals with reading and the other with writing, and Parry points to subtle contradictions between what is stated in the passages and what is implied by the tasks.

Parry then presents the responses of individual Nigerian students to the test material, relating these responses to information about the students' social and cultural background. She demonstrates how the students, in drawing on their own experience, compounded their specifically linguistic difficulties as they struggled with unfamiliar vocabulary and complex syntax. In particular, she shows how their interpretations of the passages and responses to the tasks were governed by their oral experience of language in a multilingual environment, an experience that is at odds with the activities described in the passages and with the approach that is required by the tasks.

In Chapter 5, 'Adult education in the United States: adapting material for reading tests', Clifford Hill and Laurie Anderson also consider test material from the test takers' point of view. They analyse narrative material drawn from the Test of Adult Basic Education (TABE), which is the most widely used test of adult literacy in the United States. They begin their chapter by showing how test makers adapted material from the California Achievement Test (CAT) designed for children, but failed to take account of pragmatic inferences that adult readers may make in responding to this material. As a consequence, one of the tasks that follows the material elicits a sharply contrasting set of responses: certain readers focus on a single local detail and select the target response; others deal with the holistic pattern and select a distractor.

Hill and Anderson then present the results of a large-scale experiment with native speakers and non-native speakers of English. Under particular conditions that foster rapid reading, the non-native speakers were more likely to focus on the local detail and thus select the target response, whereas the native speakers were more likely to apprehend the holistic pattern and thus select the distractor. The authors are thus able to demonstrate that this test material, ironically, rewards the more limited comprehension that the non-native learners were able to manage under the experimental conditions.

This section highlights problems with reading tests in both British and American traditions. These problems are direct consequences of the autonomous model of literacy that test makers assume in constructing these tests. As long as this model remains the unquestioned premise of such tests, the problems remain largely unrecognised and so are not seriously addressed.

2 The Test of English as a Foreign Language: developing items for reading comprehension

Bonny Norton Peirce

The purpose of this chapter is two-fold. First, I wish to share the insights that I gained about test development while working in the Languages Group of the Test Development department at the Educational Testing Service (ETS) from 1984 to 1987. Second, I wish to describe the creation of a particular reading comprehension test I prepared for a TOEFL (Test of English as a Foreign Language) administration in 1986. I will begin the chapter with a brief description of the TOEFL as a whole, introduce readers to some basic terminology used in psychometric testing, and discuss some of the procedures I followed in the development of a TOEFL reading comprehension test. Thereafter, I shall use a passage I assembled, reviewed, and pre-tested for a TOEFL reading test to illustrate some of the debates that arise in the process of test development and to show the kind of information that is provided by a statistical analysis of individual items in a reading comprehension test. Additional analysis of the passage and items can be found in Peirce (1992).

The TOEFL

The TOEFL, first developed in 1963, is used to assess the English proficiency of candidates whose native language is not English, and scores are used by universities in the United States and Canada to determine whether a candidate's level of proficiency in English is acceptable for the institution in question. The test is administered by ETS on a monthly basis in more than 1250 test centres in 170 countries around the world (ETS 1992). The number of candidates taking the TOEFL test is increasing rapidly. In the 1988–89 administration year, 566 000 candidates registered to take the TOEFL; in 1989–90 this figure jumped to 675 000 – climbing again in 1990–91 to 740 000 (ETS 1990, 1991, 1992). ETS does not determine passing or failing scores; the decision on which students are accepted by a particular institution is dependent on the policy makers of each individual institution. Policy varies from institution to institution, often depending on the kind of programme a student has applied for and whether the institution offers supplementary courses in English. Any given TOEFL form is used only once, and the Test Development staff at ETS produce a new TOEFL form for each monthly administration. The test itself has a multiple-choice format and is divided into three sections: Section 1, Listening Comprehension; Section 2, Structure and Written Expression; Section 3, Vocabulary and Reading Comprehension. The TOEFL Test of Written English, a short essay test, is included in five TOEFL administrations a year. The TOEFL Policy Council, comprising a Committee of Examiners, a Research Committee, and a Services Committee, is responsible for different areas of programme activity.

A short description of the pre-testing process in the TOEFL helps to explain how one form of the TOEFL is made equivalent to another form. All TOEFL questions (items) are pre-tested on a sample TOEFL population. The experimental or 'pre-test' items are inserted into what is called the 'final form' of a TOEFL test. The final form contains all the items that have already gone through the pre-testing process and been approved for use in a TOEFL administration. TOEFL candidates are tested on the inserted pre-test items in the same way that they are tested on the final form items (candidates do not know which items are being pre-tested). The pre-test items are scored alongside the final form items, but the results on the pre-test items are not calculated into the sample population's final TOEFL score. An item analysis is then conducted on each of the pre-tested items. The purpose of the item analysis is to determine the level of difficulty of each item as well as its discriminating ability; it also helps to pinpoint potential problems with the item. When the pre-tested items are ultimately used in a TOEFL final form, the statistics from the pre-tested items help a test developer assemble a final form with a level of difficulty equivalent to that of previous TOEFL tests. Items that have little discriminating ability are revised or discarded.

The language of multiple-choice items

A number of psychometric terms will be used in the course of this chapter. The following question illustrates many of these terms:

The answer in a multiple-choice question is referred to as

(A) an item
(B) a distractor
(C) an option
(D) a key

(A), (B), (C), and (D) are all referred to as *options*. The answer to the question, (D) in this case, is referred to as the *key*. The incorrect answers, (A), (B), and (C) in this case, are referred to as *distractors*. The question itself ('The answer to a multiple-choice question is referred to as') is called the *stem*. The stem plus options are collectively referred to as the *item*. A reading comprehension passage combined with a number of items is referred to as a *set*.

The TOEFL reading comprehension section

Because the data in this chapter is drawn from the reading section of the TOEFL,[1] it is necessary to describe this section of the test in some detail. In Section 3 of the TOEFL, the Vocabulary and Reading Comprehension section, there are 30 vocabulary items and 30 reading comprehension items and candidates are given 45 minutes to complete the section. When pre-tested items are included in the test, the number of items in the section increases to 90 and the time limits are modified. While all the vocabulary questions are discrete (individual) items, the reading comprehension section is divided into about five reading comprehension passages with approximately six items per reading passage. The five passages span a variety of disciplines, from passages with a focus in the humanities to passages with a more scientific focus. Candidates are required to answer the multiple-choice questions on the basis of what is 'stated' or 'implied' in each of the passages and they must choose what they consider the best of the four options provided in each item. The *Bulletin of Information for TOEFL/TWE and TSE 1992-1993* (ETS 1992, p. 3) states that the Vocabulary and Reading Comprehension section of the test 'measures ability to understand nontechnical reading matter' in standard written English. The construct of reading that is measured in the TOEFL reading test is not made explicit.

The passages that are chosen for the reading comprehension section are expository texts that have been drawn from academic magazines, books, newspapers, and encyclopaedias; they are not written specifically for the TOEFL. Test developers are discouraged from changing the words used by the author, although deletions are permitted. The rationale for such a policy is that TOEFL candidates should be exposed to what is called 'authentic language' used by a variety of writers. Passages that are potentially offensive are excluded from the test. A potentially offensive passage (called 'sensitive' at ETS) is difficult to define, and is in fact a subject of much debate amongst members of the TOEFL test development team. At ETS, topics on politics, religion, or sex are considered to be sensitive. One of the main criteria whereby a passage is judged to be sensitive is its potential to create unnecessary anxiety for some candidates which would in turn compromise their performance on the test. A passage on birth control or abortion, for example, might create emotional stress for some candidates and lead to poor test performance. Sexist language (such as the use of the generic 'he') might be both offensive and ambiguous. In addition, topics that deal with a country other than a North American country might be perceived as giving unfair advantage to candidates who have background knowledge from the country in question. For example, a topic on the coffee industry in Brazil might be perceived by candidates from other parts of the world as giving unfair advantage to South Americans. It might also cause confusion amongst those South Americans who have a different understanding of the coffee industry than that of the author of the given text.

The test development process

Because a new TOEFL form has to be produced each month, ETS trains private individuals outside ETS to perform the first step of the test development process. These individuals, known as item writers, are given assignments to find a variety of passages of appropriate length and to develop approximately six or seven items based on each passage. Item writers are given detailed test specifications to facilitate this process. The completed assignments are forwarded to ETS where a member of the test development team takes responsibility for converting the passage and items into a publishable pre-test set. This was one of the functions I performed in the Test Development department at ETS. In the following paragraphs I shall describe the procedures I followed in the development of items for the TOEFL reading test. While many of these procedures are standard practice at ETS, they are not unique to this institution (see Madsen 1983).

When I was given an item writer's submission to develop for pre-testing purposes, I did not initially refer to the questions that had been developed by the item writer because I wished to explore my own response to the text before being influenced by the questions that the item writer had submitted. It was only after I had completed my own analysis of the text and created my own questions that I would refer to the item writer's submissions and proceed with the revision process.

First, I adopted the position of a 'reader' rather than a test developer in the initial stages of test development. I asked myself whether the text was interesting and held my attention. Where my concentration lapsed or I found myself re-reading a portion of the text for clarification, I recorded my observations. Where there were stylistic shifts in the text, interesting use of metaphor or analogy, inferences and comparisons, contradictions or ambiguities, I made a note. At this initial stage I did not refer to the test specifications. I tried to preserve, for as long as possible, my initial responses to the text. This enabled me to detect interesting nuances in the text as well as ambiguities and potential difficulties.

Second, once I had responded to the text as a reader, I began to examine the text as a test developer. One of the assumptions I made as I developed the items is that a reader's understanding of the text does not terminate once the reader has read the passage once or twice. I assumed that the longer readers work with a text, the more comprehensive their understanding of the text becomes. Indeed, a candidate's understanding of the test questions themselves also draws on the candidate's reading ability. Thus, with respect to the assessment of reading ability, there is an artificial distinction between the reading passage and the items, and I was sensitive to the fact that the test questions are an integral part of the process of reading comprehension. The main principles I followed when developing the items are summarised below.

1. Use the candidates' time efficiently

Given the fact that the candidates have only 45 minutes for Section 3 of the TOEFL, which includes a vocabulary and a reading section, and consequently less than 30 minutes for the reading section, one of my primary concerns as a test developer was to ensure that I used the candidates' time efficiently. I tried to ensure that there were as many items in a set as the passage could sustain; content that added little to the coherence of the passage and was not used for testing purposes was deleted from the text. I assumed it would be frustrating for candidates to grapple with portions of text and then have little opportunity to demonstrate their comprehension of this content. Furthermore, I tried to use closed rather than open stems. If the stem is open, that is, if there is no question mark at the end of the stem to consolidate the thought expressed in the stem, candidates have to repeat the stem each time an option is read in order to follow the grammatical logic of the option. This is time-consuming and a burden on memory.

2. Help the candidates orient themselves to the text

Because all TOEFL reading passages have been removed from one context and transplanted in another context, I tried to help the candidates orient themselves to the content of the passages being tested. Because TOEFL passages do not have titles, I tried to ensure that the first item in a reading comprehension set addressed the main idea or subject-matter of the passage. I hoped this would give candidates an organising principle to help them in their attempts to develop a better understanding of more detailed aspects of the text. I was aware, however, that many texts do not have a 'main idea' at all – they may be descriptive or narrative with little coherent argument as such. In such cases, a stem like 'What does the passage mainly discuss?' would be preferable to 'What is the main idea of the passage?' Furthermore, I assumed it would generally be helpful to candidates if the order of items in the set followed the order of information in the text itself. This would enable candidates to locate tested information with relative ease, and enable them to build on their understanding of 'old' or 'given' information in the text. I used line references as much as possible, providing they did not compromise the intent of the item (e.g. a scanning item). I was aware, however, that items which address the prevalent 'tone' of the passage cannot always be directly associated with a particular line or sentence in a passage and are best left to the end of the item set.

3. Make sure the items are defensible

There are two issues that pertain to the 'defensibility' of items: the items in combination, and the items individually. With reference to the items in combination, I tried to ensure that the items did justice to the content and level of difficulty of the text. This is where the art of test development was central to the test development process. I had to use judgement and imagination to assess interesting (and uninteresting) characteristics of the passage and develop items that gave the candidates sufficient opportunity to demonstrate their understanding of these characteristics. For example, if the text was detailed and complex, I did not wish to underestimate the candidates' reading ability by asking trivial questions. In addition, I knew the same information from the passage could not be tested twice - albeit in different forms. This would place some candidates in double jeopardy. Conversely, the stem in one item could not reveal the answer to a question in another item. For example, if the key to a particular item was 'Gold is expensive', then another item in the same set could not be worded: 'Gold is expensive because...'

With reference to individual items, I had to ensure that the stem and key of each item were unambiguous. Each stem had to contain as much information as was necessary and sufficient to answer the question posed, and each item had to have only one correct key. In addition, the options in any one item could not logically overlap in meaning. For example, if the key to an item were 'The region suffered severe drought' and one of the distractors in the item were 'The climatic conditions were harsh', there would be logical overlap between the two options as the key would be encompassed within the distractor. This would create ambiguity and confusion among the candidates and present them with two potential keys. Nevertheless, the distractors in an item needed to have some link to information in the text and they had to be plausible. Implausible distractors would be eliminated by candidates and lead them to choose the correct key by default. The distractors, however, could not be keyable. By this I mean that the distractors could not, potentially, be correct. This is an area that caused considerable debate in the test development process. Was a distractor drawing candidates because it was a good distractor or because it was ambiguous or potentially keyable? Finally, no one option could stand out as being structurally or stylistically different from the other options. Thus, if I put a definite article 'the' in front of 'key' in the example given above, (D) would stand out as different from the other options, which are preceded by indefinite articles. This could attract undue attention from candidates, who might (correctly) key it by default.

The review process

Because it is not possible for one person to offer a definitive reading of a text or avoid all the potential problems associated with test development, a comprehensive review process has been developed at ETS. There are two cornerstones of the review process: first, a series of test reviews by approximately six different test development specialists; and, second, a pre-testing process, as described earlier in this chapter. After the test developer is satisfied that the pre-test has been adequately prepared, the test goes for a Test Specialist Review (TSR). The Test Specialist Reviewer (also TSR) is a member of the TOEFL test development team; indeed, all test developers are reviewers and all reviewers are test developers. The passage and items are systematically reviewed by the TSR, who simultaneously 'takes' the test and reviews it. The reviewer notes down all the comments on a memo and returns them to the test developer. The test developer then works through these comments, makes changes to the items where he or she thinks them appropriate, and then sets up a meeting to discuss the review with the TSR. The test developer has to defend the action that he or she has taken with respect to the TSR's suggestions.

Each member of the team has his or her own style of reviewing. When

I reviewed the test of another test developer, I had to make a decision about those items that I thought were acceptable, those that were definitely not acceptable, and those that had minor flaws. Thus, reviewing a test could be quite a delicate process. On the one hand, I felt a responsibility to help create as defensible a test as possible; on the other hand, I didn't want to be unreasonable as this would compromise my efforts to defend those comments I felt strongly about. I was particularly concerned about items that I thought were ambiguous, had more than one potential key, or perhaps no clear key at all. I felt less strongly about items that were stylistically weak or had implausible distractors. If a test developer and reviewer could not resolve a problem that each felt strongly about, the issue was referred to a more senior member of the team for arbitration.

After the test has gone through the TSR stage, it goes to the TOEFL coordinator who examines all the items again, two editors who focus on stylistic problems in the test, and a sensitivity reviewer who tries to eliminate any potentially offensive material in the test. At each of these stages, the test is returned to the test developer for discussion and revision. During this entire process, the 'history' of each item can be located by any one reviewer because all the reviews are kept in a folder until the test is ready for publishing. Once galleys of the test have been made, it is returned to Test Development for a final review before being published in a TOEFL test booklet.

A TOEFL reading comprehension case study

In order to illustrate the debates that arise in the test development process, and to contextualise the comments that I will make in the latter part of this chapter, I shall draw on the experience I went through as I developed one particular reading comprehension pre-test for the TOEFL in 1986. There is nothing special about the passage and the items; they were chosen at random from a number of passages that I had developed, in collaboration with my colleagues, and which had gone through the pre-testing and statistical analysis stages. If I had not chosen to use the passage and items for case study purposes, they would have been revised for the last stage of the test development process: the final form. When I worked on the passage and the items, I had not anticipated that they would be used for the purposes of exposition. Fortunately, however, I was able to locate the history of all the reviews in the ETS archives. The passage that I have chosen to illustrate the above discussion is one that examines the farming of corn in the United States of America.

The passage

Running a farm in the Middle West today is likely to be a very expensive operation. This is particularly true in the Corn Belt, where the corn that fattens the bulk of the country's livestock is grown. The heart of the Corn Belt is in Iowa, Illinois, and Indiana, and it spreads into the neighboring states as well. The soil is extremely fertile, the rainfall is   5 abundant and well-distributed among the seasons, and there is a long, warm growing season. All this makes the land extremely valuable, twice as valuable, in fact, as the average farmland in the United States. When one adds to the cost of the land the cost of livestock, seed, buildings, machinery, fuel, and fertilizer, farming becomes a very expensive operation.   10 Therefore many farmers are tenants and much of the land is owned by banks, insurance companies, or wealthy business people. These owners rent the land out to farmers, who generally provide machinery and labor. Some farms operate on contract to milling companies or meat-packing houses. Some large farms are actually owned by these industries. The companies   15 buy up farms, put in managers to run them, provide the machinery to farm them, and take the produce for their own use. Machinery is often equipped with electric lighting to permit round-the-clock operation.

In general, all the reviewers found the passage to be acceptable for the purposes of the TOEFL. The only minor change took place when 'businessmen' was changed to the current 'business people' (line 12) in keeping with a policy that encourages non-sexist language. The TSR did raise the following two issues, and then proceeded to resolve them:

line 1 – Do we need to say 'Middle West U.S.?' Guess U.S. is in line 8

– really seems like there should be a paragraph cut-off somewhere, but I guess that's authentic language for you.

In the interests of efficiency, the comments that are made by the various reviewers at ETS are written in an abbreviated style. Each test developer soon develops a style that is accessible to other members of the team. A common abbreviation however is 'S:' This is short for 'I suggest you do the following...'. In the first comment, the TSR is concerned that the introduction to the text does not offer sufficient geographical context for the reader, but is then satisfied that 'United States' is mentioned elsewhere in the text. The second comment indicates that the reviewer would like to have the paragraph divided up for easier reading, but acknowledges TOEFL policy on 'authentic language' that discourages editorial changes in the interests of authenticity.

The items

Note that the items are numbered from 70 to 78 because they have been inserted into the final form of a TOEFL reading comprehension section (normally 60 items) and numbered accordingly. The items I am discussing are those that were presented to the Test Specialist Reviewer. The items that were finally published in pre-test form during a 'live' administration of the TOEFL are given in the appendix to this chapter.

The first item in the set is a question that assesses a candidate's overall understanding of the main topic of the passage.

70. What is the author's main point?

(A) Livestock are expensive to raise.
(B) Machinery is essential to today's farming.
(C) Corn can grow only in certain climates.
(D) It is expensive to farm in the Middle West.

The key (D) is drawn primarily from the topic sentence in the first line of the passage: 'Running a farm in the Middle West today is likely to be a very expensive operation'. This idea is also supported by the comment in lines 10–11, '...farming becomes a very expensive operation'. The comments below were written by the TSR and coordinator respectively.

70. D – neat question!
70. (A) livestock is?

While the TSR is satisfied with the item as it stands, the coordinator raises the question of agreement between the subject of the sentence in option (A) 'livestock' and the verb 'are'. It would have been simple for me to change 'livestock are' to 'livestock is', but when I took another look at the item, it became apparent to me that the word 'expensive' was used twice in the item – in both options (A) and (D). As (D) is the key, this is particularly problematic. It seemed to me that the repetition of the word 'expensive' might attract attention to these two options and candidates might key (D) by default. I therefore chose to revise option (A) completely to read 'It is difficult to raise cattle'. An alternative format could have been used to test the same information. Consider:

Which of the following would be the best title for the passage?

(A) Raising Cattle: Problems and Solutions
(B) The History of Farming: A Changing Landscape
(C) Growing Corn: The Role of Climate
(D) Farming in the Middle West: Money Matters

Item 71 assesses a candidate's understanding of information that is not given explicitly in the passage but is strongly implied by the author.

71. It can be inferred from the passage that in the United States corn is

(A) the least expensive food available
(B) used primarily as animal feed
(C) cut only at night
(D) used to treat certain illnesses

This kind of item does not rely on a candidate's background knowledge, but is drawn from information that is given explicitly in the text. Phrases used to introduce this item type include: 'It can be inferred from the passage that...', 'The passage supports which of the following conclusions?', 'The author implies that...'. The comments below were written by the TSR and coordinator respectively.

71. B – I think this only refers to Middle West corn. S: '...that Middle West corn is' – (A) only option that doesn't start w. verb. S: Sold at very low prices (for (B) could say 'grown' instead of 'used')

71. C + D where do they come from?

The issues referred to above relate respectively to the accuracy of the stem, the stylistic quality of the options, and the suitability of the distractors. The first comment indicated that the use of 'United States' was too vague, and I accordingly changed the stem to 'Middle West'. The second comment indicated that (A) was not stylistically parallel to the other options. As I examined this option more carefully, I became conscious of two other problems with the option. The first was that the word 'expensive' had been used in the previous item – as the key – and was repeated in item 75 – again as the key. This overlap was undesirable. In addition, I was aware that the use of such exclusive terms as *the least* and *only* are often perceived by candidates to be distractors rather than keys because of the unlikelihood of such extremes occurring at any one particular time. In other words, while it is plausible that corn might be an inexpensive product, it is far less likely to be 'the *least* expensive food available'. I was therefore happy to use the reviewer's suggested revision.

The TSR's final comment was written in brackets to indicate that she did not feel strongly about the comment. Nevertheless, I was happy to change 'used' to 'grown' since the verb 'used' was already present in option (D). The last comment ('where do (C) and (D) come from?') was an abbreviated way of asking how these particular distractors could be seen as plausible. I could defend (C) on the grounds that machines are used 'round-the-clock', and I thought (D) was justified because of the repeated references to the word 'operation' (lines 2, 11, 18) which has a medical connotation. It did occur to me, however, that the key to another item – item 78 – was to be revised to 'at night' and because I wanted to avoid overlap with this item, I proceeded to revise option (C). As a result of all these deliberations, which in real time would take no more than a few minutes, I changed the item to read:

It can be inferred from the passage that Middle West corn is

(A)   sold at very low prices
(B)   grown primarily as animal feed
(C)   cut in the morning
(D)   used to treat certain illnesses

It was only once I had checked the statistics that came back from the pre-testing of this item set that I realised there was a far more serious flaw in this item than any of the reviews had picked up (this will be discussed under 'Statistical analysis' below).

Item 72 assesses a candidate's understanding of particular words and phrases as they are used in the context of the passage.

In line 3, the word 'heart' could best be replaced by which of the following?

(A)   Spirit
(B)   Courage
(C)   Cause
(D)   Center

This type of item is distinct from items in the vocabulary section of the TOEFL in that all the options refer to possible synonyms of the word 'heart' in different contexts. Thus for (A) one might say that a person has a compassionate heart/spirit; for (B) that a person should take heart/courage; for (C) that the heart/cause of a problem is that ... ; for (D) (the key) that the heart/center of the Corn Belt is in ... The suggestion below, which was simple to implement, was made by the TSR.

72. D —these options need to be lower case, since they're replacing 'heart'

Item 73 tests a reader's ability to understand the use of metaphor in the text. The TSR's comment on the item is given below.

73. It can be inferred from the passage that the region known as the Corn Belt is so named because it

(A)   is shaped like an ear of corn
(B)   resembles a long yellow belt
(C)   grows most of the nation's corn
(D)   provides the livestock hides for leather belts

73. C – nice yet humorous

On reflection, it is apparent that this item is not an inference that can be drawn directly from the passage. Rather, it tests information that can only be extrapolated from the passage. In a final form, I would revise this item to read: 'It is likely that the region known as the Corn Belt is so named because it ...'

Item 74 assesses a candidate's understanding of information that is given explicitly in the passage.

74. The author mentions all of the following as features of the Corn Belt EXCEPT

(A)   rich soil
(B)   advantageous weather
(C)   cheap labor
(D)   sufficient rainfall

The form of this item is irregular because the question is phrased negatively. In order for candidates to answer this question correctly, they cannot simply focus on one option – they have to examine all four options carefully and arrive at the key by elimination. Although the stem indicates that the author 'mentions' certain features of the Corn Belt in the text, the options do not contain information taken verbatim from the text as this would make the item far too easy for the candidate population. Thus 'rich soil' must be equated with 'extremely fertile soil' (line 4), 'advantageous weather' with 'long, warm growing season' (lines 5/6) and so forth. The comments below were written by the TSR and coordinator respectively.

74. C. – (B), (D) similar – (D) is encompassed in (B). S: (B) warm weather

74. (D) in psg the rainfall is 'abundant'

The TSR drew my attention to the fact that I had collapsed options (B) and (D), thus making the item a 3-option item and reducing the attractiveness of both options. The TSR's suggested revision 'warm weather' made option (B) sufficiently distinct from (D) and I accordingly made the change. The coordinator drew my attention to the fact that 'sufficient' is not synonymous with 'abundant' and therefore might be construed as keyable. I therefore changed this option to 'plentiful' rainfall.

Item 75 calls for an understanding of information that is given explicitly in the passage:

75. According to the passage, a plot of farmland in an area outside the Corn Belt as compared to a plot of land inside the Corn Belt would probably be

(A)   less expensive
(B)   smaller
(C)   more fertile
(D)   more profitable

The answer to the question is clearly indicated in lines 7/8 of the passage, which states that the land inside the Corn Belt is 'extremely valuable, twice as valuable, in fact, as the average farmland in the United States'. The comments below were written by the TSR and coordinator respectively.

75. A – (D) inferrable, since the land would presumably cost less, hence less overhead. S: easier (or 'more mechanized'?) I wonder if (B) isn't inferrable, too? S: less tiring (?)

75. stem very wordy – any way to simplify?

Significantly, the reviewers were as concerned with what could be reasonably inferred from the passage as with what was explicitly stated in the passage. Thus they argued that the key could not be defended simply on the basis of the opening phrase 'According to the passage ...' This is generally considered a last line of defence, but is best avoided in the interests of clarity and test fairness.

As I reflected on their comments, I could see why (D) might be construed as inferrable and hence confusing to candidates. I took the suggestion that I should change the wording to 'more mechanized'. In one of the later reviews, however, one of the editors took exception to the use of 'more mechanized', saying that it was 'implausible' to call a plot of farmland mechanised. I changed the wording again to 'more desirable'. At the time, I did not agree that (B) could be inferrable. Logically, I believed that since the land outside the Corn Belt was depicted as less valuable – and hence less expensive – than that inside the Corn Belt, it was likely that the plots of farmland outside the Corn Belt would be larger and not smaller than those inside the Corn Belt. I took the position that the distractor was a good one, rather than an unfair one. I decided, however, that if another reviewer had a similar problem with (B) I would change the option. In the final analysis, I knew that a statistical analysis would tell me if (B) had presented problems to otherwise competent readers. In response to the third comment, I did simplify the stem without compromising the clarity of the question.

Item 76 presents material that is analogous to material that is presented in the passage and asks candidates to recognise this relationship.

76. As described in the passage, which of the following is most clearly
analogous to the relationship between insurance company and tenant farmer?

(A) Doctor and patient
(B) Factory owner and worker
(C) Manufacturer and retailer
(D) Business executive and secretary

It is significant that this type of item does not draw on information that is
either explicitly stated in the passage or directly inferrable from the
passage. It asks candidates to recognise a particular relationship that is
described in the text, and it does so by presenting a variety of
relationships to candidates – only one of which is analogous to the
relationship described in the text. Thus the candidates are required to
extrapolate from ideas that are given in the text. The only comment on
this item was written by the TSR.

76. B – hope vocab doesn't get in the way here (esp. 'retailer')

The TSR expressed concern that the language in the item was more
complex than the language in the text. Thus, even if the candidates could
understand the relationship between the insurance company and tenant
farmer, they would not know the equivalent relationship expressed in the
options. I could easily revise 'retailer' to 'merchant' but I could not avoid
using the term 'analogy' without compromising the item as a whole. I
was also uncomfortably aware that the relationships depicted in the
options might be unfamiliar to some candidates, though I was confident
that the vast majority of candidates would be familiar with an
owner/worker relationship. I decided to wait for a statistical analysis
before abandoning the item at the pre-test stage.

Item 77 assesses the reader's understanding of the way cohesive
devices are used in the passage to link intrasentential relationships: 'The
companies buy up farms, put in managers to run them, provide the
machinery to farm them, and take the produce for their own use.' The
only comment on this item was made by the TSR.

77. The word 'their' in line 15 refers to

(A) companies
(B) farms
(C) managers
(D) machinery

77. A – (D) only singular. S: machines

All the options are taken directly from the text since the item does not
test knowledge of vocabulary but knowledge of syntax. I was therefore

loath to follow the reviewer's suggestion to change 'machinery' to a plural form because the use of a synonym rather than the word used in the text might confuse the candidates and compromise the intent of the item.

Item 78 began its history as a straightforward item that assessed a candidate's ability to understand information that is given explicitly in the passage. The only comment in this item was made by the TSR.

78. According to the passage, some machinery is equipped with electric lighting so that it can be used

(A)   indoors
(B)   in the fog
(C)   twenty-four hours a day
(D)   while it rains

78. C – key quite a bit longer. S: (C) at night.

The TSR's comment on this item indicates concern that the candidates might choose (C) as the key because its length attracts attention and not because the candidates have understood the reference 'round-the-clock'. I therefore took the suggestion to change the option to 'at night'. On reflection however, although this revision improves the item stylistically, it makes the key weaker. The passage states explicitly that machinery is equipped with electric lighting so that it can be used 'round-the-clock'. The phrase 'twenty-four hours a day' is thus a stronger key than the phrase 'at night', which is really an inference that is drawn from the passage and not a statement that is made explicitly. However, if I had turned this question into an inference question by saying, 'It can be inferred from the passage that...' I think that all the options would have been keyable. A better revision might have been to leave the key as 'twenty-four hours a day' and then make at least one of the distractors a little longer to balance the length of the key. For example, I could have changed (D) to 'when it rains unexpectedly'.

Statistical analysis

Once the passage and items had passed through all the reviews and I had adjusted the items where I thought necessary, the test was pre-tested in a TOEFL administration (see appendix). The results of the pre-tests were forwarded to the Statistics Department at ETS who completed an analysis of each item and forwarded the results to Test Development. The task of the test developers at this stage was to assess the results of the item analyses, decide which items worked, which needed to be revised, and which needed to be discarded. How does a test developer know whether an item has 'worked'? In a test like the TOEFL, test takers, teachers, test developers, and administrators are particularly concerned with two issues: first, that the TOEFL discriminates successfully between 'good' and 'poor' candidates; second, that one form of the TOEFL is comparable in difficulty with other forms of the TOEFL. For test development purposes, a successful item is one that discriminates successfully between good and poor candidates. The level of difficulty of an item, on the other hand, is a function of the percentage of candidates who chose the correct key. The latter statistic is not difficult to compute. However, the test developer needs to be assured that the relative difficulty of the item is a function of the relative levels of proficiency of the candidates as measured by the test and not a function of a poorly constructed or ambiguous item.

In order to determine whether an item discriminates successfully between good and poor candidates, there needs to be a criterion (standard) by which to judge the item. The criterion that is used in the TOEFL reading test is the candidates' performance on Section 3 of the TOEFL. Thus, for example, an item is considered to have 'worked' if most of the top candidates in the Vocabulary and Reading Comprehension section get the item right and if candidates who choose the correct key are not randomly distributed through the sample. If the latter were the case, the item would have no discriminating power. In order to determine who the 'top candidates' are, each candidate's total score on Section 3 is computed, and candidates are given percentile rankings. On the basis of these percentile rankings, the total group is then divided into five sub–groups, ranging from the top 20 per cent to the bottom 20%. Once this information is tabulated, the performance of each individual item is determined with respect to these five groups. The index of discrimination, the biserial correlation, is a correlation coefficient that measures the extent to which candidates who scored high on Section 3 as a whole tended to get the item right, and those who scored low tended to get it wrong. The item is working successfully if the biserial correlation is above 0.5.

In the passage that I had pre-tested, all the items except one can be considered to have been successful. All the biserial correlations except item 71 were above 0.5, and the item set was judged to be of average difficulty for the TOEFL population. From easiest to most difficult, the items ranked as follows: 72, 74, 78, 70, 77, 76, 73, 75, 71. What, then, was the problem with item 71, which had in fact been revised considerably? In the population on which my reading comprehension passage was pre-tested there were 1280 candidates, all of whom were divided into five different groups of 256 candidates based on percentile rankings. (See Table 2.1, a simplified form of an ETS item analysis.) Note that by the time item 71 was pre-tested, 9 candidates in the two weakest groups had dropped out, which explains the slight discrepancy in the 'Total' row at the bottom of Table 2.1. A candidate who has 'dropped out' is no longer attempting to answer any questions; a candidate who 'omits' an item is still nevertheless attempting to answer all questions and is therefore included in the 'Total' figures.

71. It can be inferred from the passage that Middle West corn is

(A)   sold at very low prices
(B)   grown primarily as animal feed
(C)   cut in the morning
(D)   used to treat certain illnesses

As a preliminary analysis of item 71, compare the candidates who chose option (A), a distractor, with those who chose option (B), the key. A large number of candidates in the weakest group chose the distractor (A) as the key (85 in all), while a smaller number (57) in the strongest group chose the distractor (A) as the key. Significantly, the situation is reversed for (B), the key: while only 95 of the weakest candidates correctly chose (B) as the key, 196 of the strongest candidates correctly chose (B) as the key. A cursory glance indicates that the item is working quite well: 52 per cent of the candidates chose the correct option: 664 out of a total of 1271 candidates – a moderately difficult item. It is clear that option (A) was the most attractive distractor as 459 of the total 1271 candidates chose this option as the key; 52 candidates chose option (C); 81 chose option (D).

Despite these apparently favourable results, there are some disturbing issues that arise from the analysis: an uncomfortably high number of candidates chose (A) as the key – 160 of whom were in the top two groups – and 15 candidates omitted this item – 6 of whom were in the top two groups. It was for these reasons that the biserial correlation fell

Table 2.1 Responses to item 71

| | Percentile rank | | | | | |
	0–20	21–40	41–60	61–80	81–100	Total
Omit	4	0	5	4	2	15
A	85	105	109	103	57	459
B (Key)	95	110	120	143	196	664
C	27	15	5	4	1	52
D	37	25	17	2	0	81
Total	248	255	256	256	256	1271

Table 2.2 Responses to item 75

	Percentile rank					
	0–20	21–40	41–60	61–80	81–100	Total
Omit	3	4	0	1	1	9
A (Key)	66	101	149	191	222	729
B	62	44	41	29	21	197
C	73	61	41	22	6	203
D	39	43	24	13	6	125
Total	243	253	256	256	256	1263

below 0.5 to 0.35 and I carefully scrutinised the item. As I re-examined the key in item 71 and the information in the passage from which it was drawn, it became clear to me that the key, strictly speaking, was inaccurate. The passage states that most of the livestock in the United States is fed on corn that originates in the Corn Belt. This does not imply, however, that Middle West corn is grown primarily as animal feed. Although this may indeed be the case in the United States, such an inference cannot be drawn from the passage per se. For example, the corn could be grown primarily for export purposes, even though it is the staple diet for livestock in the United States. In a TOEFL final form, the item would need to be revised or excluded from the item set.

By way of comparison, consider the statistical analysis of item 75 (see Table 2.2). The item reads as follows:

75. According to the passage, a plot of farmland in an area outside the Corn Belt as compared to one inside the Corn Belt would probably be

(A)　less expensive
(B)　smaller
(C)　more fertile
(D)　more desirable

In item 75, which had a biserial correlation of 0.55, only 66 candidates in the weakest group correctly chose (A) as the key, while 222 in the strongest group correctly chose (A) as the key. In contrast, 62 of the weakest group incorrectly chose (B) as the key, while only 21 in the strongest group incorrectly chose (B) as the key. Similar comparisons can be drawn with options (C) and (D). In total, 9 candidates omitted the item, only 2 of whom were in the top two groups. The percentage of candidates who chose the correct key was 58 per cent (729 of a total 1263) – thus the item was of average difficulty. The remaining candidates were relatively evenly divided in their choice of distractors. Nevertheless, it was still a little disturbing that 50 candidates in the top two groups incorrectly chose (B) as the key. The comment of my TSR reviewer had been validated. This distractor would have needed revision before it reached the final form stage.

Conclusion

The above discussion has highlighted a number of important issues in the development of the TOEFL reading test at ETS. First, test development is always a collaborative effort in which test developers work with colleagues to enhance the quality of the reading test. Such collaboration gives test developers the opportunity to subject the passage and items to alternative readings and minimise ambiguity in individual items. Second, the pre-testing process and the statistical analysis of pre-tested items provides a different set of checks and balances for the test developer: it may confirm the reservations that the test developer has had about a particular item; it may draw attention to aspects of the item that have been overlooked; it may help to resolve disputes about the fairness and suitability of the item. However, despite the rigour with which the TOEFL reading test is developed, important questions have been raised both within and outside ETS about the validity of the TOEFL reading test. While it is not within the scope of this chapter to address these questions, the reader may refer to Peirce (1992) for an analysis of some of the debates. As Robert Altman, the vice-president of ETS, argued in his plenary address at the International TESOL convention in Vancouver in 1992, machine-scorable standardised tests may not adequately reflect what students really know.

Acknowledgements

I would like to acknowledge the members of the Languages Group, Test Development, ETS, for the diverse ways in which they have contributed to the production of this chapter; in particular, Barbara Suomi, Valerie Richardson, and Ellie LeBaron for their part in the case study. I would also like to thank Susan Chyn and Jackie Ross for their comments on an earlier draft of the chapter, and ETS for providing access to TOEFL archives and TOEFL copyright material.

Note

1. Large sections of this chapter were drawn from the author's article published in *TESOL Quarterly*, 1992, 23:4, p. 665-691, 'Demystifying the TOEFL reading test'. The author wishes to thank *TESOL Quarterly* for permission to reprint these sections.

Appendix 2.1: A TOEFL pre-test item

Questions 70–78

Running a farm in the Middle West today is likely to be a very expensive operation. This is particularly true in the Corn Belt, where the corn that fattens the bulk of the country's livestock is grown. The heart of the Corn Belt is in Iowa, Illinois, and Indiana, and it spreads into the neighboring states as well. The soil is extremely fertile, the rainfall is abundant and (5) well-distributed among the seasons, and there is a long, warm growing season. All this makes the land extremely valuable, twice as valuable, in fact, as the average farmland in the United States. When one adds to the cost of the land the cost of livestock, seed, buildings, machinery, fuel, and fertilizer, farming becomes a very expensive operation. Therefore many (10) farmers are tenants and much of the land is owned by banks, insurance companies, or wealthy business people. These owners rent the land out to farmers, who generally provide machinery and labor. Some farms operate on contract to milling companies or meat-packing houses. Some large farms are actually owned by these industries. The companies buy up (15) farms, put in managers to run them, provide the machinery to farm them, and take the produce for their own use. Machinery is often equipped with electric lighting to permit round-the-clock operation.

70. What is the author's main point?

   (A) It is difficult to raise cattle.
   (B) Machinery is essential to today's farming.
   (C) Corn can grow only in certain climates.
   (D) It is expensive to farm in the Middle West.

71. It can be inferred from the passage that Middle West corn is

   (A) sold at very low prices
   (B) grown primarily as animal feed
   (C) cut in the morning
   (D) used to treat certain illnesses

72. In line 3, the word 'heart' could best be replaced by which of the following?

   (A) spirit
   (B) courage
   (C) cause
   (D) center

73. It can be inferred from the passage that the region known as the Corn Belt is so named because it

   (A) is shaped like an ear of corn
   (B) resembles a long yellow belt
   (C) grows most of the Nation's corn
   (D) provides the livestock hides for leather belts

74. The author mentions all of the
following as features of the
Corn Belt EXCEPT

(A) rich soil
(B) warm weather
(C) cheap labor
(D) plentiful rainfall

75. According to the passage, a plot
of farmland in an area outside
the Corn Belt as compared to
one inside the Corn Belt
would probably be

(A) less expensive
(B) smaller
(C) more fertile
(D) more desirable

76. As described in the passage,
which of the following is most
clearly analogous to the
relationship between insurance
company and tenant farmer?

(A) Doctor and patient
(B) Factory owner and worker
(C) Manufacturer and
merchant

(D) Business executive and
secretary

77. The word 'their' in line 17
refers to

(A) companies
(B) farms
(C) managers
(D) machinery

78. According to the passage, some
machinery is equipped with
electric lighting so that it can
be used

(A) indoors
(B) in the fog
(C) at night
(D) while it rains

3 An entrance test to Japanese universities: social and historical context

John E. Ingulsrud

Historical development

Civil service examinations in ancient China

Modern life has been so greatly influenced by western civilisation that for many people 'modernisation' is virtually synonymous with 'westernisation'; and yet, certain features fundamental to modernity come not from the west but from the east. Consider, for example, institutional bureaucracy. It was in East Asian societies that such bureaucracy first arose out of the notion that the persons who lead should be the most able. The selection of leaders, it was thought, should be based on individual worth, not on endowed wealth or status. Of course, such meritocratic ideals existed outside East Asia as well. Plato, for example, in *The Republic* describes how society should choose its 'guardians':

> ...so we must introduce our Guardians when they are young to fear and, by contrast, give them opportunities for pleasure, proving them far more rigorously than we prove gold in the furnace...And any Guardian who survives these continuous trials in childhood, youth, and manhood unscathed, shall be given authority in our state. (Plato 1987, p. 180)

Through these 'trials' individuals were to be selected for their superior attributes of mind and body.

It was only in the Chinese empire of the Han Dynasty (206BC – AD 220), however, that these ideals were actually applied on a nationwide scale. The selection process for the bureaucracy was carried out by means of tests – not of physical abilities such as archery or javelin throwing – but of abilities demonstrated through the skills of reading and writing. The civil service examinations for the imperial bureaucracy took the form of, from our perspective, an achievement test. They were based on a specific body of knowledge which consisted largely of the literary works attributed to Confucius (Reischaur and Fairbank 1960). The emphasis on Confucius rather than other ancient Chinese sages lay in his political ideology. Confucian thinking emphasised human relationships and stratified people depending on the kind of work they performed. This stratification placed the emperor at the top and the merchants at the bottom. Each family maintained a miniature version of this stratification with the patriarchal father at the top and the daughter-in-law at the bottom. An ideology of this kind maintained the people in power and offered an environment for social stability. It was thus assumed that selecting talented individuals versed in this ideology would preserve the social order.

Ironically, the examinations themselves served as a sort of check on the abuses of human relationships that Confucianism tended to foster. Confucian ethics are based on the harmonious maintenance of five relationships: (1) between sovereign and subject, (2) between father and son, (3) between husband and wife, (4) between elder brother and younger brother, and (5) between friend and friend (Bahm 1969, p. 92). Since three of these relationships concern the family, they tended to encourage certain abuses in civil life, such as nepotism. The examinations provided the state with a mechanism to curb such abuses, for they provided an independent means of selection. In fact, such independence may constitute the most powerful rationale for any use of an examination system, particularly in a society where family relationships impose strong obligations.

To pass the civil service examinations in ancient China was no easy matter. Preparation took years, since candidates were required to know thousands of logographs merely to read the classics. Furthermore, they had to memorise whole texts. On the examinations, they wrote essays about particular questions on particular texts. The form of these essays was strictly prescribed: it consisted of a rhetorical style called *baguwen* or 'the eight-legged essay'. Hu (1984 p. 13) explains:

> It was a highly formalized form of literary composition, with a terse and pithy introductory remark, followed by an equally terse elucidation of the topic and then the main text divided into eight paragraphs, forming four parallel or balanced parts, each developing the essay's theme in logical sequence and leading to a crescendo. The number of characters used was limited, rarely exceeding 600 or so.

These essays were then evaluated according to the criteria of purity, truthfulness, elegance, and propriety. These criteria were, however, so vague that candidates had little choice but to try to detect the literary preferences of the examiners as well as their tastes in calligraphy (Hu 1984).

The early civil service examinations of the Han Dynasty were by no means open. Only aristocratic candidates could compete. Beginning, however, with the Sui Dynasty (589–618) and continuing through the Tang Dynasty (618–907), the examinations were opened up to all social classes. This development allowed an unprecedented opportunity for social mobility (Miyazaki 1976). Aristocratic families still found methods of bypassing the examinations, but as Miyazaki points out, officials who did bypass them found themselves in a position of lower prestige. Less respect was given to those who failed to follow the normal paths of achievement.

Apart from the aristocratic abuses of the system, there was the problem of limited economic resources. Not every man who wanted to compete could realistically do so. The necessary training lasted for many years and was extremely expensive. No system of universal education was available to support the training. Although most candidates came from families where such resources were available, Miyazaki mentions cases where whole communities would support a promising young man.

Transmission to other societies

By the seventeenth century, information regarding the examination system for the Chinese civil service filtered to Europe, primarily by means of letters written by Jesuit missionaries (Teng 1943). During the eighteenth century, the Enlightenment philosophers began to see such a system as providing a rational alternative to the power of the European aristocracy. Support for an examination system can be found in works such as Voltaire's *Essay on Morals* (1756) as well as Adam Smith's *Wealth of Nations* (1776). Civil service examinations were subsequently developed in various countries. The British, for example, first experimented with a system in India in the 1850s and then, by the 1870s, had adopted a system for themselves (Teng 1943, pp. 299–300).

The European adoption of a civil service system was, in fact, relatively late. Nearly a thousand years earlier, Japan had borrowed the Chinese system. This system, however, was only one feature of the large-scale transmission of Chinese culture during the Tang Dynasty. Other features included the writing system, architecture, painting, Buddhism, and Confucianism. Initially, the examination system was begun in the eighth century, and according to Amano (1983), it was at first administered by experts from China. Although the system was restricted to the aristocracy, prominent clans still felt threatened, and by the eleventh century it was abolished. By that time, contact with China had weakened and Japan had embarked on a period of cultural development of its own.

From the eleventh century, Japan experienced alternating periods of political unity and fragmentation. The aristocratic warriors, the *samurai*, began to play an important role in the fiefdoms of feudal Japan. At times of unity, certain aristocratic families controlled the whole country. At times of fragmentation, competing fiefdoms battled for power. Given the lack of political stability, the civil service examination system was not able to function.

At the beginning of the seventeenth century, the Tokugawa family gained control of Japan and for 250 years the nation was united and relatively peaceful. The *samurai* began to function less as soldiers and more as bureaucrats. Culturally, scholars and artists again looked to the continent for inspiration, even though there was little direct contact. There was a revival of the Chinese classics and Confucianism was emphasised as a social ideology (Reischaur and Fairbank 1960). At the same time, limited civil service testing was started among the *samurai*. The tests, however, were not conducted on a national scale, but rather in individual fiefs and in a manner each lord saw fit. Nevertheless, the notion of a national system had been kept alive, as Amano (1983) points out, because the classical works from the continent, particularly the works of the twelfth-century neo-Confucian philosopher Zhu Xi, dominated Japanese intellectual life.

By the mid-nineteenth century, Japan was once again faced with internal political collapse with western imperial powers at its doorstep. There was a movement at this time to adopt civil service testing on a national scale. This time, however, the testing was not after the pattern of China, but more after the pattern of England and Prussia. Western learning seemed more appropriate to nineteenth-century nation building than the Confucian classics (Amano 1983).

Yet, it was not until 1887 that the open testing of the western systems was instituted. The relatively slow pace with which it was adopted was partly due to the longstanding fear of social mobility. Japan was governed by oligarchs with strong regional loyalties who tended to promote individuals from their home areas (Spaulding 1967). In fact, the adoption of open testing was partly due to the fact that it had become relatively unimportant. By this time institutions, namely, the universities, had been established and gradually they took over the role of selecting individuals for public careers.

University entrance examinations in Japan

Background

During the 1870s a few institutions of higher learning, such as the University of Tokyo, were established (Narita 1978). These institutions were the only places where people could gain access to western learning. The government needed individuals who were equipped to run a modern nation and so they looked to these few institutions. Since the students constituted the group of appropriately trained individuals, the government waived civil service examinations for the graduates (Spaulding 1967). The government as well as other employers simply assumed that the graduates were the most capable because of the stiff competition to enter these institutions (Amano 1983).

The prestige of an institution came to be valued over an individual's academic achievement. This tendency continues to a large degree today as Pempel (1978 p. 153) observes:

> Career success depends much less on actual skills than on school standing and a school's alumni connections, the entire syndrome suggesting that the university one graduates from is more important than what one learns there.

Although the number of institutions of higher learning have proliferated since the end of the Second World War, it is generally the six former imperial universities and a dozen or so private universities that form an élite group. Among these universities, the University of Tokyo has an especially privileged status. Rohlen (1983) reports that over 60 per cent of all top management positions in the government ministries are filled by graduates of the University of Tokyo. One explanation for this pattern is the alumni themselves who are eager to promote the prestige of their alma mater (Passin 1965). In fact, the prestige of a university can correlate highly with its age; an older institution has more graduates, and thus a more extensive network. Although people with special skills who do not graduate from the prestigious universities may be hired, they will not, according to Taylor (1983), advance to top management positions.

A nationwide entrance examination: The Joint First Stage Achievement Test

Initially, the universities had prepared their annual entrance examinations separately. In each university, a faculty committee was annually selected to carry out the task of preparing an exam. Soon particular types of exams began developing at different universities. There evolved, for example, a University of Tokyo-style test and a University of Kyoto-style test. The differences were primarily of format and item-type. The University of Kyoto test, for example, tended to include more subjective items such as essay writing (Sato 1979). Vogel (1979) argues that such typification allowed for a certain degree of predictability, and thus studying for the examinations was less arduous than popularly believed. At the same time, there was no control over what the tests covered. Narita (1978 p. 89) explains:

> Though the examination syllabi accord with the requirements for upper secondary graduates, the content and level of the entrance examinations are not by any means standardised.

Because these tests were locally constructed and confidential, there were no opportunities to pre-test them, to conduct item analyses, or even to check for errors. The reliability and validity of the tests depended entirely on the judgement of those faculty committee members who were responsible for preparing them.

In addition to the problem of standardising the subject-matter on the test, the annual task of preparing an entrance examination required a great deal of work. And the job was duplicated at each university. In order to reduce the redundancy of test preparation and to standardise test content, the Ministry of Education and Culture decided in 1971 to prepare a nationwide general achievement test (*Exam* 1984) and this decision resulted in the *Kyotsu Ichiji Gakuryoku Shiken* or 'The Joint First Stage Achievement Test' (hereafter JFSAT). The test was not, however, actually administered until 1979.

There were a number of reasons for the delay. First, there was a practical administrative problem: time was needed not only for planning and development, but for the entire educational system to be given ample notification about the nature of the test. Then there were political and social factors. The relatively slow pace with which a standardised test was adopted was indicative that many universities, especially the highly ranked ones, preferred to maintain their autonomy. Fujita Hidenori, an assistant professor of sociology at the University of Tokyo, mentioned that many academics opposed the test and have become bitter that it was adopted without sufficient discussion (personal communication).

In spite of this, there were efforts to preserve university autonomy. For example, the JFSAT is called the Joint *First* Stage Achievement Test, and there does exist a 'second stage' test. The two tests were intended to be equal in value. This second test is prepared and administered by individual universities, usually by departments within each university. Depending on the preference of a particular university, this test can vary widely. For example, Kyoto University has administered a test that calls for writing essays, while the University of Tokyo has administered another general achievement test (Satø 1979).

The test is administered only once annually. The five sub-tests are administered over two days on the fourth Saturday and Sunday of January. Several weeks later, the 'second stage' test is administered. The test takers select only one university before taking the JFSAT, and the basis for their choice is usually the statistical information that is provided by mock tests prepared by private publishing houses.

Since 1987, there have been some reforms in this system to allow students more choice and to give universities more autonomy. Students can now take two 'second stage' tests, which means they can attempt to enter two government-sponsored universities instead of one. Each university now has the power to determine the relative value of the JFSAT and the 'second stage' test, so some universities focus on the JFSAT, others on the 'second stage' test.

This double-testing practice preserves a degree of autonomy for individual universities, but it places an additional burden on students. Several high-school teachers have suggested that capable students find this testing procedure too demanding, and as a consequence, many of these students opt for private universities whose examination procedures are less demanding. A private university may require testing in only two or three subjects, while the government-sponsored institutions require five subjects on the JFSAT followed by two 'second stage' tests. With the increasing affluence among many Japanese families, funding a college education at a private university is becoming less of a financial burden. As a result, some regional government-sponsored universities, which are traditionally less popular, have been given the right to require only certain subtests from the JFSAT, in a bid to compete with the private institutions.

The nature of the JFSAT

The JFSAT is an 'achievement' test, not an 'aptitude' test. There is a preference, in Japanese society, for achievement tests, since hard work and perseverance are generally valued above inherent ability. Japanese schools tend to be reluctant to measure a kind of ability one cannot work towards. After all, what is the good of inherent ability if the will does not exist to act on it? There is a tendency, for example, to regard scores on intelligence tests with scepticism (Dore 1967), although personality inventories have become popular in the corporate world.

Despite the fact that the JFSAT is written entirely in a multiple-choice format and is computer-scored, it cannot be called a standardised test in the strict sense. For example, when test takers receive their scores, they receive a raw score. The scores are not 'standardised' on to a normal curve and norm-referenced. One reason for not computing standard scores is the relative stability of the raw scores. The mean score from an annual number of about 360,000 test takers has only fluctuated between 607 and 636 (out of a total of 1000) between 1979 and 1985. The reason for this relative stability, suggests Nakajima Setsuo, of the Ministry of Education and Culture (personal communication), lies in the academically homogeneous test-taker population. He points out, by way of contrast, that the population taking the Scholastic Aptitude Test (SAT) in the United States is far more academically diverse.

Another difference from conventional standardised testing is the choice of test within the five sub-tests (Japanese, mathematics, science, social studies, and foreign language).[1] For example, within the science and social studies sub-tests, the test taker chooses two subjects from a list of five for each sub-test. Although this opportunity to choose a discipline – economics, for example, over political science – may be initially appealing, it leads to the psychometric problem of calibrating the results on different tests. By 1987, choice of test within most of the sub-tests had been eliminated, thus improving the reliability of the test.

A similar point can be made concerning item point values. The items on the Japanese language sub-test, for example, have different point values. Presumably the more difficult ones have a higher point value than the easier ones. On the reading comprehension item sets, for example, the main-idea items receive the highest point value. On the English sub-test, the items in the reading comprehension section have a higher point value than the grammar and vocabulary section. This reflects the high value placed on reading ability.

What makes the JFSAT akin to conventional standardised tests is its format and administration. The multiple-choice format has been adopted for the entire test. The test is prepared, distributed, and scored at a central location: the National Center for Entrance Examinations in Tokyo. This Center began operations in 1977 and moved into its present facility in 1981. According to Imada Osamu, the executive director, the Center possesses three Westinghouse 301 scanners, which makes it one of the largest test-processing institutions in the world (personal communication).

The JFSAT as textual communication

I would now like to examine the basic structure of communication surrounding the JFSAT. In examining this structure, I shall be drawing on the framework developed by Hymes (1974) and so shall first examine the participants – the test makers and the test takers – before moving on to consider sample English texts included in the JFSAT.

The test makers.   Communication on a standardised test involves two parties: those who prepare the test and those who are required to take it. Like any other communication through writing, the writer is normally not available when the reader reads. Although text usually possesses an identified writer, the writer of test material is almost never disclosed, presumably for security reasons. Moreover, test material is ordinarily not prepared by a single individual. Most standardised tests include material written by a number of writers. These writers include those working in either a full-time or a freelance capacity. This is the situation at large test publishers such as Recruit, Inc. in Japan and Educational Testing Service in the United States.

At the National Center for Entrance Examinations in Tokyo, however, the JFSAT is not written by professional or freelance writers, but rather by committees. These committees consist of faculty members selected from the government-sponsored universities that require the test. The members serve on the committee for a two-year term. Their identities are kept confidential: only the president and department head of their respective universities know about the appointment. Presumably the appointment does not involve a great deal of time or it would be difficult to keep it a secret.

There is one test preparation committee formed for each sub-test on the JFSAT. On the English sub-test, for example, there are sixteen members, of whom two are native speakers of English. It is not known how the members divide up the responsibility or decide which items to include. Furthermore, the role of the native speakers is not clearly defined. As one who not only served on an entrance examination committee at a private Japanese institution but even chaired it, I found working with such a committee extremely difficult. Often items were selected not because of their intrinsic worth but because of the status of the person who submitted them. At other times, a contribution would be accepted from all committee members, in spite of the quality, in order to make the test a product of group effort. Whether these kinds of social dynamics are at work on the JFSAT preparation committees is something that is not known. What we do know is that half of the committee members have already served for one year and the remainder consist of those who are new to the job. While the working relationships among the committee members may vary from year to year, the two-year appointment allows for some experience to be passed on.

The final responsibility for the test does not rest with the preparation committees. There is a further screening committee that approves the tests before they are printed. This screening committee consists of individuals who have finished their two-year term on one of the test preparation committees, and it is assumed that their experience will offer continuity and quality control to the test preparation process. Because the Center is unable to pre-test the JFSAT, due to security restrictions, the only way the quality of the test is maintained is by relying on the experience of the screening committee.

Although the JFSAT is supposedly an achievement test based on the high-school curriculum, high-school teachers are not appointed to these committees. The JFSAT is considered to be a university entrance examination, so it is not considered appropriate to include a high-school teacher on the committee. This excluding of high-school teachers is a further effort at preserving the universities' autonomy with respect to entrance examinations.

After the test is administered, it is evaluated in a number of ways. First, a group of university freshmen is asked to take the test in order to assess concurrent validity followed by studies assessing comparisons with past tests. Next, opinions are solicited from various high-school teachers' organisations. These opinions are submitted in the form of reports criticising various features of the test such as the construction of items, the appropriacy of reading passages, and most important of all, breaches in the syllabus. In response to these reports, the test preparation committees write their own reports explaining their reasons for preparing the test in the way they did. Sometimes they accept the criticisms and occasionally they even make apologies. At other times, they resolutely stick to what they have written. For example, regarding the reading comprehension item sets on both the English and Japanese sub-tests, the test makers consistently do not accept the criticism dealing with main-idea items. Criticism of this kind of item seems to strike a raw nerve, for it challenges the test makers' basic interpretation of the passages.

This exchange constitutes a kind of dialogue which is then compiled and published annually as *Kyotsu daiichiji gakuryoku shiken no shikenmondai ni kansuru iken-hyoka* ('Opinions and evaluations concerning the JFSAT test items'). This publication proved to be extremely useful here, for it provided direct access to the test makers' interpretation of the items they had prepared. It is difficult to ascertain the amount of influence reports by the high school organizations have on the preparation of the test. In my interviews at the Center, I was led to believe that they have little influence, that they constituted a formality. On close examination of reports over the years, and subsequent changes in the test, there is some evidence that the reports have made a difference. For instance, with respect to the two item-sets below, one contains only two items while the other one has four. This might not appear to be a matter of much consequence, but one high-school organisation criticised the test makers concerning this imbalance. Both passages are roughly the same length and it was suggested that an item-set with fewer items is generally more difficult. There was no response to this criticism in the test makers' report, yet on the JFSAT the following year, the two reading comprehension item-sets appeared with three items each.

The test takers.   Those who take the JFSAT are individuals who want to enter government-established institutions of higher learning. These institutions are generally regarded as the most prestigious ones, so the test takers tend to consider themselves good students. They are normally high-school seniors who have completed 12 years of schooling including 6 years of instruction in English. In addition, they include students who in past years have failed to receive a desired score. These students prepare for the test, usually at coaching schools called *juku*, for a year or even longer.

Rohlen (1983), in his study of selected Japanese high schools, observes that the pressure of preparing for the entrance examinations dominates high-school life, despite the opportunities provided by the schools for non-academic activities. Although most entrance examinations follow the high-school curriculum closely, Cummings (1980) has observed that the high-school curriculum is so broad that teachers have difficulty covering the material, much less reviewing it. If parents are serious about their children entering a prestigious university, they will send them to after-school and holiday coaching schools. Students are under a great deal of pressure to complete the homework and then attend the *juku*. At these schools, students receive highly targeted special instruction and take frequent mock tests that are followed by detailed lectures analysing the tests and delineating the appropriate strategies for passing them. Moreover, students are informed, on the basis of their mock test scores, as to the probability of their gaining admission to particular universities. Often because the *juku* addresses specifically the issue of passing the entrance examinations, students take them more seriously than their regular high-school courses.

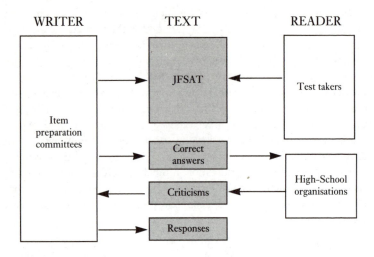

Figure 3.1 Communication surrounding the JFSAT

The intensity with which many students prepare for the entrance examinations has resulted in a number of negative social effects. Because there is little time left for social and sports activities, feelings of frustration have been found among young people. Sometimes these frustrations have been expressed in school violence and suicides (Yoshiya 1983, pp. 3–7). It goes without saying that the test preparation industry reflects economic inequalities in education: high-quality coaching is available only to those who can afford it.

In spite of these problems, there is little effort towards adopting alternatives. Procedures like interviews and letters of recommendation are considered to be more open to abuse. Entrance to a leading university is such an important factor in society, that a common examination is still the preferred practice (Taylor 1983).

Figure 3.1 is a summary diagram of the various groups involved in making and taking the test.

Sample texts. The English sub-test of the JFSAT contains items dealing with grammar, vocabulary, and paraphrase, in addition to reading comprehension; the items in the reading comprehension section have a higher point value than the others. For example, the comprehension items are worth 8 points whereas a grammar item can be worth as little as 3 points. In effect, reading skills are more highly valued. With this in mind, let us now turn to the kind of texts used as test passages.

In analysing the passages, the first task is to discover their origins. In the case of the Japanese sub-test, the passages include a reference to their sources. By doing some library research, I was able to locate the original texts and analyse how the passages were extracted from them (Ingulsrud 1988). Hill and Larsen (1983) refer to such passages as 'excerpted text' and point out how difficult it is for such text to be sufficiently self-contained. One passage, for instance, consisted of a whole subsection from a chapter of a book but appeared on the test without the sub-section heading. The key to one of the main-idea items referred to information in the heading. Hence the test taker lacked what would be a crucial element in ordinary reading. In spite of the problems that arise from using excerpted material, many test makers still prefer to do so. They select from a number of different genres in order to increase the face validity of the test (Walsh and Betz 1985). The obvious difficulty they face is to find short passages that are sufficiently self-contained.

Additional problems arise when passages are adapted. Most borrowed material has to be adapted in order to remove what might be considered racist and sexist language; or it is simplified because of syllabus restrictions in syntax and vocabulary. Once the adaptation process begins, however, problems inevitably arise. To begin with, writers have ordinarily woven the text in such a way that its syntax and vocabulary serve highly particular functions. Any adaptation, no matter how slight, may introduce problems that test makers cannot properly foresee.

Unlike the material for the Japanese sub-test, the passages on the English sub-test appear to have been written expressly for the test. Not only do they contain no references to outside sources, but they reflect stylistic features that seem to be Japanese.

Let us now examine the two item-sets from the 1986 version of the JFSAT. The first deals with ecological problems in the modern world, the second with the difficulty of understanding a familiar proverb in English. These topics are fairly typical of what appears on the English sub-test. In the case of the first passage, its topic is considered appropriate since it deals with science. One reason for the popularity of passages that deal with scientific content is that they are thought to be more neutral and thus more accessible to a diverse population. The scientifically oriented passage is as follows:

It is only during the last few years that man has become generally aware that in the world of nature a most delicate balance exists between all forms of life. No living thing can exist by itself: it is part of a system in which all forms of life are joined together. If we change one part of the natural order, this will in its turn almost certainly bring about changes in some other part.

The cutting down of forests reduces the supply of oxygen. The killing of weeds and insects by chemicals leads to the wide-spread poisoning of animals and birds. The throwing of waste products into the ocean damages life in the sea, while exhaust fumes change the chemical balance of the atmosphere and shut out some of the sun's essential life-giving rays.

And so we could go on, adding more examples, until in despair we might feel like giving up the struggle to control and keep within limits these harmful human activities. Man is very clever at changing the world around him to satisfy his immediate needs, but he is not so clever at looking far ahead, or at thinking about what the future results of his actions might be. Man may well, in his attempt to be too ambitious, destroy himself.

1. The examples given in the second paragraph are used as evidence

(A)   that it is only during the last few years that man has generally become aware of the balance of nature

(B)   that there are some living things which can exist all by themselves without change

(C)   that all forms of life belong to a system in which all the parts can be changed for one another

(D)   that we cannot affect one form of life or matter without disturbing the balance of nature.

2. The final paragraph suggests that, in his attempt to increase his immediate benefits,

(A)   man often fails to think about their future effects

(B)   man is always too ambitious in planning for his distant future

(C)   man often feels he will have to give up in despair

(D)   man is always anxious to control and keep his activities within limits.

(*Showa 61 nendo kyotsu ichiji shiken mondai shokai*, 1986b, pp. 9-10)

Appropriate material is a major concern for test makers in Japan. There are no clearly stated guidelines, but from my experience as an item writer for entrance examinations, it is considered proper to avoid subject-matter that is politically or socially controversial. Furthermore, passages that contain cultural information should be limited to information about Japan or any of the major English-speaking countries of the world, ordinarily Britain or the United States. The National Center for University Entrance Examination has prepared an internal mimeographed document called *Daigaku nyugakusha sembatsu kyotsu daiichiji gakuryoku shiken shiken mondai sakusei no gaiyo* ('The outline for the university applicant selection JFSAT test item construction'). According to this document, content for English passages is not restricted. The document does caution test writers that if ideological material is used, it should be written from a public perspective in an educational manner.

It is this 'educational manner' that sets the tone for many of the passages in English. They not only inform readers but often take the opportunity to admonish them. Consider, for example, the last two sentences in the passage presented above:

Man is very clever at changing the world around him to satisfy his immediate needs, but he is not so clever at looking far ahead, or at thinking about what the future results of his actions might be. Man may well, in his attempt to be too ambitious, destroy himself.

It seems as though the reader is being chided. This kind of moralising is not restricted to the 1986 test. All the JFSAT papers since 1979 contain passages expressing either admonition or disappointment about a particular state of affairs; this is particularly evident in the long passage on each test. In the 1985 test, for example, there is a passage about the sale of antique and second-hand goods in England. It ends with a remark that can be interpreted as reproving contemporary Japanese for their trendiness:

> In Britain, people do not buy something just because it is new. Old things are treasured for their proven worth; new things have to prove themselves before they are accepted. (Saita 1985, p. 18)

It is of interest that such moralising is not found on the Japanese sub-test. The Japanese passages, extracted from natural text, reflect a level of literary sophistication that would make such moralising seem simplistic. Perhaps on a foreign language test, where syntactic and vocabulary constraints are more of an issue, the material chosen for the passages tends to be more simplistic and thus allows for such moralising.

Let us turn to the other passage on the 1986 JFSAT English sub-test:

> There is a well-known saying that everyone seems to know – and that many people use, often mistakenly: the exception proves the rule.
> Today, the word 'prove' is chiefly used in one sense only: that is, to show clearly that something is true. As a result, many people these days seem to believe that for a rule to be true there has to be an exception. 'Ah, that is the exception that proves the rule,' they cry when someone points it out to them, and suppose that the exception is a proof of the truth of the rule. This is nonsense, for what an exception proves – in today's limited sense of the word – is that the rule cannot be true in all cases.
> One of the several meanings of 'to prove' has always been 'to test'. If you put something to the proof, you test it. Something that is 'waterproof', for instance, has been tested and found not to let water in; if a watch lets water in when it has been tested, it will be set aside as an exception. Watches that have passed the test, though, can then be depended upon.
> An exception will, in fact, test a rule. If there are exceptions, however, a rule cannot be taken as being universally true – nor should the saying be taken to mean, as it so often is these days, that for a rule to be true there has to be an exception. Only after the exception has been set aside, can we depend upon the rule and then use it.

1. According to this passage, the saying, the *exception proves the rule*, tells us

(A)   that all exceptions to a rule can be depended upon
(B)   that for a rule to be true it must have one exception
(C)   that the truth of a rule will be tested by an exception
(D)   that any rule needs an exception before it can be proved to be true.

2. If a room is 'sound-proof', we can suppose

(A)   that sound is easily able to pass into or out of the room
(B)   that sound cannot pass into or out of the room
(C)   that people will not be able to hear anything at all within the room
(D)   that people in the room will have to work in silence.

3. A rule can be thought to be universally true

(A)   only if no exception can be found to it
(B)   only if there is at least one exception to prove its truth
(C)   only if it is put to the proof and found in most cases to be true
(D)   only if we find out that it can never be put to the proof

4. One conclusion the writer seems to suggest is

(A)   that some sayings are sometimes exceptions to the rule
(B)   that we must always try to use old sayings in present-day circumstances
(C)   that well-known sayings often prove to be excellent guides in daily life
(D)   that when we use familiar sayings we should think hard about what they
      mean.

(*Showa 61 nendo kyotsu ichiji shiken mondai shokai*, 1986b, pp. 10-11)

This passage had mixed reviews by the high-school critics. Some felt
that this kind of passage was appropriate, especially for the final item-set
(suggesting that the English sub-test should end on a difficult note).
Another report, however, called this passage an *akubun* ('wicked text'),
because the point of the text is deliberately obscured.

Several Japanese adults whom I interviewed, observed that this
passage was probably written by a Japanese rather than a native speaker
of English.[2] One test taker explained her reasons for this observation in
detail. Her first reason was the condescending style in which the material
was presented. The passage dealt with a mistake, according to the writer,
that Japanese people make in English. She, however, felt that the text
was not difficult. In fact, she thought it was like reading Japanese. When
I asked her for her reason, she said:

The passage is arranged as *ki-sho-ten-ketsu*, so it doesn't flow in an American
manner.

Ki-sho-ten-ketsu is a traditional rhetorical pattern in Japanese writing.
In this kind of rhetorical pattern, *ki* introduces the topic; *sho* develops it;
ten introduces a related but tangential topic; *ketsu* ties all the topics
together (Hinds 1983). This pattern originated as a poetic style in China
during the Tang and Song Dynasties and subsequently was borrowed by

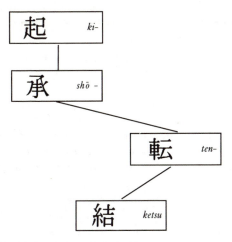

Figure 3.2 The *ki-sho-ten-ketsu* rhetorical pattern

the Japanese. It was often used as a pattern for making chain poems among drinking courtiers, and as a result, its origins are in the oral tradition. In the last hundred years, the pattern has been applied to expository writing (Kobayashi 1984).

This four-part pattern fits rather neatly with the four paragraphs of this passage. In the first paragraph (*ki*), the proverb is introduced. The reader is also informed that the proverb is misunderstood – the theme of the passage. The second paragraph (*sho*) explains a possible reason for the common misunderstanding, the different ways of interpreting the word 'prove'. It thus develops what was presented in the first paragraph. In fact, this second paragraph actually suggests a solution to the problem of an appropriate understanding – the exception does not prove the truth of the rule, but the fact that it cannot be applied absolutely. Thus, the passage could have ended here. A kind of red herring is, however, presented in the third paragraph (*ten*). The proverb itself is not referred to, but rather an explanation, with an example, of another sense of 'prove'. It is not entirely clear, at this point in the passage, how this explanation relates to the proverb at hand. The final paragraph (*ketsu*) does finally relate the explanation to the theme; it does so by pointing out that this special meaning of 'prove' is, in fact, the key to understanding the proverb.

Although the origin of the English passages is not known, the moralising style and the native-language rhetorical pattern suggest that they may well have been written for the test. While the inclusion of such texts might avoid the problems associated with adapting excerpted text, they obviously create new problems of their own: students are forced to read unnatural English text, which, of course, calls into question the face validity of the test. We should, however, bear in mind that the JFSAT is, in a very real sense, an achievement test, and these kinds of passages may represent rather well the material used in Japanese schools.

Conclusions

An examination system was originally developed in ancient China to select the most able individuals for positions of leadership in government. A primary motivation for developing the system was to provide a means of selection that could operate independently of traditional means such as family influence. The system was thus designed to provide a check on abuses such as nepotism and corruption that had become widespread throughout the empire.

This examination system, from our modern perspective, would be best described as oriented towards achievement rather than intrinsic ability. Candidates were expected to spend many years mastering not only a prescribed set of Confucian texts but a strict essay form that they were to use in writing their exams. We can surmise that this focus on achievement was important in ancient China, for it meant that, in principle, any individual, with hard work, could be successful in the exams. Moreover, it meant that individuals, who lacked certain physical abilities, such as horsemanship, could still take part in the exams. In this way, the system was opened up to a much wider population and could thus be perceived in the larger society as a more equitable means of selecting individuals for the civil service.

This examination system eventually spread to many different parts of the world and is considered one of the major legacies of ancient China. It has had a particularly long history of influence in Japan. At various periods of its history, Japan maintained some form of a civil service examination system transplanted from China. In the last 100 years, however, this system has been gradually eclipsed by entrance examinations to major universities; and in the last 20 years a single entrance examination to the most prestigious universities has emerged. This exam, known as the Joint First Stage Achievement Test (JFSAT), serves much the same function that civil service examinations once did. In selecting individuals for major universities, it ensures that they will one day occupy positions of leadership in the society. The particular university that students attend has a great deal to do with their career. A prestigious university does not necessarily offer a high-quality education, but it does ensure access to an extensive alumni network for job placement and advancement.

In modern Japan, the JFSAT serves much the same function that the civil service examinations did in ancient China – providing an independent means of selecting individuals for important positions. They are considered to be much less subject to abuse than other means of selection such as interviews and letters of recommendation. At the same time, the JFSAT emphasises achievement rather than ability. It is designed to measure qualities such as hard work and perseverance. Indeed, from the Japanese perspective a quality such as innate ability can be viewed as somewhat nebulous. The preference for achievement-oriented exams provided one of the two major rationales for initially developing the JFSAT. Perhaps the primary reason was efficiency: a single exam would lighten the burden on individual universities since each had to prepare and administer its own exam. At the same time, the JFSAT was developed to be more closely aligned with the high-school curriculum.

In spite of this effort, the National Center of University Entrance Examination does not invite high-school teachers to participate in preparing the JFSAT. The test is ultimately considered a university entrance examination and so only university faculty are viewed as appropriate for this task. This seeming élitism is one way in which the government-sponsored universities, which use the JFSAT, have sought to protect their autonomy from encroaching government bureaucracies. Another way they have maintained their autonomy is to require a 'second stage' test prepared by individual universities. This double testing has, however, proved burdensome, and many capable high-school students, instead of submitting to this process, have begun to opt for private universities, which, with the exception of half a dozen or so, are generally considered less prestigious than the government-sponsored ones. The new affluence in Japan enables them to attend these private universities even though they are rather costly. Some government-sponsored universities have been forced to respond by giving less weight to one or other of the two tests, depending on what each university perceives as its best interest. In this way, they are attempting to lure back some of the more capable students.

For students who are serious about entering a highly ranked university, a considerable amount of coaching is normal in preparing for the entrance examination. High-school students spend evenings, weekends, and even vacations preparing for the test at the various *juku* that provide a range of coaching services. Supplemental education of this kind costs a good deal of money, and yet students and their families are willing to make such sacrifices. If they do well on the JFSAT, for example, they are assured of a place in a prestigious university, which, in turn, leads to a successful career in business or government. One is reminded of the situation in ancient China where candidates would spend long years and considerable sums of money in preparation for the civil service exams.

It has been shown that the *juku* are effective in preparing students for the test. If they pass the test, however, does this necessarily indicate that they are able to perform the tasks ahead? According to the well-known Chinese writer Lu Xun, the civil service examinations in China were not relevant. Even at the beginning of this century, they still required students to master the Confucian classics. For Lu Xun, mastery of such material bore little relation to the tasks of running a modern state. The final years of the Chinese civil service examinations – they ended in 1905 – exemplify particularly vivid contradictions between exam material and the realities faced by those who passed it; and yet test makers in all societies are faced with some form of this contradiction – just what is the relation between the test material and what individuals are expected to do? Indeed, the problems of predictive validity are among the most intractable that test makers must deal with.

In the case of the JFSAT, various subject areas are tested to ensure that those who enter university possess a certain level of general knowledge. Moreover, it is designed to ensure a certain level of reading competence in both the native language and a foreign language – ordinarily English. This commitment to biliteracy is apparently based on the contemporary demands of Japanese society. On the Japanese sub-test, for instance, literary and scholarly texts are included, perhaps appropriately predicting the kind of material that students will have to read in university and beyond. On the English sub-test, however, the gap seems to be greater between the test material and what students will be expected to read. The passages included on the test often do not resemble what can be found in books or periodicals. Rather, they seem to form a peculiar genre of their own, one that reflects a good deal of Japanese influence. They include not only overall rhetorical patterns such as *ki-sho-ten-ketsu* but particular kinds of content such as the moralising statements often used to bring closure in Japanese writing. Such hybrid writing calls for a peculiar kind of biliteracy, one in which students have to manage Japanese rhetorical patterns within English texts.

It is not altogether clear why such texts end up on the English sub-test, but they may, to some degree, simply be a by-product of the test-making process itself. As committee members work together, they may be forced to work out compromises that lead to hybrid texts. My own experience on entrance exam committees in Japan provides certain evidence for this view: it is as if multiple authors were being forced to write a single short story together.

Despite these problems in the test-making process, mechanisms have been set up to deal with them. A screening committee made up of former test preparation committee members must approve the test. Since there is no pretesting process, the quality of the test is very much dependent on the experience of the committee members. There exists another, perhaps even more significant, mechanism of quality control: each year organisations of high-school teachers are set up to review the test after it is administered (as mentioned, these teachers are not allowed to serve on the test-making committee itself). After these organisations submit their reports, the test makers are required to respond to them. This exchange, at times, smacks of mere formality, but it is clear that certain of the teachers' suggestions have been implemented on subsequent tests. Hence, this process of review may be viewed as constituting a kind of public dialogue around the exam. Many other societies are now attempting to create such public discourse and could profit from examining the institutional form that it has taken around the JFSAT. Certainly such dialogue is vital in helping to achieve the goal of those who first introduced the civil service examination system in imperial China – to develop an independent and equitable means of selecting individuals for responsible positions in society.

Acknowledgement

I would like to thank the National Center for University Entrance Examination in Tokyo for kindly providing information regarding the construction, administration, and research of the Joint First Stage Achievement Test.

Notes

1. Close to 99 per cent choose English, even though a test in German or French can be chosen.
2. The individuals that I interviewed were not drawn from the target population (i.e. those who are preparing for university entrance examinations). It would have been easy to find high-school students in Japan to interview, since there is so much public interest in the JFSAT. It would not have been easy, however, to find students who had not studied past tests of the JFSAT, particularly the English sub-test. The JFSAT becomes a public-domain document once it is administered. In fact, the test items are printed in the major newspapers the day after it is administered. Consequently, past tests are available for study, even for those students bound for private universities.

4 The test and the text: readers in a Nigerian secondary school

Kate Parry

A major legacy of colonial rule in Africa has been a division of each national economy into a traditional rural sector that depends mainly on subsistence farming and a modern urban sector that provides opportunities for salaried employment. For several generations, ambitious young people have sought to move from the first to the second, and the main route by which they have done so has been western education. The evidence of this education is in certificates issued to those who have passed exams at various levels, the most important of which are the exams taken at the end of secondary school. In anglophone West Africa these exams are collectively known as the West African School Certificate, or WASC, and are closely modelled on the School Certificate exams that used to be administered by the Cambridge University Local Examinations Syndicate. Though the WASC can be taken in a number of different subjects, by far the most important is English Language; it is the one subject that all students must pass in order to be admitted to a college or university or, indeed, to be eligible for many jobs – reasonably enough, it would seem, since English, throughout anglophone Africa, is the lingua franca of the modern sector.

A failure in the English Language is therefore tantamount to a failure in education more generally, and there is accordingly great concern where large numbers of students do not pass this exam. Such is the situation in northern Nigeria: by the late 1970s and early 1980s pass rates were regularly less than 30 per cent. Such poor performance was recognised as a serious problem, and there were frequent lamentations in the newspapers about the 'declining standard of education', but there was no investigation of what these results meant in terms of students' actual competence, particularly as readers. Why did students do so badly? Was it that they simply could not read – or could not read in English – at all? Or was it rather that they could not handle the particular demands of the test? And was the students' acquisition of literate skills hampered by specifically linguistic difficulties as well as by the obvious administrative ones occasioned by the rapid expansion of the education system? In this chapter I report a study that attempted to address these questions. It was an examination of the interaction between a group of Northern Nigerian students and a selection of texts that represented the reading components of the WASC English Language exam.

Methodology

The study was conducted at Saint Peter's Seminary, a small secondary school run by the Roman Catholic mission in Yola, Gongola State,[1] for boys who were considering becoming priests. There were major advantages in doing the research at this school: Saint Peter's could give me smaller classes and a lighter teaching load than any other school in the region, and I already knew the students, having taught them four years previously, in 1979–80, when they were in Form 1. Moreover, since I had also trained primary and secondary school teachers in the area, I was familiar with the education system through which the students had been taught, and I knew many of the small towns and villages in which they lived before they came to Saint Peter's. Thus, even before I started, I had considerable background information about the students whose reading I was about to examine. This information was supplemented by data collected specifically for the project. I interviewed all the students individually, with the help of a questionnaire, to find out basic facts about the languages they customarily used at home and the extent of their exposure to English texts; I asked them to keep journals of their activities, especially of their reading, during their Christmas holidays; and I assigned, as part of their regular work for English, essays about their lives at home and at school. Finally, I consulted the school's records, and, wherever possible, visited the students in their homes during the school holidays. These various forms of data helped me to construct a detailed if not complete picture of the knowledge the students were bringing to bear on the material they were given to read.

As for the texts, they were selected from the most recent past exam papers and were of two kinds. First were what I shall call *comprehension units*, each of which consisted of a short passage (about 200 words) together with tasks directed at the meaning of particular words or phrases; there were two such units on each exam, but we dealt with them in class only one at a time. Second were what I shall call *summary units*, each of which consisted of a longer passage (about 500 words) and tasks eliciting its main points; there was only one such unit on each exam. The tasks were always open-ended, so that students had to produce a good deal of language to deal with them in either type of unit. Every week I administered one of these units to the students as practice for the exam, alternating between comprehension and summary types. During these practice sessions, exam conditions were replicated as closely as possible: no dictionaries were allowed, there was, of course, no talking, and the time was limited to about what they would have available in the WASC (20 minutes for a comprehension unit and 40 for a summary). The students wrote their answers in duplicate, using carbon paper, so that I was able to mark the copy and return it while retaining the original for further study; they also recorded any words from the passage that were new to them, initially on their answer sheets and then later by handing in their question papers with the words underlined. I marked their answers immediately, using a marking scheme that I devised on the basis of experience with similar exams. The answers were recorded, in abbreviated form, in a notebook so that different students' responses could be easily compared.

The next stage of the weekly routine was interviewing the students individually. All were invited for interviews, and to begin with everyone came; at a later stage numbers fell off somewhat, but until the very last session there were never fewer than four students who discussed their answers with me. Each interview lasted about half an hour, and the general pattern was as follows:

1. The student read the passage aloud; I noted all instances of miscues, hesitation, and self-correction.
2. The student was asked to comment on the unit: how difficult it was and whether there were any words or phrases that caused particular problems.
3. We went over the questions together, with the student giving his answers orally (they usually corresponded to what he had written down, although I did not at that point let him see his answer sheet); and he explained as best he could how he had come to each answer. If he had difficulty in doing this in English I would invite him to use Hausa, which was a second language for all the students and the one they most commonly used among themselves.

Notes were made during the interview and it was also recorded on tape for subsequent transcription.

Sometimes in the course of the interviews a point would come up that suggested a general difficulty. In such cases I would conduct a small experiment with the whole class by requesting the students to give a written answer to a question that focused on the problem under consideration. I would also occasionally do such experiments before presenting a unit if I anticipated a general problem. Then, as a pedagogical follow-up, I would invariably go over the tasks in class: we would construct a set of answers together, and these would be written on the board for the students to copy down in notebooks supplied for the purpose. From the students' point of view this may have been the most important aspect of the project, for this was how they developed new techniques for responding to the various kinds of task.

More important from the point of view of a researcher, however, was the analysis of the data that had been collected. This was done under four headings: *lexis, syntax, rhetorical structure*, and *schemata*, each being taken as a different level of processing – although an important theme of the study was the constant and complex interaction between them. Under the first heading, the texts themselves were put through a computer program that identified any lexical item that was not on the General Service List (West 1964; the program was devised by Kenneth Cripwell at the Institute of Education, London University); and the results were compared with the students' own statements about which words had caused them difficulty. Then, under the second heading, the texts were subjected to a syntactic analysis that enabled me to measure the length of T-units and constituents at the sentence level, as well as of sentences as such; it also showed what was the dominant sentence pattern in any particular passage, and pointed up any sentences that were irregular or unusual (the syntactic model used was *sector analysis*, as described by Allen (1972) and Deakins (1985)). Again, the results of this analysis were compared with whatever syntactic difficulties had been suggested by what the students had written or said. The texts were also examined in terms of their rhetorical structure, especially as indicated by an analysis of their cohesion (Halliday and Hasan 1976), and the students' responses were studied to see whether the rhetorical structure had been apparently perceived and used. Finally, under the heading of *schemata*, the assumptions underlying the texts were considered in relation to those that the students seemed to be making; and a factor borne in mind throughout the analysis was how such high-level schemata interacted with the interpretation – or misinterpretation – of low-level linguistic cues.

The results of the whole study are reported elsewhere (Parry 1986). Here I shall concentrate on just two texts, one intended to test comprehension, and the other to test summary skills. These texts are particularly interesting because their subject-matter – reading in the one and writing in the other – is precisely those skills that the English Language exam is meant to assess. So discussion of the passages produced interesting remarks from the students about what they thought was involved in reading and in writing, and what they considered to be their own difficulties with text.

A comprehension unit: Reading

The text

The *Reading* comprehension passage and the items that go with it are as follows:

> Private solitary reading, which takes in words through the eye <u>at a fast rate</u>, is obviously very well suited for many kinds of material. Newspaper articles, for example, are written to be <u>gulped down in this fashion</u>; taken slowly, they become <u>intolerable</u>. But the more meat there is in what we read, the less <u>effective</u> we find this <u>silent skimming</u>. In a novel, for instance, we read fast and silently during long stretches, but at <u>crucial</u> moments – during important dialogue or memorable description – we slow down to something approaching the speed of the speaking voice. Nobody tells us to do this; we do it because, if we are enjoying the story, and <u>imaginatively entering the author's world</u>, we need to savour what he is giving us.

(a) Replace the following with words or phrases that mean the same and will fit in the context:
    (i)   at a fast rate
    (ii)   gulped down
    (iii) in this fashion
    (iv) intolerable
    (v)   effective
    (vi) crucial.

(b) Quote, from the passage, the three words that suggest that reading provides food for the mind.

(c) State in your own words two reasons why one will read slowly, according to the writer.

(d) What do you think the writer means by:
    (i)   silent skimming
    (ii)   imaginatively entering the author's world?

This passage, taken from the November 1981 exam, is typical of those used for the WASC comprehension units. To consider it first at the lexical level, it consists of 136 words, as compared to an average length of 192 over all the comprehension passages studied. Of these words, 17, or 12.5 per cent, are outside the General Service List; this proportion is close to the average for all the comprehension passages in the corpus – and it is noticeably higher than the 9.3 per cent found in the London newspaper, *The Times* (Cripwell 1984). The implication is that, considered in terms of one major factor in readability formulae (Klare 1963), this comprehension passage, like others in the corpus, is difficult. But a frequency count alone is an inadequate indicator of lexical difficulty, for often the most serious problems arise from frequent, and therefore familiar, items that are used in unusual and therefore unfamiliar ways. In this passage there are several instances of such usage, for there is a large number of common words that are used figuratively. There are three metaphors, the first being based on the image of food: reading, we are told, is an activity which 'takes in' words, newspaper articles are 'gulped down', but sometimes a text may contain 'meat', in which case readers will want to 'savour' it. Then there is the travelling metaphor: reading may progress 'at a fast rate' or 'slowly', it may continue over 'long stretches', the reader may 'slow down' and 'approach the speed of the speaking voice', and is likely to do this especially if 'entering the author's world'. Finally there is the central word of the whole passage – 'skimming' – though the image on which it draws, skimming milk, is not a familiar one to modern readers. The use of metaphor like this is not at all unusual in these comprehension passages – of the seven examined for this study there was only one that did not have at least one instance of such figurative language.

In syntax, also, the passage is not unusual for the WASC. The sentences are long, certainly, with an average length of 27.2 words, but this is typical, the average over all the comprehension passages being 27.1 words. The long constituents, like the subject of the first sentence ('solitary silent reading, which takes in words through the eye at a fast rate') and the adverbial clause at the end of the last ('because, if we are enjoying the story, and imaginatively entering the author's world, we need to savour what he is giving us') are again not unusual. Also characteristic of the whole corpus are the long inserts, such as 'during important dialogue or memorable description', that are included in this passage. These are all features of a complex and formal, even hyperliterate, style which the writers of the WASC seem to think are important for the students to be able to interpret. Again, passages in this corpus often contain, as this one does, a central sentence that follows an unusual pattern:

> But the more meat there is in what we read the less effective we find this silent skimming.

Here the normal order of syntactic constituents is reversed; it is the only sentence of this particular pattern in the entire corpus, but it is far from being the only unusual one used.

This sentence is significant not only because of its own structure but also because it marks a turning point in the rhetorical structure of the whole passage. An analysis of the cohesion shows that the passage is clearly divided into two parts. The first presents the notion of reading fast: 'solitary silent reading, which takes in words through the eye at a fast rate'. This notion is picked up in the following sentence by 'newspaper articles, for example, are written to be read in this fashion'. Then, with the sentence quoted above, the idea of 'this silent skimming' is rejected, the rejection being signalled by the contrastive 'but', and the unusual structure of the sentence itself gives added emphasis to the point (consider how much weaker it would be if phrased, 'But if there is meat in what we read we do not find this silent skimming effective'). The next sentence exemplifies this point: 'In a novel, for instance ...', and the remainder of the passage is devoted to the idea of reading slowly. Obviously, to obtain a clear representation of how the passage works as a whole, it is necessary to appreciate the significance of the conjunctive and reference items by which its rhetorical structure is marked, and particularly to understand that central sentence which can be described as a hinge on which the whole passage depends. But that sentence may be the most difficult, both in its complex parallel construction and in its balancing of a positive statement against a negative one; and it also employs two of those metaphors on which I have already commented. On the other hand, if the structure and the cohesive signals are correctly perceived, many of the potential lexical problems are solved: 'silent skimming', for example, is explained, for those who can use the clue, by the anaphoric reference, signalled by 'this', to 'solitary silent reading which takes in words through the eye at a fast rate'.

So much for what can be seen in the surface structure of the text; but equally important are the ideas underlying it, for, as studies of schema theory have shown, if these ideas run counter to readers' expectations, the text will be extremely difficult for them to interpret. In this case, the passage is about an activity that is necessarily familiar to anybody reading it; it can therefore be expected, if understood at all, to evoke associations based on the reader's previous experience with text. Such experience, however, varies from one culture to another, and it will be noticed that this passage represents the perspective of a culture that is deeply influenced by print. It refers to many different kinds of reading material, assuming a diversity that has only been made possible by the printing press; it deals particularly with newspapers and novels, both of which owe their development to the technology of printing; and it states that much of this material deserves only cursory treatment – an attitude that might be considered impious in a society where written material is not readily available. Thus while the content of this passage is obviously based on an activity familiar to the students for whom it is intended, it is expressing an attitude towards that activity which, while deeply embedded in mainstream English-speaking cultures, is not necessarily shared by all those who use writing.

The passage, however, is not the whole text: in a reading test the passage must be considered in conjunction with the tasks, for these will condition its reading, and the necessity to produce tasks may strongly influence its writers, the test makers, as well. Certainly, this passage looks as if it was written specifically for the exam, for it is hard to imagine such a text as part of a larger whole; and all the other comprehension passages in the corpus are similarly self-contained. Further, it is a striking fact that those features that make the passage unusual are precisely those points on which tasks have been set. At the lexical level, for instance, the ability to process the metaphors is explicitly called for: (a) (ii) requires the students to provide a substitute for 'gulped down' – presumably an answer such as 'taken in' or 'read' is expected, rather than the more literal 'swallowed'; in (b), on the other hand, the students are asked to interpret the images in their literal sense, so as to provide 'gulped', 'meat', and 'savour'. Such metaphors and idioms are a regular feature of WASC comprehension passages, and where they are included there are invariably corresponding tasks. As for the other tasks, (a) (iv), (v), and (vi) all require the replacement of low-frequency vocabulary, thus emphasising those words that the students are least likely to know; the effect is likely to be a fragmented view of the text, as a collection of words which the reader may or may not be fortunate enough to have come across before. Tasks (c) and (d) are more holistic, but there are problems with these too. In the case of (c), which requires the student to 'state ... two reasons why one will read slowly, according to the writer', there are more than two possible answers:

– because there is important dialogue
– because there is memorable description
– because we are enjoying the story
– because we are imaginatively entering the author's world.

It is impossible even for an accomplished test taker to tell which two the test maker had in mind. As for (d), while part (i), which asks for an explanation of 'silent skimming', can be answered correctly if the cohesive cues are used, it does, like all of question (a), target a possible vocabulary problem, and so may encourage much more low-level processing; and part (ii) requires the explanation of 'imaginatively' entering the author's world – yet another metaphor, though one that seems less contrived and may be more easily related to the student's own experience.

Altogether the tasks on this passage seem designed to turn the act of reading into a puzzle whereby one targets certain low-level elements of the text and either shows one's knowledge of possible substitutes or else uses the clues provided by such elements to explain other individual words or phrases. There is little opportunity to show an understanding of the text as a whole. Again, this is characteristic of the comprehension units throughout the corpus. 'Comprehension' seems to be understood by the test makers as being primarily knowledge of individual (and usually infrequent) words, knowledge that includes the ability to provide syntactically correct substitutes and to interpret figurative extensions of meaning. Even those items that allow of a more holistic response emphasise the use of particular signals of cohesion rather than the construction of what have been called macro-propositions (Van Dijk 1977). So this comprehension unit is, in effect, assessing reading of a specialised kind – one that is, I might add, totally different from either of those described in the passage.

The students' responses

Having considered the text, let us now turn to its readers. As test takers they performed badly: of the 16 who did this exercise, only 2 scored more than half marks, and the average score was 25 per cent. These scores were not unusual. Although there was some improvement in the course of this project (the average score for the last of the comprehension units was 33 per cent) the students were never able as a group to do particularly well; and on those few occasions when I was able to administer the same unit to a parallel class in another school, the results were not very different. The message that these students were conveying to the test makers was that they were, effectively, illiterate in English. Was this an accurate representation? And if it was not, why was such a distorted message getting through?

That all the Saint Peter's students could 'read' in the sense that they could render orally what was written on the page, there was no doubt: in this passage, as in others, there were occasional mispronunciations and miscues – reading 'saviour' for 'savour', for instance – but basically there was no problem, to use Kenneth Goodman's term, with orally 'recoding' the text (1967, p. 13). There were, however, numerous problems with lexis. In this passage, as in others, most of the students found three or four words they did not know: of the 10 who were interviewed only one claimed to have seen them all before. Among the 9 others there was also considerable unanimity as to which words constituted the problem: 'crucial' was identified by them all, 'gulped' and 'skimming' by 8 of them, and 'solitary' by 5. There is thus one simple explanation for the students' poor performance in tasks (a) (ii), (a) (vi) and (d) (i); they could not supply appropriate substitutes or definitions because they did not know the words.

But the problems at the lexical level were not confined to the fact that some of the words – admittedly important ones – were unfamiliar. The interviews showed that for several students quite as many difficulties arose from the words they did know as from those they did not. One student, for example, was totally mystified by the passage's use of the word 'meat'. 'Is the spelling correct?' he asked, 'M-E-A-T? ... It made the sentence ununderstandable for me.' The fact that he could translate 'meat' correctly as the Hausa 'nama' was no help at all, for he evidently could not see any connection between 'nama' and reading. For other students 'meat' itself was not such a problem – they interpreted it figuratively as 'important points' – but 'effective', appearing in the same sentence, proved very hard to interpret. There were none who said they did not know this word, but the limits of their knowledge were suggested by the examples they gave of its use, as well as by their answers to item (a) (v). One, for example, said of the word,

> This 'effective' is an adjective of the word 'effect'. Then 'with an effect from – with an effect the staff – will have meeting – on Monday'.

He had obviously heard the expression 'with effect from (a certain time)', but this knowledge was not much help in interpreting the word as used here. But he quickly realised this point and so tried to think of 'a better example':

> This 'effect', 'effective', it may have different – many meanings. 'Effect' on the other hand can mean what happened to something that resulted to something. 'The less effective we find this silent skimming' – the less problem we find – in this silent skimming ... The less problem it affect the skimming.

Accordingly, he wrote 'problem' as his substitute for 'effective', an answer for which he did not get a mark. Another student gave a response that was similar in that he also interpreted 'effective' in a negative sense. The definition he offered when interviewed was 'something that will affect someone – something very harmful', and he gave as an example the sentence 'Insecticides are very effective'. His answer therefore for (a) (v) was 'harmful', so that he, too, did not get a mark. Other students did not impute this negative sense to the word, but their interpretations were equally inexact: the answers they gave included 'troublesome', 'active', 'serious', and 'important'; none gave acceptable forms like 'useful', 'helpful', 'valuable', or 'productive'. These interpretations of 'effective' illustrate a common problem, one that occurred throughout the study: the students often considered that they 'knew' a word, but what they had was only a limited sense of its meaning, a sense derived from coming across it in a narrow range of contexts. Such a limited understanding made it difficult, if not impossible, for them to use familiar words to infer correctly the meanings of those that were totally new to them.

Such lexical problems were, moreover, constantly interacting with syntactic difficulties. Even when the students could put a correct semantic interpretation on a particular word, the substitutes they provided in tasks like (a) showed some shakiness with regard to its syntactic function – or else to the syntactic functions of the words they supplied. In the case of (a) (i), for instance, which solicits a substitute for 'at a fast rate', only four students failed to produce one that included the notion of speed, but a further eight gave answers that did not fill the syntactic slot correctly – answers like 'in a quick time', 'very quick', 'quick speed', or 'quick glance'. According to the WASC examiners' reports, this kind of mistake is penalised; so again there is a simple explanation for the fact that students scored badly in items like (a) – the problem was often an inaccurate use of syntax rather than a failure of comprehension.

But difficulties with syntax were involved in genuine comprehension difficulties too. One of the students put it well. When asked if any of the words in the passage were new to him, he replied,

> I've heard of them but the only thing they're mixed with complicated sentences.

This was particularly true, of course, of that sentence which I have described as a 'hinge' sentence. Another student gave a clear indication of what a puzzle this sentence was to him:

> The more point in what – what is read, the less important we find the – [here he shook his head].... That the more point in what is read, the less important it becomes – the less important the silent skimming is found. [He shook his head again.] What I'm saying does not make sense to what is written.

For another – the one who was so mystified by 'meat' – the inverse variation expressed in the sentence caused considerable difficulty. What he said it meant was,

> The more we read, the less knowledge we get from what we have read.

He explained the apparent lack of logic in this by drawing the moral:

In other words too much of everything is bad.

It is clear that the unusual structure of the sentence did indeed present a problem; but it is also clear that the problem was interacting with the students' uncertainties about 'meat' and 'effective'. So I then gave the students a further task to see the extent to which they could cope with the syntactic structure when it was not complicated by vocabulary difficulties. I constructed sentences of the same pattern which included only common vocabulary, and asked the students to explain, in writing, what they meant. Some of these sentences expressed ideas that the students would expect, for example:

> The more passengers there are in the taxi, the less pleasant we find the journey.

All of the 17 students present that day interpreted this sentence correctly. But the following sentence, presented at the same time, expressed a less obvious idea:

> The more workers there are in an office the less efficient we find the work.

In this case only 11 students gave a correct interpretation. It seems that while such a complex sentence as this could be understood if it made obvious sense, the pattern was not sufficiently well grasped – at least, not by all the students – for the syntax to act as an effective guide to interpretation when the sense was unexpected. It is small wonder, then, that when this pattern was used together with metaphor and imprecisely understood lexis, it should prove, as one of those quoted above put it, 'ununderstandable'.

The difficulty in inferring accurately the meaning of individual words was exacerbated by the failure of several students to make appropriate use of rhetorical signals. A striking example of misinterpretation at this level occurred with regard to the following sentence:

> Newspaper articles, for example, are written to be gulped down in this fashion; taken slowly they become intolerable.

One student, when reading the passage aloud, and again when quoting from it in discussion, rendered the sentence like this:

> Newspaper articles, for example, are written to be gulped down in this fashion: taken slowly. They become intolerable ...

By dropping his voice and pausing as he said 'slowly', he showed that he was interpreting 'this' in the phrase 'in this fashion' cataphorically. And so, he said,

> I think [newspaper articles] are to be read slowly so that they can be understood.

Thus his ignorance of 'gulped' (in (a) (ii), he provided the substitute 'noted') interacted with his misinterpretation of 'this' to reverse completely the meaning of what he read.

Another, and more widespread, example of failing to use cohesive cues was in the interpretation of 'this silent skimming'. 'Skimming' was among those words that nearly all those interviewed said they did not know; and they were asked to say what it meant in item (d) (ii). Of the 12 students who wrote answers to this, 10 described 'skimming' as a kind of reading, but only 2 said that it was fast. The others, it seems, missed the links between '*this* silent skimming', 'gulped down in *this* fashion', and 'solitary silent reading which takes in words through the eye *at a fast rate*'.

So, in dealing with this passage, the students were labouring under a number of disadvantages: first, they did not know several key content words; second, they had a somewhat limited and imprecise understanding of others; and, third, they were apparently insensitive to several important syntactic and rhetorical cues. But over and above all this, and perhaps more important than anything, was the fact that the students came to the passage with their own clear idea of what reading involved – and it was an idea quite different from that assumed by the text. When they came to secondary school in 1979, their experience of reading was extremely limited: few of them had books in their homes, and in their primary schools they were lucky if they had as many as two or three textbooks. As for newspapers and magazines, they were seldom to be seen in the small towns and villages from which most of these students came. On reaching the school in Yola, they did, of course, come across more reading matter. The school had a small library consisting mostly of reference books, they had had a class library, when they were in Form 1, of about 50 simplified readers, and the local newspapers, like the *New Nigerian* and the *Daily Standard*, were quite readily available. Nevertheless, the quantity was still small by western standards, and the variety was limited. Moreover, all these materials were in English: most of the students read nothing at all in their first language, and few of them read anything in Hausa. So reading for them was always done in a foreign language and was closely associated with school work. It was natural, therefore, that the students should expect to read slowly, whatever the material; and they did in fact do so, as I found when I timed their reading of a familiar passage: the highest speed achieved was 192 words per minute, while the average was 161. Consequently, the main issue with which this passage deals – whether one should read quickly or slowly – was not an issue at all as far as these students were concerned. That is, I believe, a major reason why they missed the significance of the phrase 'at a fast rate' and failed to pick up the references to it in the subsequent text; so they could not possibly infer the meaning of the other words suggesting speed, 'gulped down' and 'skimming'.

Besides this, there was another issue which did seem important to these students, and which they could see as the theme of this passage: namely, whether one should read aloud or silently. Again, there is plenty in their background to explain the importance of this issue to them. They were not Muslim, but they had all seen Quran schools where children recite the text from script written on small wooden boards. They had also experienced in their own primary schools a similar approach to text: a common teaching method, especially appropriate when books are in short supply, is for the teacher to read out a sentence and for the students to repeat it in chorus. Then the children take turns reading aloud (and, of course, those who have memorised the text do best). It was quite a shock for these students, therefore, to find when they came to Saint Peter's that they were expected to read silently, and that I, as their teacher in Form 1, would tell them not even to mouth the words. Given this background, it is not surprising that most of the students took this passage to be about 'silent reading' as opposed to 'the speaking voice' – both of which phrases are present in the text.

Just how widespread this interpretation was is indicated by the students' answers to (d) (ii), which asks what the writer means by 'silent skimming'. Twelve students answered this question, but only two responses suggested that the phrase implied speed; two others interpreted it as referring to material to be read rather than to the act of reading ('the news given in the newspapers' was one, and 'important points' was the other); and the other eight were as follows:

– reading silently to oneself
– he means a private reading
– silent skimming mean, reading in silent carefully and understanding
– without motion or sound
– the silent skimming means the silent reading
– silent skimming – silent reading or use your eyes only
– quite [quiet] reading through either a newspaper or a novel
– quiet method or way of doing something, e.g. method of reading.

Thus 50 per cent of those who read the passage, and 75 per cent of those who responded to this particular item, misinterpreted the phrase in the same way. The fact suggests strongly that the interpretation was not idiosyncratic – the product of individual ignorance of particular linguistic items – but was based on assumptions about reading that were common to the students' community.

The students' failure with (d) (i) contrasts strongly with their generally successful responses to (d) (ii), which asks for an explanation of the phrase 'imaginatively entering the author's world'. Here are extracts from some of their papers:

> He means that we can understand what the author writes in his passage.

> Imaginatively entering the authors world means as we read the story and imagine how the author tells the story as if you are the one, you will know what he means.

> 'Imaginatively entering the author's world.' Means, while reading the passage which interest us, we try to know why the author wrote the passage for, what was in his mind, that he put it down on paper for us to assimilate. To know what mood the author was in, while writing the passage.

> When we get into the right story of the author that is the true or main aim of the story.

> Imaginatively – to understand fully what the author is trying to tell us.

> Understanding what the author is talking about. For instance, in a dialogue, if you enter the man who is talking with's mind, you understood what he is talking about.

> Understanding what the author is saying.

Indeed, only two students failed to provide at least an approximately correct answer to this question. The students obviously had little difficulty with this particular metaphor, primarily, I would suggest, because it reflected the way in which they themselves were accustomed to reading.

However deviant the students' answers may have been from the test maker's point of view, they were evidently based on real experience with text – a point that was amply demonstrated by what was said in the interviews. Several students referred to the set books they were studying that year for the WASC Literature in English, *The African Child* and *Julius Caesar*. The latter, indeed, was one which they knew well, as they showed when watching a video-tape of the play, by reciting the lines along with the actors. Others spoke of novels they had read on their own, often with enthusiasm. One, for example, cited Chinua Achebe's *Things Fall Apart*, as a story that might be 'very enjoyable for you', because it was about a great wrestler who was 'widely known'. Another spoke even more enthusiastically about *Animal Farm,* and in so doing gave an intriguing demonstration of how the schema for skimming as 'silent reading' affected his interpretation of that hinge sentence,

> But the more meat there is in what we read, the less effective we find this silent skimming.

This is what he said:

> If I'm reading novels sometime ... I will read that line loudly then I will come to myself again and start reading silently.... I was reading *Animal Farm* and then I experience it ... where there was contradiction between Jones and animals – where they revolted against him. [It was] very very exciting.

It is clear that he was indeed 'entering the author's world', to the point that he, as he put it, became 'less serious' (his interpretation of 'less effective') about reading silently, and began instead to say the words aloud. Another student extended his consideration of reading beyond novels to poetry, and described eloquently the feeling of identification with the author that can be attained:

> When we were reading that poem concerning *Night Rain*,[2] ... how the poem, the poet presents the poem, it's – as we Africans now we are ... familiar to the kind of building he was talking about – the experience. So you feel as if it is – if you were just together with the author there, the way the author presents the story.

One noticeable feature of these responses is that they are all placed firmly in an oral framework: text is compared to talk, and the greater the reader's involvement, the more like talk it is. This points again to the social environment in which literacy, for these students, is practised. They grew up among people who, for the most part, do not read at all; and even among those who do read, any really important and urgent communication is conducted orally . Text is certainly used, even among the uneducated, but it is for formalising decisions, for recording transactions, for making formal – and respectful – requests, and for expressing and transmitting religious teaching. With these uses of text the students at Saint Peter's had no difficulty; and, as the responses quoted above show, they had also, through school, gone beyond these to perceiving text as a means of communicating with authors and of participating in, and enjoying, the experiences described. They had not, however, learnt to treat text with the contempt that is suggested in the first part of this passage; nor had they learnt to dissect it in the manner required by the tasks. So most of them got scores which, if replicated in the final exam, and not countered by particularly strong scores in other sections, would ensure that they would not get their West African School Certificate in English Language; thus they would be officially designated as unworthy of entering the literate élite. Fortunately, however, this comprehension unit only represents a portion of the exam. Reading is also tested by means of summary, and it is to this part of the exam that we now turn.

A summary unit: Writing

The text

This unit is taken from the WASC exam of June 1981:

> There is no easily learnt set of rules or directions that will help you to become an effective writer. As in the development of any skill, learning to write is a matter of diligent practice. It is useful to have a critic (most often an instructor or teacher) close at hand to point out where you are unclear or clumsy, where your organization of ideas can be improved, and where your choice of words is inappropriate or misleading. But far more important is the development of the habit of self-criticism. A great deal of the labour of writing is editing – examining closely what you have written as if you were the reader for whom you are writing. Put yourself in the reader's place to see if you have communicated your ideas successfully. When you do, you will see very often that your first choices were not always the best. You may want to revise some sentences in order to make them more emphatic; a whole paragraph may have to be shifted in order to make the logic of your thoughts clearer; and words that had previously seemed adequate may no longer be found to say exactly what you meant. Changing, shifting, even erasing – these are all part of the work of editing. It is not easy, but it is essential if you want to develop your ability to write in a manner that is concise, lively and clear.
>
> One way to increase your capacity for self-criticism is to examine closely the work of other writers. In your daily reading – newspapers, magazines, novels, other books – stop from time to time to ask these questions: What idea is the writer trying to convey in this paragraph? Has he made it clear? Why did he choose this word over other possibilities? Could I make the same point more effectively? Occasionally you will come upon a paragraph that strikes you because of its vividness and clarity; you instinctively recognize it as 'good writing'. At such times you should stop and examine it with particular care to see how the writer has managed to make this impression upon you, the reader.
>
> During your analysis of the work of other writers, you will notice that the most successful writers are the most careful ones. First of all, they are sure of their facts; they know that no amount of decoration will disguise a slight knowledge of their subject. They also have a clear sense of structure; their ideas follow a logical and consistent pattern from beginning to end. Finally, they use words with a sense of authority; they know what words will be the most effective for the purpose they have in mind. The sense of

'appropriateness' is perhaps one of the clearest marks of the careful writer. As your knowledge of English grows, you will find that for every situation you wish to describe or for every argument you wish to present, a wide variety of choices is open to you.

(a) State briefly and clearly the author's remarks on:
    (i)   What self-criticism consists of
    (ii) How self-criticism may be attained.
(b) State the five qualities of the good writer which the passage further mentions.

Your answers should be as short as possible and free from unnecessary material.

Like the *Reading* unit, *Writing* is typical of its kind. The passage is 486 words long, which is in the middle of the range for the seven summary passages in the corpus. Of these words, 49 are not on the General Service List; but this figure includes 12 that are either repeated or obviously closely related to others that are used. So the proportion of 'difficult' words (just over 10 per cent if one counts all the instances of repetition) is considerably smaller than it is in the *Reading* passage. Also, those words that are identified as not being on the General Service List are by no means as difficult as one might expect: they include 'instructor', 'labour', 'closely', and 'writer', all of which, on the basis of ordinary experience, seem common enough. Moreover, 'writer' or 'writers' appears seven times; when these two forms are excluded from the count the proportion of 'difficult' words is reduced to little over 8 per cent. Nor are there instances of such idioms and metaphors as are so marked a feature of the *Reading* passage. In all these respects the passage is representative of the corpus: over all the passages used for this study, the average proportion of words outside the General Service List is 11.1 per cent, and while the vocabulary is formal, there is no deliberate inclusion of metaphorical and idiomatic expressions.

On the syntactic level, too, the passage would appear to be easier than the *Reading* one. Average sentence length is 20.3 words, as compared with *Reading's* 27.2; and 20.3 is only a little less than the average of 21.6 over all the summary passages. Nor, since the passage is longer, does it depend so heavily on a single and easily misinterpreted sentence. There is, it is true, one unusual sentence, in which the normal order of subject and complement is reversed:

But far more important is the development of the habit of self-criticism.

But it is not nearly as long as the sentence that caused such trouble in *Reading*, nor is the difficulty compounded by the presence of figurative vocabulary.

As is generally the case in this corpus, this unusual sentence structure serves to mark a point that is of rhetorical significance. The passage begins with a statement of the topic – how 'to become an effective writer', a comment on that topic – it is 'a matter of diligent practice', and a concessionary point – 'It is useful to have a critic ...'. Then the sentence in question, introduced as it is by 'but', and with the complement coming first, alerts the proficient reader to what is the main point to be noticed – it is, in fact, a thesis statement. The remainder of the paragraph is devoted to a discussion of what self-criticism is.

The next paragraph is more straightforward in that the topic sentence is the first one and is also simpler syntactically:

> One way to increase your capacity for self-criticism is to examine closely the work of other writers.

The remainder of the paragraph explains how this is to be done. The paragraph, in short, follows standard rhetorical form, with its theme introduced as rheme in its first sentence (Fries 1981).

The third paragraph is similar, opening again with a topic sentence, and with the theme of the paragraph appearing here as rheme:

> During your analysis of the work of other writers, you will notice that the most successful writers are the most careful ones.

The structure of this paragraph is made still more explicit, however, by the use of the connectives, 'first of all', 'also', and 'finally'. Each of these introduces a statement detailing one way in which writers are careful; and then that statement is explicated further in a sentence connected to it by a semicolon. The effect is almost pedantically canonical: students who have been taught explicitly about English rhetorical devices should, it seems, have no problem with this passage.

With its careful use of rhetorical signals it may be that this passage is the product of just such careful editing as is its subject-matter. One can imagine that 'changing, shifting, even erasing' did indeed take place; and the writer obviously made a great effort to 'follow a logical and consistent pattern' and to 'use words with a sense of authority'. 'Authority' is, indeed, a key concept here. The writer as test maker does, of course, have enormous authority, and writes with the certitude of one in that position.

Note, however, how different that perspective is from that of the test takers who are the readers for whom the passage is designed. These test takers are, by definition, people who are learning the language; they may not be able to 'instinctively recognize ... good writing', and they may not have the self-confidence necessary for criticising the writing of others as the passage says they should. Again, as in the *Reading* unit there is a curious contrast between what appears in the text, and what is implicit in the situation in which it is to be read. 'Put yourself in the reader's place' is what the text says, but it is plain that the test maker is not putting himself[3] in the test takers' place, nor is it possible for the test takers, who must respond as writers to this piece, to put themselves in that of the test maker.

When one considers the items as part of the whole text there is a still more problematic contradiction. The first one, (a), demands a fine and not easily perceived distinction between (i) 'what self-criticism consists of' and (ii) 'how self-criticism may be attained'. Test-wise students can make the distinction by looking for the answer to (i) in the first paragraph and the answer to (ii) in the second – it is a strategy that often, though not always, works in these summary units. The difficulty is that this strategy requires the equation of the phrase, 'to *increase* your capacity for self-criticism' with 'how self-criticism may be *attained*'. Given the emphasis that the passage puts on the precise use of words, the necessity for such an equation of an incomplete action with a complete one seems rather odd.

Question (b) presents a still greater difficulty. Like many questions in the summary units it requires the production of a given number of points:

State the five qualities of the good writer ...

A good test-taking strategy is to look for answers to successive questions in successive paragraphs; accordingly, the answer to this, the third question, can be found in the third paragraph:

First of all, they are sure of their facts; they know that no amount of decoration will disguise a slight knowledge of their subject. They also have a clear sense of structure; their ideas follow a logical and consistent pattern from beginning to end. Finally, they use words with a sense of authority; they know what words will be the most effective for the purpose they have in mind.

But, whichever way one counts them, these points do not add up to five. Either one follows the signals, 'first of all', 'also', and 'finally', in which case one arrives at three qualities; or one counts each of the main clauses, in which case one arrives at six. It would seem that the test maker is not, after all, such a careful writer and has constructed an item for which it is impossible for even the most proficient reader to know what is the expected response.

Another problem with the items for this unit, one which is common to all the summary units in the corpus, is the vagueness of the instructions. Test takers are asked to 'state' what is said in the passage, and then there is the additional rubric:

> Your answers should be as short as possible and free from unnecessary material.

It is rather difficult to determine what exactly this means. Is it permissible to select words and phrases from the text, or is paraphrasing required? How is one to determine which textual material is 'unnecessary'? How brief is 'brief'? The exercise of self-criticism, even when supported by extensive and critical reading, will not in fact help much in solving these particular writing problems. What one needs is a teacher who, either through marking exams or from reading examiners' reports, is familiar with the conventions to which test takers must conform. Thus again, as in the *Reading* unit, we see a contradiction between the assertions of the passage and the requirements of the tasks.

The students' responses

The overall scores for this unit were significantly better than those for *Reading*, the average here being 43 per cent. This is partly because the students worked on this text relatively late in the project: it was the fifth of the seven summary units they did, whereas *Reading* was only the second of the seven comprehension units. But it also reflects the fact that the students generally did much better on summary than on comprehension: over the whole corpus the average score for the former was 40 per cent, whereas for the latter it was only 29 per cent. These averages, however, disguise wide differences in the performances of individual students. Some in this unit did extremely well, with scores up to 70 per cent, but others did poorly with scores as low as 10 per cent.

Because this unit was done much later in the project, the data collected were in some respects even richer than they were for *Reading*. First, since I anticipated similar problems to those encountered in that unit, I collected some preliminary information by asking the students, a day or two before they worked on this one, to write for 10 minutes on 'How to improve my written composition'. This gave me some indication of how they viewed the writing process when they were not yet influenced by the passage. Second, the students were recording the unfamiliar vocabulary more systematically than at first – by underlining it in their copies of the passage rather than by listing it separately – and thus I obtained a more complete record of those words with which they felt uncomfortable. On the other hand, the novelty of the project had worn off by this time, so that fewer of them came to discuss their responses; indeed only four were interviewed on this passage. These four, however, represented well the range of success achieved in the class as a whole, having scores of 58, 45, 18, and 10 per cent.

In contrast to the *Reading* unit (and to the comprehension units generally) few of the difficulties with *Writing* can be clearly attributed to problems at the lexical level. Although a fairly large number of words – 25 – were reported by one student or another to be unfamiliar, the average number of such words per student was only 6, that is, less than 2 per cent of the total. In most cases, moreover, those words were not generally considered to be difficult, for they were underlined by only two or three individuals; so the passage does seem to be easier at the lexical level than *Reading*, as the analysis above suggests that it should be.

This is not to say that there were no difficulties with lexis, but the interviews suggested that the difficulties had more to do with words the students knew in some sense but interpreted inaccurately in this context. There was, for instance, the phenomenon, noted in the responses to *Reading*, of students ascribing too restricted a meaning to particular words. One, for example, considered 'erasing' to mean 'using an eraser' – which, of course, it may mean, but it suggests a much less global kind of editing than is intended here. Another had a similar problem with the word 'editing' itself. He related it explicitly to the word 'editor', who was, he said, 'one who publish newspaper ... who collects ideas and then arrange them'.

There was also a more widespread, though more subtle, problem with the related pair of words: 'critic' and 'self-criticism'. Two of the students who were interviewed seemed to interpret the parenthetical remark that follows 'critic' in the text – 'most often an instructor or a teacher' – as a definition of the word, so that, as one of them put it,

'Self-criticism' is to train yourself. Or a teacher training you – an instructor to correct you,

or, in the other's words,

You are supposed to correct your mistakes.

This is close to the description of 'self-criticism' in the first paragraph of the passage, but it has lost something of the latter's range, focusing, as it does, on the correction of mistakes. The first of these students, indeed, seems to have thought that 'criticism' has a definitely antagonistic meaning since, in discussing the verb 'criticise' (which he said he knew, whereas 'self-criticism' he did not), he suggested that it might come up in this kind of context:

> Maybe you may quarrel with [somebody] ... I utter a word of who he – annoy him or what. So he say, 'Don't criticise me'.

Another of those interviewed seems to have seen the same antagonism implicit in the word:

> If you see that others are criticising your work you, the author you won't like .. others to criticise it in such a way. So to avoid such you'd better form the habit ... of criticising your work.

And again he saw 'self-criticism' narrowly, as the correction of mistakes:

> While reading it you have to be careful on your tense, and also the punctuation marks.

The interpretation of the fourth was similar. To 'criticise', for him, meant to

> speak against either of one's character, what he's doing is good or bad.

And 'self-criticism' was, he thought, recommended because

> no matter how you write you will make some mistakes so it is good to read through your work to correct your errors before you give it to the person that is correcting them.

Clearly all these students had some understanding of these words; but there was for all of them a degree of distortion which could interact with other difficulties to create serious problems.

Two of the students also demonstrated a certain difficulty with the procedural vocabulary used in the items. The problem lay in the word 'quality' as used in item (b):

> State the five qualities of the good writer which the passage further mentions.

One said that he knew the word 'quality'. For him, it meant

> something that is either good or bad. We have good qualities, we have bad qualities.

But when it came to the phrase 'the qualities of a good writer' he seemed to get confused, saying that it meant 'the important of the writer', and launching into a long discussion of the advice given in the passage to those who aspire to write. So, trying to draw on more familiar material, I asked him to tell me the qualities of a good student. He again gave a list of specific activities rather than of characteristics; he obviously had some sense of the word 'quality', but it was a distorted one, and the distortion was sufficient to make it hard for him to produce acceptable answers to question (b). The second student had similar difficulty in defining 'quality': 'It is the standard of a person,' he said, and when I asked him to illustrate what he meant by telling me the good qualities of people we both knew, he said,

> Corper [one of the teachers] has good quality ... of geography,

and also,

> [The Rector] has a quality of games ... He knows the rule of many games.

He seemed to be associating the word 'quality' with 'qualification', and so it is not surprising that he, too, had difficulties in responding to item (b).

These vocabulary difficulties, however, were not nearly as great as those with the *Reading* text. Moreover, there seemed to be much less interaction in the students' interpretation of this passage between unfamiliar vocabulary and confusing syntax. Indeed, only one student gave clear evidence that he had incorrectly processed a syntactic structure. The trouble arose with the unusual sentence discussed above:

> But far more important is the development of the habit of self-criticism.

He had failed to see the point made here that self-criticism is more important than having a teacher, and he explained this failure by saying,

> But 'far' is the word that confused me from that. I thought that 'far from the point'. ... When they put 'but' I thought they change everything. ... It confused me, this part.

He does, indeed, seem to have been confused, apparently thinking the sentence meant that self-criticism was irrelevant; but he was the only one to misinterpret the syntax in this way.

Rhetorical cues, on the other hand, seem to have been more generally missed. With the sentence just discussed, for instance, many students failed to see its rhetorical function, although they did apparently understand its structure. The need for an instructor or teacher was a recurrent theme in their responses, suggesting that they had not understood how the sentence is intended to underplay the importance of teachers and focus the reader's attention on self-criticism.

There were also several students whose written responses showed clearly that they did not perceive the relationship between the paragraph structure of the passage and the design of the items. For task (a), for example, three put material from paragraph 2 in their response to number (i), while another had material from paragraph 3 here; and in answering (a) (ii), one student drew on the third paragraph, while another took his answer from the first as well as the second. Similar problems were encountered by the students in their responses to item (b). One, for example, took his material for this from everywhere but the last paragraph (the number given in square brackets after each response indicates the paragraph from which it seems to have come):

> The five qualities of the good writer which the passage mentions are:
>
> i. the development of any skill in writing, [1]
> ii. to have a teacher or instructor to point your mistake and bad expressions, [1]
> iii. reading many books or different books and copying the writers form of writing,[2]
> iv. read your own written words and see your mistake and [1]
> v. studied the paragraphs the writer made and his chose of words at the beginning of each sentence. [2]

This student was one of those who had difficulty in interpreting 'qualities', a fact which must have played a large role in his producing such deviant responses; but he might have overcome this difficulty if he had had a stronger sense of the structure of the text as a whole, and especially if he had been alerted by the words 'first of all', 'also', and 'finally'.

But such problems were by no means universal. In the course of our work on the previous four summary units, we had talked a good deal about how paragraph divisions, connectives, and topic sentences were important guides in responding to the tasks, and in this unit many of the students applied these lessons. Seven of them scored more than 50 per cent – a reputable score in this examination system, where the usual pass mark is 35 per cent – and in each case their success can be attributed primarily to the fact that they obtained their responses to each item from the appropriate portion of the text. Consider, for example, this set of answers:

> (a) The writer remarked that self-criticism consists of a great deal of writing editing, – changing, shifting and even using and eraser.

Self criticism can be attained by examining closely the work done by other good writers either through reading the newspapers – magazines novels or other interesting books.

(b) The five qualities of a good writer are: –

(i)   They know their facts
(iii) They make sure that they have a clear sense of structure
(iii) Their notions follow point by point and consistent pattern from the starting point to the end.
(iv) They use words with sense of authority.
(v)   The sense of being appropriate.

There are mistakes here, certainly, but it is clear that the student understood the basic structure of the passage. Moreover, he was consciously using that understanding. The mistake in his numbering of the second 'quality' for task (b) is explained by the fact that he had just previously written, and then crossed out,

(ii) They are sure that no amount of decoration will disguise a slight knowledge of their topic.

His rejection of this point was almost certainly because he realised, as soon as he had written it, that it was a subordinate one, whose purpose was to explicate the quality that he numbered (i). During his interview, he answered the question again, without seeing his written responses, and he explained his thinking thus:

'First of all, they are sure of their facts.' That's the major point, and this one is to support it 'They know that no amount of decoration will disguise a slight knowledge of their subject.' That is one ... 'They also have a clear sense of structure.' This is the main sentence. Then the point supporting it: 'their ideas follow a logical and consistent pattern from beginning to end' ... 'Finally, they use words with a sense of authority; they know what words will be .. the most effective for the purpose they have in mind.'

Here, of course, he got into trouble, for he had exhausted all the 'main points' and had not got the five required by the item – so he added 'the sense of appropriateness is perhaps one of the clearest marks of the careful writer' for the fourth, but found that for the fifth he was forced to elevate one of his 'supporting' points. This difficulty, however, was not his fault; indeed, from this discussion it appears that his sense of structure was clearer than the test maker's.

This student, and those others who scored more than 50 per cent, had performed a considerable feat of imagination in following the text with such success. For while it proved considerably easier than *Reading* at the levels of lexis and syntax, it was no less difficult in terms of its underlying assumptions or schema. The passage, as we have seen, explicitly plays down the role of the teacher in the formation of a good writer and emphasises instead the development of the writer's own critical faculties. The students, however, were strongly inclined to the opposite view, as they showed in the pieces they wrote, before reading this passage, on 'How to improve my written composition'. One of these pieces is worth quoting in full:

How to improve written composition

It is very worth improving on writing compositions, so I have taken this opportunity to lay out my emphasis on writing good composition.

My brother, the best way I think we can improve in writing composition is: first, to learn what good english text books have got to teach us.

Secondly, it is very beneficial to listen to your teacher and any one you think that knows english better so as to learn how to speak good english. From listening and practicing how to speak good english, writing good compositions can be improved.

Thirdly, if you can afford the time to read novels, newspapers, magazines and other articles, good composition and better writing could be improved.

A noticeable point in this description is the total absence of the idea that improving one's composition can be a reflexive process, by which writers become their own readers and revise their texts according to their perceived needs in this new role.

Although there was considerable variation in the students' responses to this topic, this absence of reflexivity was common to them all. Four others explicitly suggested that improvement in writing would come from an external source – receiving instruction from a teacher, reading textbooks, or listening to the radio; a further four presented a formula for what they deemed to be a satisfactory composition; another six referred more to the process of writing, but their emphasis was on understanding the topic, planning an appropriate response, and avoiding errors (one, indeed, recommended avoiding the use of tense – like other learners of English, these students had considerable difficulty with the English verb system). Only two said that one should actually read one's own work, and even these two did not seem to be thinking of 'self-criticism': one recommended it for the sole purpose of correcting 'mechanical errors', while the other said it was to be done only after the teacher had marked the work so that the writer might learn from the latter's corrections.

It seems clear that the idea of self-criticism was foreign to these students and was difficult for them to grasp. This is understandable when we remember that writing, like reading, was for them always done in English, a foreign language. They knew that their command of it was limited and that, as one put it, 'Dole ne mutum ya yi kuskure', ('It's certain that a person will make mistakes'). The excerpts from their work that have been quoted here amply illustrate his point; and while the students could, with prompting, see an error and correct it, they had no confidence in their ability to do so unaided. It is not surprising, then, that more than half of the class, on seeing the remark in this text about the usefulness of an instructor or teacher, should interpret it as saying what they would expect it to say – that a teacher is, in fact, necessary for people who want to improve their writing.

This interpretation also fitted into the students' broader frame of reference. An important principle of social relations throughout Nigeria is the notion of seniority, and the authority that goes with it. In traditional society children are taught from their earliest years to respect their elders, and when they come to school, this respect is transferred to senior students and still more to teachers. It is shown in countless small ways – in gestures of greeting, in forms of address, and in errands that junior students, especially, are asked to do. The authority of those senior to oneself is thus constantly reinforced, and for senior students, like those I was teaching, the way to assert themselves was not so much to try to become independent of their teachers as to assert their own authority over those junior to them. In such a social situation, it is natural that the instruction of the teacher, or, in one student's words 'someone that has learned more than you', should be seen as more important in a writer's development than the writer's own efforts at self-improvement.

A final factor to consider is the circumstances in which these students usually wrote. Their main reason for writing, as it is for many others across the world, was to demonstrate to teachers or examiners that they knew how to do it, or that they knew particular facts in some academic area since most other WASC subjects are examined by means of essay tests. Thus, the act of writing was in itself an expression of the students' subordinate status in the hierarchical structure of modern Nigerian society. That this was the perception of at least several of the students in my class is shown, again, in their pieces on 'How to improve my written composition', which I quote here with my own emphasis added. One student wrote,

> To improve my written composition I have to keep on constant practise so that I may familiar with writing composition whenever it comes out in any *examination*.

Another was still more explicit:

> I should proceed to think twice over the topic and ask myself what the *examiner must have wanted me to do*.

The examiner appears even more prominently in the following:

> When coming to the next paragraph you need not repeat the same expression
> (here) you talk of the main point so as to draw *the attention of the examiner* of
> what you have to say ...
>   In conclusion you conclude the composition with the main topic and sweet
> oration *so as to bring home of the examiner* what you are doing.

This summary unit is, of course, itself an expression of the students'
subordinate position as writers. Its very terms deny them any autonomy
or opportunity to be critical, for the rubric, 'Your answers should be ...
free from unnecessary material', requires them to repeat what the test
maker says, and not introduce any ideas of their own. The fact illustrates
well a point we have made elsewhere about the conflict between the
'inner context' of the text – that is, the context one must infer if one is to
interpret it – and the 'outer context' of the test – that is, the situation,
including the surrounding units, in which the passage is actually being
read (Hill and Parry 1989). For while the text posits reflexive, critical,
and independent writers, the test has the effect of confirming the
dependence of the students on their teachers, and still more on the
judgement of the test makers.

Conclusions

This study has shown that the poor results of the WASC can be
attributed partly to the inadequacy of the reading components used. The
two units presented here illustrate difficulties that recurred regularly
throughout the corpus: there are ambiguous questions for which it is
impossible to tell what responses the test makers had in mind; the
language is extremely formal, and in the comprehension passages there is
a contrived use of idioms and figures of speech – and the tasks are so
constructed as to penalise students heavily for not knowing them; there
is also in the comprehension units, a demand for syntactic accuracy that
goes well beyond the requirements of normal reading; and in both kinds
of unit students have to produce a great deal of language themselves so
that their productive difficulties may obscure a fairly good understanding
of the text. As for the content, while it is obviously chosen for its
relevance for West African students, it is presented from a European
perspective: the suppositions behind *Reading* are those of people reared
in a print culture, and the difficulties addressed in *Writing* are those of
people trying to develop a style in their first language. The two kinds of
unit are not equally unsatisfactory – those designed to test summary

skills were found to distinguish far more effectively between students, and to reflect more accurately their overall performance – but there is evidently a strong case for re-examining both of them, and for developing new reading components that would be more appropriate for the modern student population. Nor, perhaps, does this apply only to the WASC, for the testing model used here is a legacy of the British Empire, and it may be that in places as far apart as India, Jamaica, and Hong Kong, the reading components of decisive exams are similarly inappropriate.

But the Saint Peter's students' difficulties cannot be blamed entirely on the tests, for during the interviews they often demonstrated that they had severe problems with the language itself. In the comprehension units these problems were made particularly apparent by those items that demanded lexical substitution. Among the words targeted in these items there were few that all the students knew, and often there were one or two that were unfamiliar to nearly everyone; but, given the low frequency of these words this was not in itself indicative of a general linguistic deficiency. The problem was more in the only partial knowledge that the students had of the surrounding words, a knowledge that often led them to infer meanings for the unknown ones that were quite wrong. This tendency to misinterpretation was compounded by a weak grasp of the syntax, and a frequent failure to perceive and use low-level rhetorical cues. The result was that the students often proved capable of constructing whole interpretive edifices on the foundation of a few misinterpreted words; the point of the passage could thus be missed entirely.

That the students could be so drastically misled was not, however, merely a function of ignorance. Frank Smith maintains that text can only be understood by 'having meaning brought to it' (1982, p. 75), and that is indeed how the texts used in this study were understood by these students. But the meaning that the students brought was quite different from what the test makers presumably had in mind. The two units discussed here, being themselves about text, illustrate the point dramatically. The students were by no means ignorant of text: they had their own opinions about it, based on their experience, in primary school, of mainly oral reading, and then, in secondary school, of exercises like these test units as well as literature set books and textbooks for other subjects. But the passages do not refer to such learners' experience; they present text from the perspective of one who has read widely in the western tradition and who has also written much himself – a kind of person these students seldom had occasion to meet, especially among their fellow Nigerians. Consequently, to handle either text successfully they had to adopt a position that was radically different from their normal stance – not only to learn a language other than their own, but to accept the view of life associated with it.

There is, moreover, another dimension of complexity, in the relationship to text that is implicit in the testing situation. The units here presented are markedly different in form from the American ones studied by Fillmore and Kay (1983) and Hill and Larsen (1983), but, like the American ones, they reflect characteristics that are perhaps common to all test discourse. There is the same insistence on 'the very words' and the same demand that test takers ignore pragmatic considerations. This is an approach to language that Olson and Hildyard have asserted is peculiarly literate, and learned only through western modes of schooling (1980); but I would claim that it represents only a particular kind of literacy, one among many. This kind of literacy is especially privileged in western society, and it is one that most of these students did not have. Yet they could and did interact with text, as they showed especially in their comments on *Reading*. Several of them were, indeed, extraordinarily inventive in treating the somewhat turgid texts of these exams as instruments of communication. In so doing these individuals were showing an important linguistic ability, for they were constructing meaning by applying their own experience to a limited range of graphic cues. With the tests as they now stand, however – and perhaps with any sort of reading test – this ability goes unrecognised and unrewarded.

Acknowledgements

This article is based on work done at Saint Peter's Seminary, Yola, Nigeria. I could not have done it without the help of my students in that school, or without the support of the Rector, the late Reverend Damian Loughran, OSA, of the Bishop of Yola, the Right Reverend Bishop Patrick Sheehan, OSA, and of many others who work in the dioceses of Yola and Maiduguri. I should like to thank all these people for their help; and I should also like to thank my friends and colleagues at Teachers College, Columbia University, for the advice and encouragement they have given me and Sam McCarter of the Institute of Education, London University, for his help in analysing the texts.

Notes

1. Since this research was done, Gongola has been divided into a number of smaller states. Yola is now in Adamawa.

2. The poem is by John Pepper Clark and is published in Senanu and Vincent (1976).
3. The masculine pronoun is used here because nearly all WASC examiners are men.

5 Adult education in the United States: adapting materials for reading tests

Clifford Hill and Laurie Anderson

In this chapter[1] we address two related questions: What kinds of textual inconsistencies emerge as test makers adapt material for use on a reading test? What kinds of constructive processes do test takers engage in as they deal with adapted text? The first question is important in any volume on testing and assessment since test makers are so dependent on text adaptation. This dependency comes from their commitment to using varied samples of actual text in a standard format. In constructing passages for different levels, test makers must take into account such matters as number of words used and degree of vocabulary difficulty. The second question is important because constructive processes are virtually ignored in current approaches to testing. One reason for this neglect is the difficulty of documenting such processes in any reliable way. Our own methods of documentation are quite varied, and certain of them may prove useful to those concerned with the reform of testing and assessment.

In relating text structure and reader response, we work within a theoretical framework developed by Van Dijk and Kintsch (1983). Adapting their framework, we use *text base* to refer to information either in the text surface (i.e. that represented in, to use Olson's phrase, 'the very words') or supplied by *automated inferences* (i.e. inferences strictly entailed by the text surface).[2] We use *situation model* to refer to information supplied by all other inferences that readers make. We use two terms to describe these other inferences: (1) *invited inferences* which are directly evoked by the text base but not, strictly speaking, entailed by it; and (2) *extended inferences* which are not directly evoked by the text base. Extended inferences do, however, elaborate the situation that the text base represents (see Geis and Zwicky 1971 and Harris and Monaco 1978 for further discussion). These various distinctions will be illustrated as we deal with adapted test material.

Background

The adapted material that we analyse is drawn from the 1976 edition of the Test of Adult Basic Education (TABE), which is a test published by

CTB/Macmillan/McGraw-Hill.[3] The TABE is the most widely used test in adult education throughout the United States. It was originally developed for use with native speakers of English, but the majority of those who now take it are non-native speakers. In New York City, for example, non-native speakers constitute about two-thirds of those enrolled in adult education programmes.

The TABE contains three major components – reading, mathematics, and language – all administered at three levels – easy (E), medium (M), and difficult (D) – and, since 1987, at an advanced (A) level. These three components are further divided into sections, as shown in Figure 5.1.

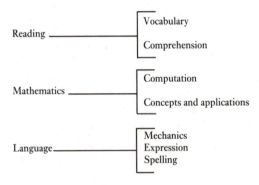

Figure 5.1 Three components of the TABE

The adapted material that we analyse is drawn from the comprehension section of the reading component.

In developing material for the 1976 edition of the TABE, test makers drew on the 1970 edition of the California Achievement Test (CAT), a test that is widely used with children at the elementary level. Consider, for example, the material from the mathematics component of the two tests shown in Figure 5.2 (the CAT material is on the left, the adapted TABE material on the right).

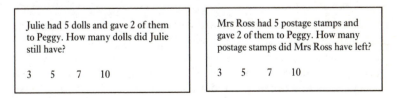

Figure 5.2 A passage in the CAT and the TABE

As can be seen, the CAT material is only minimally adapted for use on the TABE: the dolls become postage stamps and Julie a married woman. In characterising such shifts, the *Examiner's Manual* states that

> adaptation of the CAT ... items was generally limited to changing the language and content of the items to reflect adult usage, experience, and interests. The item content, test organization, and format remained essentially intact. (1976, p. 1)

It is interesting to observe to what degree this manual description fits what the test makers did in adapting material for the reading comprehension section. Consider, for example, the materials shown in Figure 5.3.

The children in Mrs Kim's room were talking about how to make scrapbooks. Eva said, 'I will bring some pictures'. 'I will bring some scissors' Monty said. Marie said, 'And I will bring some paper'. The children decided they would need more paste than they had. To make paste they would need water, flour, and salt. Eva said, 'I will bring a pan to mix them in'.	The men in Mr Smith's office decided to build a model boat. Sam brought some tools from home. Joe brought some wood. Pete brought some string. Mike brought some pictures. The men decided they would need some glue. To make the glue they needed glue powder and water. Joe brought a pan in which to mix them.

Figure 5.3 A passage in the CAT and the TABE

Hill and Parry point out how the 'language and content' of this passage show little evidence of the 'adult usage, experience, and interests' mentioned in the manual. As they observe with respect to its language,

> there are occasional shifts in wording (e.g., 'paste' to 'glue') that are presumably designed to reflect adult language, but they are at such a superficial level that they merely call attention to the fact the language of the adapted passage (e.g., the short sentences) is still best suited for children. (1988, p. 13)

With respect to its content, Hill and Parry point out how the project that the men undertook strains credibility: though adult males do strange things, they don't ordinarily get together in their lunch hour to build a model boat. In fact, when one of the authors of this chapter first encountered this material, she did not know that it had been adapted from a children's test. She immediately exclaimed that this passage must have come from something about children in some teacher's classroom.

For her, this material was clearly trailing a child's world.

Hill and Parry examined a range of adapted material in their review of the two editions of the TABE. On the basis of their review, they concluded that text adaptation often results in internal contradictions that are likely to engender a wide range of reader responses. It is for this reason that we have decided to examine a particular adaptation in greater depth to determine how readers from different sociocultural backgrounds respond to it. We shall be particularly concerned with contrasting how native speakers and non-native speakers respond to this material.

In Figure 5.4 we present two versions of this material – the original CAT passage is on the left, the adapted TABE version on the right (in Appendix 5.1 we present the two versions of the tasks that accompany the passage).[4] As can be seen, the original passage is changed only minimally. The two most obvious features that have been altered are

(1) the number of characters in the story
     (Al has replaced Benny and Al)
(2) the nature of the desired object
     ('black shoes' has replaced 'shiny skates').

Moreover, the tasks that follow the passage have been left intact, except for these two features. In task 19, for example, 'Al' replaces 'The boys' in the stem, and among the choices 'shoes' replaces 'skates'. It is thus

The big store looked very far away. Benny and Al wondered if they would ever get there. It was very hot and crowded on the sidewalks. They had to squeeze between the people as they ran. At last they came to the big glass doors. The doors swung open and they were soon inside the cool building. They rushed down the stairs to the toy shop. Right in front of them were the shiny skates which they had come to buy.	The big store looked very far away. Al wondered if he would get there in time. It was very hot and crowded on the sidewalks. He had to squeeze between the people as he walked. At last he came to the big glass doors. The doors swung open and he was soon inside the cool building. He rushed down the stairs to the shoe department. Right in front of him were the black shoes that he had come to buy.

Figure 5.4 A passage in the CAT and the TABE

| Benny and Al were in a hurry to get to the store because they were

excited   late
hungry   tired | Al was in a hurry to get to the store because he was

excited   *late*
hungry   tired |

Figure 5.5 A task in the CAT and the TABE

surprising to discover a shift in target response for task 20 – as indicated by the italics in Figure 5.5, it is 'excited' for the CAT version, but 'late' for the TABE version.

Given the close parallelism of the two passages, how did the test makers end up with a different target response for what appears to be the same task? In responding to this question, we can speculate on how the adaptation process itself might have forced test makers to make this shift. In following their scheme for adapting CAT material, they first stripped the passage of any objects associated with a child's world – clearly the shiny skates in the toy department had to go. They were then faced with the problem of finding an appropriate replacement for the skates. Presumably they decided that shoes are a commodity that reflects 'adult usage, experience, and interests' (we suspect that they coloured the shoes *black* as a further means of activating an adult world). This change, however, created a problem: in an adult world men do not ordinarily shop together for shoes; and if they do, there may be a hint of something in the air that test makers wish to avoid. They may have thus felt pressure to reduce the two characters to one, and it is not surprising that Benny was the one to go since the name itself suggests a child.

Having made these changes, the test makers faced a problem if they wished to retain task 20 within the larger set. The shopping expedition no longer conveyed the same sense of excitement. Once the shiny skates were gone, the world of play was no longer present; and once Benny was gone, the sense of shared adventure disappeared as well. As indicated by the *Examiner's Manual*, however, the test makers were committed to maintaining the integrity of the test format, i.e. they were committed to keeping 'item content, test organization, and format ... essentially intact' (1976, p. 1). In order to maintain test stability, they had to re-establish congruence between the passage and the task.[5]

The test makers thus needed to build a case for 'late'. They were now dealing with an adult world where the critical phrase in the task stem – 'Al was in a hurry' – could be readily assimilated to a choice of 'late' (i.e. adults are more concerned than children with being on time). Hence the test makers presumably decided to adapt the passage even further so that it would be more closely aligned with 'late' than 'excited'. They thus replaced the word 'ever' with the phrase 'in time' in the second sentence:

Al wondered if he would ⟶ Al wondered if he would get
ever get there.   there in *time*.

Once this change was in place, a reader would simply have to align 'late' in the task with 'in time' in the passage:

sentence 2:
Al wondered if he would get there   *in time.*

task 20:
Al was in a hurry to get to the store because he was   *late.*

This solution for task 20 does not, however, work as smoothly as the test makers might have anticipated. For many readers, as we shall shortly show, the adapted text is sufficiently continuous with the original one that they still prefer 'excited' to 'late'. In order to investigate this preference, we need to examine more closely the narrative structure that was carried over from the original. To begin with, we can examine certain features that are distributed throughout the passage. These features, constituting what we can describe as an *excited-youth gestalt*, are of two kinds. First are those having to do with narrative point of view. The story opens with the sentence 'The big store looked very far away'. The fact that the world is magnified, in size as well as distance, suggests a diminished point of view, which is evidenced, once again, when Al arrives at 'the big glass doors' of the store. Second are stylistic features that suggest an excited youth. The final sentence begins with a frontshifted locative phrase – 'right in front of him' – providing a vivid sense of Al coming upon the black shoes he had rushed to the store to buy. Apart from this local feature, global features such as simple vocabulary and short sentences suggest not only a story written for young people but, for many readers, a story written *about* a young person. Moreover, the narrative structure itself conveys a sense of anticipation: readers are continuously forced to draw on later information to make sense out of what is going on: in the first sentence, for example, the use of 'looked' sets up a narrative point of view, but it is only in the second sentence that the one who possesses this point of view is named. One reader described this anticipatory structure in this way:

As I read each sentence, I felt as if I was being propelled through space, moving closer and closer to those black shoes. I had the distinct feeling that Al was anticipating something.

The attraction to 'excited' can be traced not only to the excited-youth gestalt but to a certain fit between the two major elements of the narrative. The initiating element, which we can describe as 'getting to the store', contains the elliptical phrase 'in time' that calls for readers to make some kind of inference:

> Al wondered if he would get there in time Ø.

When readers first encounter this phrase in the second sentence, the only information that they can work with is 'the big store'. As a consequence, they are led to make what we call an invited inference (i.e. one directly evoked, though not strictly entailed, by the text surface):

> Al wondered if he would get ⟶ Al wondered if he would get
> there in time Ø.   to the store before it closed.

When we presented only the first two sentences of the passage to 40 readers and asked them to expand 'in time', all but one of them made the above inference. We can refer to this inference as *locally based*.

Once readers move on to the culminating narrative element, which we can describe as *finding the black shoes*, they come across information that they can use to reinterpret 'in time'. To begin with, they discover that Al continues to hurry even when he is inside the store (i.e. 'he rushed down the stairs to the shoe department')[6]; hence his hurrying seems to be motivated by more than just getting to the store before it closes. Once Al reaches the shoe department, readers discover that he wants to buy a particular pair of black shoes. Working with this additional information, they can go back to the initial narrative element and provide a new interpretation of 'in time' – Al was hurrying in order to get to the black shoes in time to buy them:

> Al wondered if he would get there ⟶ Al wondered if he would get
> in time Ø.   to the store before the black
>   shoes he wanted were gone.

We can refer to this inference as *globally based*.

To determine whether experienced readers, when reading the entire passage, interpret 'in time' locally or globally, we presented the task shown in Figure 5.6 to a second group of 40 students.

Among the 40 students, 32 expressed a preference: 23 preferred the first interpretation (the locally based one) and 9 preferred the second interpretation (the globally based one). Moreover, readers who made the

Here is the second sentence of the passage:

> Al wondered if he would get there in time.

Which of the following interpretations of 'in time' seems more appropriate to you? If you do not have a preference, you do not have to respond.

(1) Al wondered if he would get there before the store closed.

(2) Al wondered if he would get there before the shoes he wanted to buy were sold.

Please explain the reasons for your choice.

Figure 5.6 Experimental task based on an elliptical sentence

local interpretation tended to choose 'late', and those who made the global interpretation tended to choose 'excited', as shown in Table 5.1.

Table 5.1 Two interpretations of 'in time' related to the choice of 'late' or 'excited'

	'late'	*'excited'*
Local interpretation	16 (70%)	7 (30%)
Global interpretation	2 (22%)	7 (78%)

It is interesting to speculate why readers favour the local interpretation. To begin with, the phrase 'in time', taken in isolation, suggests a fixed reference point such as the store closing. To use linguistic terms, a fixed reference point (e.g. 5 pm) is *unmarked,* an indeterminant reference point (e.g. reaching a goal) is *marked.* Readers will tend to work with an unmarked reference point unless the context forces them to establish a marked one. Moreover, readers tend to maintain an interpretive frame once it is in place and accommodate new information to it. Such perseverance is even stronger if they have the sense of dealing with a text that is not itself well integrated. In the case of the text under consideration, the very process of adapting it led to such fragmentation that many readers were apparently discouraged from attempting to integrate it. A number of them expressed surprise that Al should be in such a rush to buy a mere pair of shoes. As one Japanese woman put it,

> I don't understand why Al was in such a hurry to buy a pair of shoes. It seems to me that buying shoes isn't an urgent matter. I think he could wear the ones he already had if he could not get a new pair on that day.

Probably the most crucial factor in readers' failure to integrate the text was their knowledge that they were dealing with test material. In handling task 20, many were content to do a surface matching of the target response 'late' with the phrase 'in time' in sentence 2. Once they had aligned the two, they did not need to deal with 'in time' any further. In fact, many readers reported that when they were reading the passage, they did not even notice that this phrase is elliptical. As one of them put it,

> I never even noticed that something should follow 'in time'.

In effect, the low-level matching called for by test material leads to a surface style of reading, one in which textual elements are not actively chunked together.

We would like to point out a certain irony here: readers who interpret 'in time' globally are, in fact, more text-based than those who interpret it locally. As readers integrate the two narrative elements, they can restrict themselves to the text base and thus discard the invited inference they initially make. By way of contrast, readers who interpret 'in time' locally hold on to this inference, which, strictly speaking, goes beyond the text base. These patterns contradict those that are ordinarily evidenced on test material: as Hill and Parry point out in Chapter 1, locally oriented readers tend to restrict themselves to the text base, globally oriented readers to work off the situation model.

We cannot be certain how this contradiction came about but suspect that it has to do with the fundamental conflict between what the test makers imported and the indigenous material they left untouched. In order to further explore this conflict, we designed a series of small-scale experiments in which we presented the original CAT material and the adapted TABE material with the crucial detail 'in time' first present and then absent. We presented the resulting four versions, accompanied by task 20, to different groups of 40 readers. Table 5.2 shows the proportion of readers who selected 'late' and 'excited' for each of the four versions.

Table 5.2 Four versions of the test material related to the choice of 'late' or 'excited'

	'late'	'excited'
(1) CAT passage	0 (0%)	40 (100%)
(2) TABE passage without 'in time'	5 (12.5%)	33 (82.5%)*
(3) CAT passage with 'in time'	14 (35.0%)	26 (65.0%)
(4) TABE passage	22 (55.0%)	18 (45.0%)

* Two respondents chose 'tired'.

As can be seen, the proportion of readers selecting the target response 'late' steadily increases across these four versions. Presumably this proportion would further increase if we were to remove the excited-youth gestalt from the TABE passage: 'in time' would then be left to do its work unimpeded. The strength of this detail can be illustrated by comparing the results for versions (2) and (3). When 'in time' is removed from the TABE passage in version (2), the choice of 'late' substantially decreases. When it is inserted in the CAT passage in version (3), the choice of 'late' substantially increases. These results provide further evidence that experienced readers, when dealing with this test material, ascribe greater weight to this single imported feature than to the entire gestalt of indigenous features that support the sense of excitement.

This series of experiments indicates how delicate text adaptation can be, particularly where it involves importation of new elements. To our way of thinking, those involved in such adaptation do not take sufficient account of the conflict between imported and indigenous elements. This is certainly the case with test makers who often use naturally occurring text in developing test material. Since they work with rather strict constraints in adapting this material (e.g. passage length and level of vocabulary), they often produce what Hill and Larsen (1983) have described as 'hybrid text'. This kind of text is also commonly produced by those who adapt material for second language teaching; as teachers and textbook writers adjust material to fit certain levels of language ability, they, too, produce text with a good deal of internal contradiction. One question that particularly interests us is the degree to which non-native learners are aware of such contradiction. It is for this reason that we decided to carry out a large-scale experiment in which we compare native and non-native responses to the adapted material.

Experiment with native and non-native speakers

Methodology

Subjects. The experiment was conducted with 365 students at Columbia University:
(1) 95 native speakers of English
(2) 270 non-native speakers of English
    (a) 135 speakers of Japanese
    (b) 135 speakers of other languages.

The native speakers were graduate students at Teachers College, the non-native speakers were students in the American Language Program, a university-wide programme designed to help foreign students prepare for academic work. In addition to speakers of Japanese, there were speakers of 28 other languages (e.g. African languages such as Igbo and Swahili, Asian languages such as Chinese and Korean, Middle Eastern languages such as Arabic and Hebrew, European languages such as Dutch and Italian). All the non-native speakers were at intermediate or advanced levels of the programme. We selected non-native speakers at these levels after we discovered that at lower levels many students were not able to respond meaningfully to the material we presented (e.g. they chose 'hungry' as a response to item 20 and wrote down little or nothing on the recall task that we presented).

Materials. The materials consisted of the adapted passage and three tasks:
(1) a recall task
(2) task 20
(3) an age-estimate task.
The last two tasks each consisted of two parts: on task (2), students first responded to task 20 and then explained their choice; and on task (3), they first estimated Al's age and then explained their estimate.

Procedures. Students were given the test passage to read for 45 seconds. The passage was then removed and students were given only the recall task (the instructions were 'to write down what they had read'). They were then given the other two tasks in sequence: first, they responded to item 20 and explained their choice, and second, they estimated Al's age and then explained their estimate (they did these tasks without access to the passage or their own recall of it).

Once the materials were administered, the following kinds of coding were performed on the written protocols that we obtained:

(1) RECALL TASK: The protocols were first coded according to the passage details they contained. Details were coded at two levels:
(a) word level
      noun ('shoes')
      adjective ('crowded')
      verb ('rushed')
(b) phrase level
      noun phrase ('black shoes')
      locative phrase ('right in front of him')

Some latitude was allowed in coding passage details: for example, a synonym such as 'distant' was accepted for 'far away'.

The protocols were then analysed for inferences according to the framework adapted from Van Dijk and Kintsch (1983):

(1) *text base*
   automated inferences

'Al would like to buy a black shoes at a distant department store'. (Filipino who inferred that Al wanted to buy the shoes)[7]

(2) *situation model*

   (a) *invited inferences*

'He thought he might be too late and was anxious to get to the store'. (American who inferred that Al was anxious)

   (b) *extended inferences*

'There is a big store of shoes. Everybody want to go inside the store and in the end the people reach the store and go inside and the man buys shoes'. (German who inferred that everybody wanted to enter the store)

The coding of these inferences was relatively parsimonious (i.e., it focused on exact wording such as 'anxious' contained in the protocols).

(2) TASK 20: The particular choice that students made was first recorded. The explanations were then coded for textual details and inferences according to the scheme used on the recall task. In addition, extended inferences, which were much more frequent in the explanations than in the recalls, were further categorised as

(a) normative reasoning

'You run in crowds only if you are to late'. (German who chose 'late')

(b) narrative expansion

'Because he had appontment of his customer, but shoe was broken so he have to buy new one as soon as possible'. (Japanese who chose 'late')

(c) self-comparison

'I identified with Al completely, putting myself in his place (shoes) by the final sentence. I was excited and identified with his emotion. I recall being in a similar situation and was extremely satisified by the resolution'. (American who chose 'excited')

(d) stylistic features

'The vivid descriptions of his actions with relatively short sentences made me believe he was absorbed in buying the shoes'. (Japanese who chose 'excited')

(3) AGE-ESTIMATE TASK: The estimates of Al's age were coded as
(a) youth (up to 18 years)

(b) adult (24 years or above)
(c) in–between (19–23 years)

We used the in–between category to provide a buffer between the youth and adult categories. The adult category was further sub-divided into 55 years or above. This more specific category was used to determine whether viewing Al as older was related to the choice of 'tired'.

The explanations were then coded for textual details and inferences according to the scheme used on the previous tasks. In addition, extended inferences involving normative reasoning were further divided into youth norms and adult norms (as illustrated by the examples below, these norms were stated both positively and negatively):

(a) youth norms
     positive:

'Because of this age boys regularly want to look great just like their friends.' (Italian who estimated '15 years')

     negative:

'Rushing, running albeit tired – someone older wouldn't so readily be bothered to suffer all this for a pair of shoes.' (American who estimated 'teenager')

(b) adult norms
     positive:

'Because he was not sure if he could reach the shoe store – and his eyesight was not very good.' (Persian who estimated 55)

     negative:

'He was rushing to buy a pair of shoes. Kids wouldn't have such a sense of urgency.' (American who estimated '30 to 50')

The coded data were then submitted to two kinds of statistical analysis:

(1) cross-tabulation analysis for all three tasks
(2) linear discriminant analysis for the recall task.

In conducting these analyses, we focused on the ways in which readers choosing 'late' and those choosing 'excited' on task 20 differed in

(1) explaining their choice on this task
(2) recalling the passage
(3) estimating Al's age and explaining this estimate.

In addition, we analysed these differences in relation to the major groups of readers: native speakers versus non–native speakers (and in the case of non–native speakers, speakers of Japanese versus speakers of other languages).

Results

Task 20. In presenting the results of the experiment, we shall begin with the second task, the one in which readers first responded to task 20 and then explained their choice. The choices that the native and non-native readers made are shown in Table 5.3.[8]

Table 5.3 Choice of 'late', 'excited', or 'tired' by native and non-native speakers of English

	'late'	'excited'	'tired'
Native speakers	51 (54.3%)	32 (34.1%)	11 (11.6%)
Non-native speakers	173 (64.1%)	65 (24.1%)	32 (12.8%)

As can be seen, a larger proportion of non-native speakers were able to select the target response 'late' ($p < 0.05$). Table 5.4 shows the results when the Japanese are separated from the other non-native speakers.

Table 5.4 Choice of 'late', 'excited', or 'tired' by native speakers, Japanese speakers, and other non–native speakers

	'late'	'excited'	'tired'
Native speakers	51 (54.3%)	32 (34.1%)	11 (11.6%)
Non-native speakers			
Japanese	78 (57.8%)	36 (26.6%)	21 (15.6%)
Other non-native	95 (70.4%)	29 (21.5%)	11 (8.1%)

The difference between the two groups of non-native speakers was not significant, but the Japanese speakers, as can be seen, fall between the native speakers and the other non-native speakers. As we report results for the various tasks, we shall continue to keep the Japanese separate from the other non-native speakers. It will be seen that they often fall between the two groups, even though differences may not reach a level of significance.

Our primary focus, however, will be on the difference between native speakers and non-native speakers: how can we explain the fact that native speakers were less able to select the target response on task 20? We can provide no ready answer to this question but we can piece together a plausible explanation by examining reader response to the various tasks.

Let us begin by examining how readers explained their choice on task 20. They either recycled details from the passage or drew inferences from it. Those choosing 'late' tended to justify their choice with

(1)   the detail 'in time'

> 'There was a sentence that he was wondering if he would make there in time'. (Korean)

(2)   the invited inference that the store was closing

> 'It would be unlikely that he would hurry on such a hot day unless he feared the store would be closing shortly'. (American)

Those choosing 'excited' tended to justify their choice with

(1)   the automated inference that Al wanted to buy the shoes

> 'Because the only reason Al wanted to get there was to buy the black pair of shoes'. (Persian)

(2)   extended inferences that expand the narrative such as
        (a) enabling condition for Al buying the shoes

> 'Because she was given pocket money by his father and he would to buy the black shoes that he has wanted to buy before'. (Japanese)

        (b) motivation for Al's wanting the shoes

> 'I guess he came to buy a black shoes for a graduation party'. (Japanese)

As Table 5.5 shows, in all three groups readers choosing 'late' and those choosing 'excited' contrast sharply in the explanations they offer (all numbers in this table – and in all the tables that follow – represent percentages; within this table all the differences between those choosing 'late' and those choosing 'excited' are significant ($p < 0.05$) except for the category of extended inferences).[9]

In evaluating these results, we need to bear in mind that readers explained their choice on task 20 without access to the passage (or, for that matter, the recall they had just made). Hence the frequent use of the detail 'in time' is especially striking. More than half of the native speakers (and nearly 40 per cent of the non-native speakers) choosing 'late' mentioned it; and in all the groups, about one-quarter of those choosing 'late' wrote down only this detail, as though the mere mention of it were self-explanatory. By way of contrast, 'in time' was hardly mentioned by those choosing 'excited' in the three groups. As for the invited inference that the store was closing, more than two–fifths of the native speakers choosing 'late' mentioned it (the proportions were

Table 5.5 Details and inferences in explanation task related to choice of 'late' or 'excited' across the three groups

	Native speakers		Japanese speakers		Other non-native speakers	
	L	E	L	E	L	E
Detail						
in time with other details	52.2	0.0	37.7	2.9	38.8	3.3
in time alone	23.9	0.0	26.1	0.0	21.3	0.0
Invited inference store closing	43.5	6.9	24.6	2.9	35.0	16.7
Automated inference Al wanting shoes	6.5	65.5	2.9	55.9	6.3	56.7
Extended inferences	28.3	44.8	27.5	41.2	18.8	60.0

somewhat lower for the non-native speakers). Once again, in all three groups those choosing 'excited' used this inference infrequently (this was particularly the case with the native speakers and the Japanese).[10]

As for the automated inference that Al wanted the shoes, readers in all three groups frequently used it to justify the choice of 'excited' (nearly two-thirds of the native speakers and more than half of the non-native speakers used it). Predictably, those choosing 'late' in all three groups made little use of this inference. As for extended inferences, in all three groups readers choosing 'excited' used them more frequently than those choosing 'late'. This result suggests that certain readers choosing 'excited' were more prone to construct a situation model too rich for test-taking. This seems to be particularly the case for non-native speakers who tended to expand the narrative in unexpected ways. Here, for example, is how one reader constructed the enabling condition for Al buying the shoes:

> He is very eager to get to the store in time, very excited about buying the shoes. Probably he had to ask his parents 50 times for the money. He didn't have easy access to money, and finally got it. (Dutch)

The same spirit of expansion was evidenced by those who focused on Al's motivation for buying the shoes:

> He likes music. His favourite musician will come his town. They will make a concert. (Japanese)

It is as if these non-native speakers are not aware that a test-taking situation constrains the kinds of inferences that they can make. Let us now move on to consider a more text-based source of attraction to 'excited' for native speakers.

Recall task. Within the experimental design, the recall task had a special status since it was presented first: while responding to it, readers did not know that they were going to respond to task 20 (or, for that matter, the age-estimate task). Hence it is not surprising that the detail 'in time' is not particularly prominent (as it is when readers are asked to explain their choice on task 20). As can be seen in Table 5.6, this detail is in the eighth position when we rank passage details according to the frequency with which they were recalled by native speakers (only those details that were recalled by at least one-third of the native speakers are included).

Table 5.6 Rank ordering of passage detail on recall task across the three groups

	Native speakers	Japanese speakers	Other non-native speakers
crowded	77.8	73.6	76.3
black shoes	74.1	55.7	58.5
hot	71.6	57.1	43.7
cool	61.7	30.7	31.9
far away	46.9	57.1	57.8
squeeze	42.0	37.1	37.8
rush	38.2	32.9	37.0
in time	33.3	42.1	44.4

The poor showing of 'in time' among native speakers is surprising since they recalled most details with greater frequency than non-native speakers (this greater frequency is, of course, a direct consequence of the fact that their recalls were much fuller). Their relative lack of attention to 'in time' provides further evidence for a point we made earlier: native speakers were more focused on the indigenous narrative gestalt than on details that the test makers imported.

This sharper focus on the indigenous gestalt becomes particularly salient if we separate readers selecting 'late' from those selecting 'excited'. Table 5.7 presents these two groups in relation to how frequently they recalled just those details in the excited-youth gestalt. We present these details in the order in which they appear in the passage

Table 5.7 Excited-youth gestalt details on recall task in relation to choice of 'late' or 'excited' across the three groups

	Native speakers		Japanese speakers		Other non-native speakers	
	L	E	L	E	L	E
big store	6.7	18.5	51.9	27.5	25.3	27.6
far away	37.8	63.0	58.2	60.0	63.2	34.5
big doors	6.7	18.5	8.9	2.5	12.6	13.8
deictic focus on shoes	15.6	44.4	3.8	7.5	5.3	3.5

(such ordering strongly constrains a recall task – readers generally report narrative details in the order in which they occur).

Here we can see an important pattern that was obscured in Table 5.6, which presented only overall frequency of recall: it is the native speakers choosing 'excited', as opposed to those choosing 'late', who recalled with greater frequency the details belonging to the excited-youth gestalt. For the non-native speakers, however, the recall of these details does not discriminate between those choosing 'excited' and those choosing 'late'. In fact, certain details were apparently recalled more frequently by those choosing 'late' (e.g. 'big store' for the Japanese and 'far away' for the other non-native speakers).

The patterns in Table 5.7 become even more salient if we examine the structure coefficients of a linear discriminant analysis. These structure coefficients rank details on the recall task according to the degree to which they correlate with the discriminant function that predicts choice on task 20. For all three groups, we list only the six details that most strongly correlate with the discriminant function. In the case of the native speakers, it is the four details central to the excited-youth gestalt – joined with one other – that predict the choice of 'excited'.

As table 5.8 shows, the deictic focus on shoes – the culminating detail of the excited-youth gestalt – predicts most strongly the choice of 'excited'. The other three details belonging to this gestalt are also present along with one other detail: recalling the shoes but not mentioning that they are 'black'.[11]

By way of contrast, only 'in time' emerged as strongly predicting the choice of 'late'. Hence this detail, though not recalled with particular frequency by native speakers, outstripped all others in its power to predict the choice of 'late'. The native speakers who managed to keep this detail in play during the recall task were better able to select the

Table 5.8 Passage details on recall task that best correlate with the discriminant function predicting native-speaker choice on task 20

Passage detail	Correlation with discriminant function (structure coefficients)	
	L	E
deictic focus on shoes		0.50807
far away		0.38241
in time	0.34895	
big doors		0.28195
shoes (with no mention of 'black')		0.22960
big store		0.16502

target response 'late'. It is as if the phrase itself, if retained, is poised for alignment with 'late'.

In the case of the non-native speakers, the detail 'in time' best predicted the choice on task 20. As Table 5.9 shows, the detail 'in time' strongly predicts the choice of 'late' for both groups. This correlation is

Table 5.9 Passage details on recall task that best correlate with the discriminant function predicting non-native choice on task 20

Passage detail	Correlation with discriminant function (structure coefficients)	
	L	E
Japanese speakers		
in time	0.54830	
big store	0.41224	
crowded	0.30886	
squeezed	0.26897	
big doors	0.20855	
hot	0.17816	
Other non-native speakers		
in time	0.69084	
far away	0.37902	
hot	0.24500	
squeezed		0.24002
shoes (mentioned without 'black')	0.19474	
crowded		0.13056

particularly strong for the other non-native speakers (0.69) which was the group choosing 'late' most frequently (70 per cent). For neither of the non-native groups is there a distinctive set of details strongly correlated with the choice of 'excited': in Table 5.9, for the Japanese, there are no such details and for the other non-native group only 'squeezed' and 'crowded' – neither belonging to the excited-youth gestalt.

Age-estimate task. In responding to the age-estimate task, readers first estimated Al's age and then gave reasons for their estimate. Let us first examine the proportion of readers in the three groups who estimated that Al was an adult or a youth (we distinguish, once again, readers choosing 'late' from those choosing 'excited').[12] The numbers are given in Table 5.10.

Table 5.10 Response to age-estimate task related to choice of 'late' or 'excited' across the three groups

	Native speakers		Japanese speakers		Other non-native speakers	
	L	*E*	*L*	*E*	*L*	*E*
Youth	41.3	65.5	31.4	50.0	15.3	40.7
Adult	39.9	10.3	28.6	11.1	47.1	31.3

If we read across the rows, we can, once again, observe what seems to be a contrasting pattern for all three groups: those viewing Al as an adult are more likely to choose 'late', those viewing him as a youth are more likely to choose 'excited'. It is only, however, as we examine columns within Table 5.10 that differences emerge which reach the level of significance ($p < 0.05$). Among the native speakers and the Japanese, those choosing 'excited' are much more prone to view Al as a youth. The fact that this tendency is particularly strong for the native speakers lends further support, albeit indirect, to the notion that they had greater access to the excited-youth gestalt.[13]

If we examine how readers explained their estimate of Al's age, we find further evidence for the gestalt. As we examine Table 5.11, we can see that native speakers choosing 'excited' were especially prone to use what we call *youth norms* to justify their estimate (e.g. 'He must have been a young boy by the way he was hurrying in the street').[14]

Native speakers choosing 'excited' were also prone to draw on stylistic features in explaining their estimate: 37.7 per cent of them drew on such features whereas only 17.4 per cent of those choosing 'late' did (among

Table 5.11 Explanation of age-estimate related to choice of 'late' or
'excited' across the three groups

	Native speakers		Japanese speakers		Other non-native speakers	
	L	E	L	E	L	E
Youth norms	37.0	75.9	40.6	50.5	52.5	36.7
Adult norms	41.3	3.4	23.2	11.8	28.8	23.3

non-native speakers the use of stylistic features on this task was
practically nil). In examining the nature of these features, we discovered
that they were largely those we earlier associated with the excited-youth
gestalt (e.g. 'I estimate that Al is young – 10 or so – because of the
grammatical structure of the sentences and the formation of the
paragraph').

Summary of experiment.

Having analysed all three tasks, we are now able to piece together the
larger story of why native speakers are not able to select the target
response 'late' as effectively as non-native speakers: they have much
greater access to the excited-youth gestalt and so are more attracted to
the choice 'excited'. Various kinds of evidence have been used to support
this claim:

(1) those choosing 'excited' were better able to recall the details
    belonging to this gestalt
(2) those choosing 'excited' were more text based in justifying their
    choice (globally integrating the two major narrative elements)
(3) those choosing 'excited' were more likely to view Al as a youth and
    to justify this view by
    (a) the use of normative reasoning about what a youth is likely to do
    (b) the use of stylistic features belonging to the excited-youth gestalt.

The cumulative weight of this evidence is imposing, particularly when
viewed in relation to the actual protocols of native speakers choosing
'excited'. We present here some samples of how they responded to the
recall task (as indicated by the italics, the details belonging to the
excited-youth gestalt are very much in evidence)[15]:

The *big building* looked *far away*. It was hot and crowded and he had to
squeeze through people to get to it. Once he got to the *big glass doors*, he went

downstairs to the shoe department and the black shoes he wanted were *right there in front of him.*

The department store seemed *far away.* Al had to squeeze through the hot and crowded street to get there. The *big doors* swung open. He was soon inside the cool building. He rushed down the stairs. *There in front of him* were the black shoes he had come to buy.

Even when native speakers choosing 'excited' included the transplanted detail 'in time', it did not seem to offset the weight of the excited-youth gestalt (note the strong tendency to recall this detail as 'on time'):

The store looked very *far away.* He wondered if he would get there 'on time'. He *squeezed* between people on the crowded street. It was hot outside. He went through the *big glass doors.* It was cool inside. He went downstairs to go to the shoe department. He saw the black shoes he wanted *right in front of him.*

The *big building* looked *far away.* Al wondered if he would get there 'on time'. It was hot. He got to the building and went in. It was cool. He ran down the steps to the shoe department. The black shoes which he wanted were there.

The second protocol omits the final detail in the gestalt but it does contain another critical detail: that Al continued to hurry even when he was inside the store (i.e. 'He *ran down* the steps to the shoe department'). As we claimed in the first section, it is precisely this detail that allows a reader to integrate the two sections of the narrative: if Al continues to hurry inside the store, it is plausible that the same goal motivated his earlier hurrying outside the store – to get to the shoes he wanted to buy.

Native speakers choosing 'excited' demonstrated their access to the excited-youth gestalt not only on the recall task but on the other tasks as well. Here is the complete protocol of one native speaker who chose 'excited':

(1) recall task

The *big store* seemed *very far away.* Al had to walk through a crowd to get there. It was hot & sticky out. At last he came to the *big glass doors* and opened them to step into the cool building. Then he went downstairs to the shoe department and saw *in front of him* the black shoes he wanted to buy. [italics added]

(2) task 20

– excited

– It seems as though he is anxious to reach the store and that getting the shoes is his goal. Everything seems magnified – like a kid sees the world when he is excited.

(3) age-estimate task

  – about 10

  – Story details (e.g. the building is big) give the feeling of a child and his perceptions.

Clearly this reader captured the details belonging to the excited-youth gestalt: 'big store', 'very far away', 'big glass doors', and even the front shifted 'in front of him'. Moreover, she even managed to spell out what lay behind those details – a child, especially when excited, perceiving the world as magnified. The reading skill exemplified in her protocol is quite remarkable when one considers the situation in which she demonstrated it: after reading the test passage for only 45 seconds, she was able to provide a relatively complete reconstruction of it. Not only did she manage to write down all the important details but she was able to keep them in the right sequence. Moreover, she was able, as indicated by her response to the last two tasks, to infer an appropriate narrative point of view. That a reader of such skill would be marked wrong on task 20 is difficult for us to accept.

Conclusions

The various studies that we have conducted show how difficult text adaptation can be for test makers, particularly when they are importing new elements into existing material. As indicated, they undertake such adaptation for good reasons: they want to ensure that each test contains samples of real-world text and that these samples are at an appropriate level of difficulty for those taking the test. Unfortunately, their approach to adaptation does not take sufficient account of the delicacy of text structure: as material is imported into a text, it comes into conflict with what is already there. In our own experience as writers, we find that a text must often be reconstructed in order to absorb the new; it is seldom that a local change does not have larger ramifications. Consider, for example, the apparently innocent introduction of 'in time' in the adapted test material. Once this phrase was in place, it led readers to pose the question 'in time for what?'. As we pointed out, this question can be answered in two ways: if readers approach it locally, they respond, 'getting to the store before it closes'; but if they approach it globally, they respond, 'getting to the black shoes before they disappear'.

In analysing test discourse over the years, we have often encountered the kinds of problems we have here described. From our own perspective as discourse analysts, test makers have been too facile in their approach to text adaptation. We can only speculate on the reasons for this. One possible explanation is that their academic training does not sufficiently alert them to the kinds of problems we have dealt with in this chapter. Many of them come from certain fields in psychology where texts are manipulated for experimental purposes (e.g. particular bits of text are inserted or removed to determine how this affects reader response). Such manipulation should, in principle, alert those doing it to the delicacy of text structure. But when one reads the results of these experiments, there is often a sense that such delicacy has not been properly attended to.[16]

There is another aspect of test-making that may contribute to this problem. The tasks that test makers construct must sufficiently discriminate among test takers: if a task does not, it will not be included on a test since it cannot pull its own weight. As Hill and Larsen (1983) suggest, a hybrid text can provide fertile conditions for creating tasks that discriminate among test takers. The more internal contradictions within a text, the greater its potential for producing a differentiated set of responses to the tasks that accompany it. Those readers who attend to local detail tend to select the target response, those who attend to holistic pattern a distractor. We are not suggesting that test makers deliberately adapt text as a means of constructing such tasks. Rather, our claim is that the various constraints with which they operate lower their vigilance about the effects of the adapted material they produce.

As we have suggested, the problems that result from text adaptation are not confined to test makers. Those who produce materials for second language learning face these problems as well. They, too, draw on children's material in creating text for adult learners. Such material is seductive for it reflects an appropriate simplicity in language structure. The situation that it represents may, however, reflect an inappropriate simplicity. In reading the adapted material in this study, many adults were puzzled about why Al was so intent upon buying a particular pair of shoes. As one Nigerian put it, 'So what's the big deal about buying a pair of black shoes?'.

The banality of this situation led certain adult readers to construct a quite different motivation for Al. Here is an excerpt from a think-aloud protocol of a Haitian, newly enrolled in an adult literacy programme in New York City:

> Before it was very hot. He go to buy shoes but it is not real. He would like to have a fresh air. And when he goes to the...to the store, maybe sometime in my country I was hot. I did same like Al. When I was hot, I go to the big store. Inside have 'air conditionné' and I say, 'How much is this?' It's not true. I ... I go to the store for ... I was hot before. I take a new fresh air. Maybe Al come to the store. It's not real because he's very hot and very squeeze outside. He go inside the store for only take a fresh air.

It is obvious that this young man is an inexperienced test taker, for he draws massively on personal experience in responding to the passage; yet his response is attuned to a crucial dimension of the represented situation: Al rushing from the hot crowded streets into a cool store. Moreover, since a mere pair of shoes does not seem to justify such rushing, he draws on his own experience to construct a plausible explanation – Al was really wanting to escape from the heat and was just pretending to buy a pair of shoes. Adults, even when they are inexperienced readers, are able to engage in sophisticated reasoning about psychological matters such as motivation. It is the very stuff they work with in making sense out of everyday life, and so they naturally draw on it in interpreting text.

From a pedagogical perspective, this kind of reading should be valued for it shows a mind actively at work. From the perspective of testing and assessment, however, it raises complicated questions: how are we to evaluate the situation that the young Haitian constructed? Is it sufficiently congruent with the text? Certainly it was an unexpected response, and it may be unduly related to his own experience; and yet once it is in place, it does help to resolve the problem of Al's motivation. It fits with a pattern of human behaviour that we can all recognise, for many of us have fabricated just such reasons for entering an air-conditioned store on a hot day.

If we are committed to assessing the constructive processes in which readers engage, we must be willing to face these kinds of questions. We have no ready answers, but we would like to suggest certain guidelines that those reforming testing need to bear in mind when dealing with constructive processes. First of all, a multiple-choice format is ill-advised since it provides the very inferences that the readers themselves should make. Consider, for example, a multiple-choice task that legitimately focuses on an important detail in the adapted test material under consideration:

Why do you think Al wanted to buy a particular pair of black shoes?

(A)   All the other shoes in the store were white.
(B)   These shoes had been advertised at a good price.
(C)   These shoes were the first ones he saw in the store.
(D)   There were many pairs of these shoes in the store.

The most plausible choice is (B), which is built around a shoe-sale scenario that many readers constructed when explaining their choice of task 20. If, however, this scenario is provided, test takers are deprived of the opportunity of actually constructing it.

For this reason, multiple-choice questions may be replaced with those that require a short answer. If this replacement takes place, we must be willing – and here we introduce a second guideline – to accept different kinds of extended inferences. In constructing a shoe-sale scenario, certain readers, as in the multiple-choice task above, focused on price, as illustrated by what a Chinese said during a think-aloud protocol:

> He found the price was cheaper than he found in the other stores. He thought the sale was going to be ended soon. If the shoes can be found anywhere or the price is all the same, he doesn't have to endure such a hot weather. So I think he must have already compared many stores and finally decided to rush back to that one before the sale is ended.

Other readers focused on scarcity, as indicated by the response of a Croatian reader:

> The shoes Al wanted to buy were probably the last pair. He really wanted to have them so he was excited and in a hurry to get to the store.

Still other readers constructed a different scenario, one built around a fashion-conscious teenager. In estimating Al's age, a Japanese reader explained:

> I think he is 16–18 years old. Because he seems to be interested in fashion.

Once we are committed to accepting different kinds of inferences, we may even decide to use methods that elicit more flexible responses from readers. Indeed, our goal might well be to determine whether individual readers can construct multiple situations that are congruent with a text. If we do come up with such ambitious goals, then our methods of assessment must necessarily shift. We can use an oral interview, such as the one discussed by Cummins and Jones in Chapter 9, or a think-aloud protocol, which, as illustrated by the Haitian and Chinese examples, we used to good advantage in our own research.

In focusing on readers' capacity for flexibility, we must not, however, overlook their capacity for discrimination. It is at this point that we can introduce a third guideline: in assessing readers' constructive processes, we need to distinguish between extended inferences that are textually based and those that are experientially based. Certainly personal and cultural experience is operative as readers construct textually based inferences; indeed, we can detect hints of such experience in the Chinese focus on a 'cheaper price', the Croatian focus on 'the last pair', or the Japanese focus on 'fashion'. Nevertheless price, scarcity, and fashion are values which, in principle, can be used in any culture to account for the crucial textual detail – Al's quest for a particular pair of shoes.

Contrasting with these broadly constructed explanations are those anchored in culturally specific experience. Consider, for example, how certain Japanese readers evoked a fashion-conscious teenager in estimating Al's age:

> 15 – they were black Reeboks. Familiar because of my experience.

> Teen, because he rushed down the stairs to the shoe department. And black color is popular among Japanese teenagers.

There is no textual evidence that the store Al was rushing to was located in Japan, and so any appeal to fashion preferences among Japanese teenagers is not motivated. In order to minimise such unmotivated inferences, it is important that the material used in reading assessment be appropriately contextualised. If Al had been rushing to a store in a well-specified location, readers' unwarranted use of personal and cultural experience would have been reduced. To coin an aphorism, vague text leads to vague interpretation.

In discussing readers' inappropriate use of their own experience, we would like to mention what may be considered the opposite problem – active resistance to the use of experiential knowledge. This problem can be illustrated by describing research that one of us conducted on the adapted test material in Nigeria. In analysing the results of the experiment described above, we discovered that student responses to task 20 and the age-estimate task were not strongly correlated (i.e. 'excited' did not correlate with youth and 'late' with adulthood). In analysing the data more closely, we discovered an obvious explanation for this lack of correlation: Nigerian students, whether choosing 'late' or 'excited', tended to view Al as youthful. When explaining their reasons for this estimate, many students pointed out that an adult would not squeeze through a crowd in a public space. We were intrigued by this appeal to normative behaviour since it runs counter to what we have observed in Nigeria, or, for that matter, in other parts of the world. When this point was raised with the students, they pointed out that what they read on a test is best understood according to how people should behave rather than how they actually do. We can observe here a rather dramatic effect of testing on how students respond: they actively suppress what they know so that they can make an appropriate response.

It is just such guarded responses that led Hill and Parry (1992a) to call for a major reform of testing in Nigeria. They argue for an assessment model that elicits readers' experientially oriented responses as well as textually oriented ones. We do not have space here to consider this comprehensive approach – it is summarised in the concluding chapter to this volume – but would like to note its fundamental premise: to develop in students greater awareness of the varied range of responses they make to text. They need not only to distinguish among the text-based inferences – automated, invited, and extended – described in this chapter but to distinguish such inferences from those involved in experiential evaluation of the situation model represented by the text. Cultivating such awareness within readers is crucial if we are to fulfil the most fundamental goal of any assessment activity – developing students' capacity for monitoring their own experience of text.

Acknowledgements

This chapter is based on a research project that we conducted with Stratton Ray and Yasuko Watt. Their energies, insights, and research skills are evidenced in all that we have written here. We would like to thank the many graduate students in Applied Linguistics at Teachers College, Columbia University, who helped us conduct interviews and think-aloud protocols. We would also like to acknowledge the New York State Education Department for funding the research.

Notes

1. This chapter uses material that was published in a research report entitled *Reading Assessment in Adult Education: Local Detail versus Textual Gestalt*, 1989, LC Report 89-2, The Literacy Center, Teachers College, Columbia University (the authors of the more extended report were Clifford Hill, Laurie Anderson, Stratton Ray, and Yasuko Watt).
2. Van Dijk and Kintsch themselves use the term *bridging inferences* (Clark and Clark 1977).
3. There is also a 1987 edition of the TABE, though the earlier edition is still used (see Hill and Parry 1989 for a detailed comparison of these two editions).
4. It is difficult to include the tasks here because there are ten of them. Unlike certain standardised tests, the number of tasks per passage is not stable on the TABE (1976 edition): it varies from 2 to 11.
5. This concern with stability was not altogether benign since the statistical norming for the 1970 edition of the CAT was directly transferred to the 1976 edition of TABE.
6. In adapting the CAT version, the test makers changed the initial verb of motion from 'ran' to 'walked' (i.e. the one that describes movement on the sidewalks). They did not, however, change the expression 'in a hurry to get to the store' in the stem of task 20. Using this information, readers still view Al as hurrying both outside the store and within it.
7. The passage does not actually state that Al wanted to buy the shoes (nor, for that matter, does it state that he bought them, even though the stem of task

27 reads 'The things Al bought were' (see Appendix 5.1).

8. The fourth distractor 'hungry' is not included here. Only one non-native speaker at the intermediate level selected it.

9. We shall no longer include 'tired' in the tables since we wish to focus on the contrast between 'late' and 'excited'. We should point out, however, that the choice of 'tired', though relatively infrequent, did correlate strongly with certain responses to the other two tasks. On the recall task, more than three-quarters of those choosing 'tired' included the detail 'hot'; and on the age-estimate task, more than half of those choosing 'tired' estimated Al to be 55 years or older. The diminished point of view, inferred from the magnified world, can be associated with age as well as youth.

10. In justifying their choice of 'late', readers tended to use either the detail 'in time' or the invited inference that the store was closing. The likelihood of the two occurring together in an explanation was nil for both native speakers and Japanese speakers and less than 2 per cent for the other non-native speakers. It is as if readers in all three groups, when providing a parsimonious explanation, viewed these two as virtually indistinguishable.

11. The predictive power of this detail provides a certain negative evidence for a claim we made earlier: the fact that the shoes are black leads readers to view Al as older which, in turn, leads them to choose 'late'. Hence it is not surprising that the recall of shoes without colour is related to the choice of 'excited'.

12. As mentioned in the methodology section, we excluded responses that fell between 18 and 24 years. It is of interest that considerably more non-native responses were in this range (more than a third, as compared to only about a fifth of the native speakers). It is as though non-native readers had some access to the excited-youth gestalt, but not enough to pull their estimate of age down into the child/teenager range.

13. The fact that this tendency is also strong for Japanese speakers may help to explain why they fall out between the native speakers and the other non-native speakers. Japanese speakers choosing 'excited' were much more prone than other non-native speakers to view Al as young. By way of contrast, it was only among the other non-native speakers that those choosing 'late' were prone to view Al as an adult.

14. When we examine how non-native speakers justify their choice of 'excited', we can see, once again, that the Japanese are much closer to the native speakers. In fact, for the Japanese choosing 'excited' there was a significant relation between choice of 'excited' and use of youth norms ($p < 0.05$). It seems evident that the Japanese who chose 'excited' tended to work with some notion of Al as young, even if they were not able to recall actual details of the excited-youth gestalt. It is as if they had some kind of receptive access to the gestalt but little capacity to reproduce its details.

15. Note the stability of the opening sentence. Certain readers varied its form, emphasising even more that the size and distance was a matter of appearance (e.g. 'The store loomed "big" and "far" from him').

16. Psychologists who have taken a constructivist approach to text demonstrate a much richer awareness, as illustrated by the work of Van Dijk and Kintsch (1983) that we cite in our introduction.

APPENDIX 5.1: Two versions of the test material

CAT Version (1970)

The big store looked very far away. Benny and Al wondered if they would ever get there. It was very hot and crowded on the sidewalks. They had to squeeze between the people as they ran. At last they came to the big glass doors. The doors swung open and they were soon inside the cool building. They rushed down the stairs to the toy shop. Right in front of them were the shiny skates which they had come to buy.

18. Benny and Al were in
    5. a big city
    6. a small village
    7. the country
    8. the mountains

19. Benny and Al went to the store to buy
    1. clothes
    2. groceries
    3. shoes
    4. toys

20. Benny and Al were in a hurry to get to the store because they were
    5. excited
    6. hungry
    7. late
    8. tired

21. On the sidewalks it was
    1. cold
    2. hot
    3. wet
    4. windy

22. Benny and Al saw lots of
    5. horses
    6. people
    7. trains
    8. trees

23. The store had big doors made of
    1. glass
    2. metal
    3. wire
    4. wood

24. Benny and Al went to the department that sold
    5. books
    6. shoes
    7. tools
    8. toys

25. The inside of the building was
    1. cool
    2. damp
    3. dark
    4. hot

26. To get to the right department, Benny and Al used the
    5. elevator
    6. escalator
    7. sidewalk
    8. stairs

27. The things that Benny and Al bought were
    1. bent
    2. black
    3. broken
    4. shiny

TABE Version (1976)

The big store looked very far away. Al wondered if he would get there in time. It was very hot and crowded on the sidewalks. He had to squeeze between the people as he walked. At last he came to the big glass doors. The doors swung open and he was soon inside the cool building. He rushed down the stairs to the shoe department. Right in front of him were the black shoes that he had come to buy.

18. Al was in
    5. a big city
    6. a small village
    7. the country
    8. the mountains

19. Al went to the store to buy
    1. clothes
    2. groceries
    3. shoes
    4. toys

20. Al was in a hurry to get to the store because he was
    5. excited
    6. hungry
    7. late
    8. tired

21. On the sidewalks it was
    1. cold
    2. hot
    3. wet
    4. windy

22. Al saw lots of
    5. horses
    6. people
    7. trains
    8. trees

23. The store had big doors made of
    1. glass
    2. metal
    3. wire
    4. wood

24. Al went to the department that sold
    5. books
    6. shoes
    7. tools
    8. toys

25. The inside of the building was
    1. cool
    2. damp
    3. dark
    4. hot

26. To get to the right department, Al used the
    5. elevator
    6. escalator
    7. sidewalk
    8. stairs

27. The things that Al bought were
    1. bent
    2. black
    3. broken
    4. shiny

PART III

LITERACY ASSESSMENT

This part also falls into two sections, with Chapters 6 and 7 describing alternative reading tests and Chapters 8 and 9 presenting assessment practices that go well beyond testing.

In Chapter 6, 'English education in Zimbabwe: testing communicative competence', Kate Allen addresses a practical problem: the need to evaluate the competence of junior secondary school students in Zimbabwe so as, on the one hand, to certify their literacy skills for the practical purposes of employment, and, on the other, to indicate their ability to proceed to a senior secondary education. She first discusses the reading section of the existing Zimbabwe Junior Certificate exam, which was developed within the British tradition and was effectively used to exclude most students from senior secondary education. The exam no longer has an official gate-keeping function, but it is still taken by all Zimbabwean secondary school students, and Allen argues that its effects are damaging because it is at variance with the communicative syllabus introduced in the schools. She discusses the principles on which a new test should be based, and she points out the practical constraints within which the test developer must work in the Zimbabwean context. She then presents test material that is based on these principles while taking account of the constraints: it includes authentic texts – such as newspaper articles, advertisements, bureaucratic forms – together with multiple-choice or short-answer tasks that untrained teachers can easily mark. She describes how she pilot tested and evaluated this material, combining statistical analysis of test takers' responses with discourse analysis of interviews conducted with representative students. She concludes by recommending that this more comprehensive method of developing and evaluating test material become standard practice.

In Chapter 7, 'English for academic purposes in Brazil: the use of summary tasks', Andrew Cohen deals with a test designed to assess proficiency in reading English in a Brazilian university context. The test consists of newspaper and magazine articles in English, which the students are asked to summarise in Portuguese. Cohen demonstrates the validity of this form of test by examining closely how students arrived at their responses, and he reports the students' evaluation of the test in relation to what they had done in an English course and in the context of their regular English reading habits. He also, however, considers the problem of test reliability by analysing how two different test raters evaluated the students' summaries.

Both of these studies demonstrate the advantages as well as the difficulties of alternative testing. In both cases the passages and tasks constitute an improvement on traditional tests in that they reflect much more closely students' everyday uses of text; and so such tests can be expected to have a beneficial effect on classroom teaching. The reliability of the tests proved, however, to be a problem. In Allen's case, the material she used and the need to keep tasks in an easily marked form so limited the range of questions she could ask that the resulting test proved to be too easy. Thus it did not satisfy psychometric standards of reliability and it did not discriminate sufficiently between the students for gate-keeping purposes (though she argues that it would be quite appropriate for basic certification). In Cohen's case, his raters differed significantly both in the scores they gave to the same summaries and in the general features they rewarded and penalised. He concludes that, to achieve reliability in scoring summaries, raters must be adequately trained and make use of carefully developed score keys.

Chapters 8 and 9 move beyond the testing paradigm and consider assessment practices that we collectively describe as *documentation*. In Chapter 8, 'An adult learner in Canada: watching assessment take place', Patrick Cummins and Stan Jones examine a particular instance of a learner being assessed for purposes of placement within a literacy programme. The assessor is an experienced intake counsellor whose concern is not only to develop an adequate description of the learner's capabilities but to help him see what he is able to do. She takes pains to avoid the traditional testing situation in which the learner would be isolated with text. Instead she presents the test that she uses in the context of a conversation that covers not only the test items but also the learner's previous experience and present goals, and the assessment consists of the documentary record of that conversation.

Like other writers in this volume, Cummins and Jones look particularly closely at the strategies that the learner uses, and one of their most interesting observations is how extensively he draws on his real world knowledge and how he depends as much on the context and physical form of a text as on the words of which it is constructed. They also examine the strategies used by the assessor. She is both experienced and thoughtful and displays considerable insight; yet her outlook is in certain respects curiously limited by her training as an elementary school teacher. As a result, her documentation of the interview reflects assumptions associated with the autonomous model of literacy and is accordingly impoverished. Cummins and Jones make a number of suggestions as to how the documentation could be enriched. They conclude by pointing out how much the assessor is able to achieve in helping the student to identify appropriate goals and to appreciate his own capabilities.

In Chapter 9, 'Assessing adult literacy in the United Kingdom: the Progress Profile', Deryn Holland and Brian Street place the assessment of adult literacy in its sociopolitical context. They begin by showing how a learner-centred approach, marginalised in traditional educational settings, has been widely used in adult literacy programmes. They then point out how government policies have recently challenged this approach by emphasising greater accountability in methods of assessing both individual and programme achievement. Adult literacy programmes are now coming under strong pressure to develop models of assessment more akin to those used in the United States.

In response to this political pressure, the Adult Literacy Basic Skills Unit has developed two methods of assessing literacy skills, one taking the form of certification of a more traditional kind and the other – the Progress Profile – representing a relatively novel approach. It is the latter model on which Holland and Street concentrate. They discuss first the central concepts on which the Progress Profile is based, namely, 'literacy' and 'progress'. Then they describe the Progress Profile itself, showing how its format reflects the principles on which it is based. Finally, they describe how the instrument has been disseminated through training sessions that Holland conducted throughout England and Wales – in which, interestingly enough, she encountered in practitioners the same kind of adherence to the autonomous model as is described by Cummins and Jones.

Both these chapters make clear that problems will inevitably be encountered in introducing new forms of assessment, even in adult education programmes, where there is more room for manoeuvre than in a school setting. Nevertheless, these chapters are instructive in that they show how the pragmatic model of literacy can be applied in practice, and they suggest that it should indeed be possible, by documenting the reading and writing in which individuals engage, to move from testing to a broader, more valid, and, for the student, more instructive model of assessment.

6 English education in Zimbabwe: testing communicative competence

Kate Allen

Background

In Zimbabwe, as in other anglophone African countries, the education system in colonial times was modelled on the one in Britain – indeed, the British model was followed particularly closely because the country's substantial settler community demanded an education for their children that was comparable to what they would have had at home. Thus, a British curriculum was followed, textbooks for all subjects were originally imported from Britain, and the examinations on which certificates were based were provided by British examining boards such as the Associated Examination Board and the University of Cambridge Local Examinations Syndicate. Needless to say, the language of instruction was English, and both curricula and teaching methods were based on the assumption that students were native speakers or had native speaker proficiency.

While such a system may have served the needs of the settler community, it was far less appropriate for the Africans who comprised the vast majority of Zimbabwe's population. The language of instruction was an obvious difficulty. As their first language, most Zimbabweans speak Shona, a significant minority speak Ndebele and other smaller groups speak a variety of other languages. None of these languages was used as a medium beyond the first few weeks of primary school, even though, in the racially segregated schools of the time, it might, in principle, have been possible. African students, therefore, had to study in a second or even third language, and it was a language that few of them encountered before embarking on their school careers. Nevertheless, they were taught the same curriculum and judged by the same standards as were the children of the British settlers.

The situation was made even more inequitable by the fact that in colonial days provision for African education was extremely limited. To begin with, indeed, the colonial government took no responsibility for it at all, leaving the teaching of African children in the hands of missionaries – it was not until 1944 that the first state primary school was established for Africans, and the first state secondary school for them followed in 1950 (Blake 1977; Meredith 1979). Competition for the few places available in African schools was severe, and examinations were used to select those who would be allowed to further their education – not only at the end of secondary school, but also at the end of primary and junior secondary school. The certificates given to successful candidates were accordingly highly valued, and the curriculum came to be dominated by tests as teachers tried to prepare their students for the various national and overseas exams.

In 1980, when an African majority government was established, one of its first priorities was to reform the education system: schools were desegregated, new syllabi were developed, and enormous numbers of new students were admitted. Between 1979 and 1985 there was a 272 per cent expansion in primary school enrolment, and over the same period, the expansion in secondary school enrolment was 677 per cent (Central Statistical Office 1985, p. 5). Today more children than ever before have access to education, and they all want to take the examinations that mark the completion of each level. Parents are even more enthusiastic and will do their utmost to find the money to pay the exam fees. All too often, both children and parents are disappointed, for the exam system, designed as it is to select a privileged élite, has not been changed, and the consequence is increasingly high failure rates.

The retention of the old exam system has also had an unfortunate effect on attempts to reform the curriculum. This is particularly true for English, which, still the official language, remains the medium of instruction and is the most important single subject. During the 1970s, much work was done by the Ministry of Education to adapt the English syllabus in the light of recent work on communicative language teaching. The intention was to develop a new English syllabus that addressed the needs of the changing school population. Unlike the old syllabus, it was not designed to assume native-like proficiency on the part of the students. It was, however, designed to provide greater continuity between primary and secondary school. Previous syllabuses had failed to bridge this gap effectively and as a result most of the first year of secondary education was spent on work that was supposed to have been covered in primary school.

In addition, the new syllabus stresses the importance of relating the language used in the classroom to the students' needs as members of modern Zimbabwean society. Thus the focus is not simply on learning rules of grammar but on learning how to apply these rules appropriately in spoken and written discourse. Lessons are less teacher-centred as the greater variety of classroom activities emphasise more pair and group work. Students are encouraged to relate information in the classroom to their own experiences as well as the outside world. Several new textbooks reflecting this approach have been introduced, and during the 1980s workshops were set up around the country to acquaint teachers with the new approach. The exams, however, remain as they were before: the Cambridge O-Level is still taken at the end of senior secondary school, and the national exams that are taken at earlier stages remain closely modelled on it. Teachers, observing the discrepancies between the old exams and the new syllabus, have reverted to the old materials and teaching methods, since it is by their students' success on the exams that the teachers themselves are judged.

The current Zimbabwean Junior Certificate

The Zimbabwean Junior Certificate (hereafter ZJC) dramatically illustrates the difficulties that confront Zimbabwean educationists as they attempt to reform the education and exam systems. It is a national exam taken at the end of the second year of secondary school, and it was formerly used to determine who would go on to senior secondary education. For a small minority of students the exam thus served as a proficiency test, indicating that they had sufficient academic ability to be considered eligible for a further two years of education. For the majority of students, however, the ZJC was an achievement test: it functioned as an official school-leaving certificate. As such, it was considered the minimum educational qualification for a number of occupations (e.g. clerical work), so it was not treated lightly, especially since students were given only one opportunity to take it. The exam was offered in a number of subjects, but English and Maths were the key ones: students who failed either of these were not given certificates.

Today, the ZJC has an ambivalent status. It is no longer officially used to select those students who are eligible for senior secondary education, since every student is now entitled to remain in secondary school for four years. There are not enough places, however, so headmasters often require students to present their ZJC passes in order to decide who can remain in their particular school. If students are not accepted, they have to find places elsewhere. Furthermore, though there is no intention of restricting access to secondary education, there is talk of using the exam to help students select various educational options so that not everyone goes on to take the academically oriented O-Level exam at the end of secondary school. Therefore, though it is no longer used officially for any particular purpose, the ZJC is still taken by every student in Form 2, and a good deal of time is spent going over past exam papers.

Such work is not, however, very effective, for pass rates have been steadily declining; in 1985, for instance, only about 50 per cent of those who took the ZJC passed. In their report on the 1985 English results, the chief examiners identified a number of problems: students did not demonstrate sufficient variation of style in relation to topic nor were they able to adapt their writing to the needs of the audience. The examiners claimed that many teachers were unfamiliar with the demands of the exam and so did not adequately prepare their students. This diagnosis may well be correct since in the expanded education system there is a severe shortage of qualified teachers: in the primary schools about one-half of the teachers are untrained, while in the secondary schools nearly one-half are untrained and a further one-quarter have only limited training. But inadequate teaching is not the whole answer, for there are also problems in the exam itself, as I discovered in analysing past papers and a sample of student scripts from the 1985 exam (Allen 1988).

The English exam as a whole assesses knowledge of grammar, writing, and reading comprehension. Students' marks are totalled and their overall score is considered to be a measure of their English language proficiency. Knowledge of grammar is measured by a set of questions that focus on problem areas for Zimbabwean students, such as the use of prepositions and verb tenses. Writing, the most important section as indicated by the number of marks allocated to it, is tested by two kinds of essays: an open essay and a guided one. There is a wide range of choices for the open essay, covering different types of writing: the most frequently set, and also the most popular ones with students across the country, are the narrative topics. In the guided essay, students are given various details that they have to combine into a single passage.

For the assessment of reading there is one passage of about 300 words followed by about a dozen questions. The passage is usually a narrative or descriptive piece extracted from a larger context such as a magazine article or novel. It is then simplified; that is, details which the examiner regards as irrelevant are deleted, and simpler vocabulary is substituted for words which the examiner considers too difficult. The resulting text is often less coherent than the original, and questions may focus on features that are no longer apparent because the relevant information has been deleted. Also because so many questions are needed, the examiner tends to emphasise minor details and to require students to recycle low-level information rather than to demonstrate an understanding of the piece as a whole. For example, the comprehension passage in the 1985 exam was taken from a magazine article (which I was able to locate) comparing the Kariba Dam in Zimbabwe with the Aswan Dam in Egypt, and the part selected focused on the problems of Aswan, namely the increase in bilharzia and in soil erosion. One of the questions requires students to say how bilharzia spread through Africa, a point which is mentioned in the text but which cannot be understood without some knowledge of the bilharzia cycle; but the information about the cycle that had been given in the original text had been excised from the exam version. Furthermore, the point about the spread of bilharzia is of minor significance in the passage as a whole, since the focus is on Aswan and not on the rest of Africa. In short, the kind of reading required by this exam does not represent what the students must do to study other school subjects successfully. Still less does it reflect what they will need once they leave school, when they are most likely to read English in such texts as newspapers, official letters, public documents, and manufacturers' instructions.

If the content validity of the exam is questionable, so also is its reliability. As far as the reading component is concerned, there are some multiple-choice questions, but the majority of the questions are open-ended and students have to write their answers in complete sentences. The marking scheme prepared by the examiner indicates what answers are to be judged acceptable; but it is clear from the 1985 scripts that markers do not always give credit for acceptable answers, and there are even examples of incorrect answers in the marking scheme. Consider, for example, the answers specified for the question about bilharzia:

5. Explain in your own words, where bilharzia began and how it spread to other parts of Africa.

Specified answers in the marking scheme:

(A)   Bilharzia started in the White and Blue Nile.
(B)   As time passed, the disease spread southwards.
(C)   As time passed, people carried the parasites to the south.

This format does not make clear that only two answers are expected for this two-part question: answer (*a*) for the origin of the disease and either (*b*) or (*c*) for how bilharzia spread throughout the rest of Africa. Moreover, answer (*b*) does not explain how the disease spread, only that it did so, and so this particular answer is not, strictly speaking, accurate. Such inaccuracies in the marking scheme, together with a lack of flexibility on the part of the markers, are evident throughout the exam; and these problems are exacerbated by the fact that much of the work must be done by inadequately trained teachers.

In view of all these problems, I was encouraged by the Ministry of Education to design a new English exam for the ZJC. In constructing such an exam, I was concerned that it reflect the new communicative syllabus as well as certify that the students leaving school possess basic English skills. To satisfy these concerns, I planned to draw on the ordinary kinds of textual material that students were expected to read in Zimbabwean society. At the same time, I had to work within practical constraints imposed by Ministry of Education policies: given the limited resources in Zimbabwe, the exam had to be relatively easy to administer and mark.

Rationale for a new ZJC

The theoretical basis for my work was the model of communicative competence developed by Canale and Swain (1980, 1981). According to this model, communicative competence has four aspects: grammatical, sociolinguistic, discourse, and strategic. Grammatical competence includes knowledge of the rules of phonology, morphology, syntax, and vocabulary. Sociolinguistic competence is defined as knowledge of the sociocultural rules of language use – that is, which utterances are appropriate in socially defined contexts. Discourse competence refers to the need for utterances to be both cohesive and coherent; it concerns not only the lexico-grammatical links between propositions but the rules which organise meaning so that it is both internally consistent and externally viable. Strategic competence deals with those strategies that may be used when there is limited competence, when communication breaks down, or when some rhetorical effect is emphasised.

This model has a number of implications for language assessment. It suggests, first, that in an ideal assessment instrument, language skills should be elicited in an integrated way rather than being treated, as they are in traditional tests, as if they were discrete. Second, in order to accommodate the sociolinguistic aspect of communicative competence, the instrument should reflect a variety of social circumstances, preferably over a number of occasions. Third, it should put more emphasis than traditional tests do on higher levels of language processing, for traditional tests tend to stress the grammatical aspect while neglecting discourse competence. Fourth, the instrument should be sufficiently flexible to reward the effective use of alternative strategies when communication is in danger of breaking down. Overall, the guiding principle should be that in responding to the instrument students should use language as they would in real life.

In designing a communicative test for Zimbabwe, however, I had to work within certain constraints. First, it was not practicable to test listening or speaking on a national scale, given the lack of trained teachers as well as a shortage of tape recorders and batteries. Nor was it possible to have students talk about the reading and writing on which they were to be assessed, since one of the essential features of the exam tradition is that students work in silence on their own. Similarly, the range of social uses of language that could be tested was severely limited, for the test had to bear some resemblance to the exam that people were accustomed to; otherwise it would not be recognised at all. Moreover, the Ministry of Education insisted on the use of multiple-choice questions; though there are no statistics for the current ZJC exam, ministry officials expected any new instrument to be evaluated in terms of psychometric measures of validity and reliability, and considered multiple-choice questions to be more reliable than open-ended ones. Finally, there were economic considerations. The exam had to be inexpensive to administer, thus precluding a battery of tests taken over various occasions; and it had to be easy to mark, since the majority of teachers who grade the ZJC have limited proficiency in English and receive only a brief training on how to do it.

Thus I was working within the framework of a single exam designed to test reading and writing only; and I had to develop questions to which the answers could be easily judged right or wrong. Nevertheless, I could make the exam more communicative than the existing ZJC by working on its content validity. I did this for both the reading and writing sections of the exam, but here I shall focus on the assessment of reading. I decided to use a greater variety of materials that would represent what students encounter outside school – that is, common local texts such as newpaper articles, bureaucratic forms, advertisements, and instruction manuals. I also presented these texts in the form that they would normally be encountered so that the students could use such clues as format and typeface in deciding how to approach them. Then, in developing the questions, I tried to test reading skills that would be useful not only in the academic context but in the outside world – skills such as scanning, analysing the organisation of a text, identifying the overall idea, and interpreting and reorganising information presented in different formats. In this way, I hoped to develop a test that would have a positive effect on what went on in the classroom, by encouraging the use of a wider and more appropriate range of reading materials and by stimulating activities in which students would learn how to make practical use of them.

Process of development

Since I was trying out a variety of texts and formats, I decided to develop two reading tests, differing both in format and in the types of text used.

The first test, Test A, was based on four different texts and used the multiple-choice format to present a range of tasks:

(1) a newspaper article [a single task that requires students to identify the main subject]

(2) a newspaper index [multiple tasks that require students to scan, make inferences, and transform information]

(3) two advertisements for local correspondence colleges [multiple tasks that require students to compare the information in each]

(4) a newspaper article [multiple tasks that require students to recognise how key points are organised and to identify incorrect information].

Test B contained six passages followed by open-ended questions that elicited short answers:

(1) an instruction manual including two diagrams and a key [multiple tasks that require students to locate specific details and transform information]

(2) an advertisement [multiple tasks that require students to skim, scan, and make inferences]

(3) a form for depositing money into a post office savings account [multiple tasks that require students to select information and distribute it into appropriate spaces on the form]

(4) a schedule for progammes on radio and television [multiple tasks that require students to search for details, compare information located in different places, and make inferences]

(5) a competition entry form [multiple tasks that require students to distribute information into appropriate spaces on the form]

(6) a set of instructions, complete with diagrams and text [multiple tasks that require students to locate specific details and interpret them].

I administered the tests in three schools, to almost 600 students across a wide range of abilities. Two of the schools were urban day schools and the third was a rural boarding school. As I had two different types of reading test and was unable to administer them both to the entire sample, the students were randomly divided into two groups, each of which was given a different test. From the total sample, I selected a smaller one, that is, every third student, to study in greater detail. This resulted in a final sample of 177 students, of whom 89 took Test A and 88 took Test B.

The tests were marked and the data entered into a computer and analysed using SPSSX and the Rasch model of Item Response Theory (Wright and Stone 1979). The SPSSX package uses traditional psychometric techniques to provide information about summary statistics, correlations, reliability, and multiple regressions. Unlike these traditional measurement techniques, the Rasch model claims to be more objective in measuring item difficulty and person's ability (Wright and Stone 1979). There was no intention to replace the classical measures, but rather to obtain additional information about the tests and the students (Henning 1984). I also had access to the ZJC exam papers of the students who took the new tests and so was able to compare their results on the old and the new.

These statistical analyses could tell me whether the items were discriminating between the students and whether the new test was easier or more difficult than the old. They could not, however, tell me whether the items were eliciting, and thereby testing, the skills I hoped to elicit; and since my purpose in designing this exam was not so much to select the best students as to encourage the teaching of appropriate skills, it was important to find out how the students arrived at their responses. I therefore supplemented the data by interviewing individually a representative number of students after they had taken the test. The interview sample was composed of 50 boys and girls who represented a range of abilities as determined by tests administered by their teachers as well as their results on the old ZJC. During the interviews, students went through each question describing which answers they had selected and explaining their reasons. In addition, I asked them some general questions in order to collect information about the social context of the ZJC: for example, what they would like to see in an English exam at this level, and what they thought of the new type of test they had just taken.

Thus, I collected both quantitative and qualitative data on each of the two types of test that I had designed. Analysing these data enabled me to assess the psychometric reliability and validity of each item as well as its effectiveness in eliciting a particular kind of reading. On the basis of this assessment, I could then determine which items should be retained and which rejected in a single exam that could replace the old ZJC.

Results

The students found both Tests A and B easy; that is, many of them correctly answered the questions as reflected in the summary statistics in Table 6.1.

Table 6.1 Summary statistics for Test A and Test B

	Mean	*Standard deviation*	*Minimum score*	*Maximum score*
Test A (*n*=89)	32.4	7.2	8	40
Test B (*n*=88)	23.6	6.4	4	32

Table 6.2 Reliability indices for Test A and Test B

	Alpha Coefficient	Person Separability Index
Test A (n=89)	0.65	0.22
Test B (n=88)	0.91	0.86

According to the traditional Spearman–Brown measure (Alpha Coefficient) and the Rasch programme Person Separability Index, the tests had varying degrees of reliability, as indicated by the results in Table 6.2 (these results differ in the way they are obtained, but they can be easily compared since they use the same scale of 0 to 1).

As can be seen, the Person Separability Index for Test A was considerably lower than the Alpha Coefficient, and it suggested that Test A was, in purely statistical terms, lacking in reliability. This result is partly explained by the manner in which the index is calculated. The sample was comprised of 89 students, 22 of whom achieved perfect scores. They are thus excluded from the calculation, reducing the sample to 67 students. A smaller number of students, whose scores were relatively close together, and the limited number of questions resulted in relatively little discrimination between the students. It was thus difficult to calculate an index based on discrimination within the sample. Even so, the reliability index suggests that the test was not as effective as I had hoped and that closer attention was needed to determine where the problems lay.

The students also found Test B easy; that is, many of them answered most of the questions correctly. Nevertheless both measures of reliability are higher for Test B than for Test A. Test B discriminated between students, who were more widely distributed across the range of marks than were the students who took Test A. One reason for the improved reliability is the added length of Test B: the increased number of questions made it easier to discriminate between student scores (Nunnally 1972).

If the tests were intended to select students for further education, they were inadequate since they did not discriminate efficiently. This problem was particularly pronounced with Test A – unfortunately since, in using the multiple-choice format, it followed more closely the criteria set by the Ministry. On the other hand, if these two tests were to be used only to certify students' competence, the tests could be considered adequate, provided that students' success in both tests did indeed indicate that the standard of English set by the new tests had been realised. The statistical analysis did not indicate how the test items functioned, what skills students used in answering questions, or whether these corresponded to those I had intended. The interviews did, however, give this information and were able to demonstrate more effectively than traditional measures of reliability the strengths and weaknesses of the tests.

An analysis of certain tasks illustrates the importance of basing any decision on a range of data. The following tasks from Test A used the index for the classified column headings from the leading local newspaper, as shown in Figure 6.1.

2. You have lost your dog. Which would be the most suitable heading to advertise for it?

(A) 8
(B) 99
(C) 5
(D) 6

3. You want to sell a house. What is the number of the heading that you would use?

(A) 37
(B) 40
(C) 38
(D) 39

Let us consider task 2, the results for which are indicated in Table 6.3:

Table 6.3 Distribution of choices for task 2

Task	(A)	(B)	(C)	(D)
2	2	3	80	4

As Table 6.3 shows, all the distractors for task 2 were selected by at least some students. It would have been preferable, however, to have distractors that attracted a larger number of students. For example, distractor (B) looks too obviously incorrect because it is the only one with double digits, and, in fact, only two students chose this distractor. A possible improvement might be to replace distractor (A), that is, the Personal Column or 8, by Pet's Corner or 95. Unfortunately, if one wants to attempt to relate the column headings to themes such as animals and location, the numbers of the column headings do not allow for much diversity. The students do need to distinguish between the Lost and Found columns, numbers 5 and 6. Although the other two distractors, Pet's Corner and Poultry and Livestock, have the disadvantage of being in the nineties, they are useful because they relate to a theme of animals. The difficulty in creating sufficiently strong distractors illustrates well the problems that arise in developing multiple-choice questions on unadapted authentic texts.

Look at the information below about classified advertisements.
Then answer the questions that follow.

CLASSIFIED COLUMN HEADINGS

Accommodation	3	Holiday & Travel	21
Aircraft	54	Houses for Sale	39
Antiques	56	Houses to Let	37
Arms & Ammunition	58	Houses Wanted to Buy	40
Bicycles	60	Houses Wanted to Rent	38
Boats & Equipment	62	Investments & Business	24
Building Materials	64	Just for Women	10
Business Premises	45	Lost	5
Caravans & Camping	66	Machinery & Tools	76
Club Notices	15	Miscellaneous for Sale	88
Coins	68	Miscellaneous Wanted	89
Creches: Nursery Schools	19	Money	23
Domestic Appliances	70	Monumental Masons	4
Entertainment & Social	13	Motor Sundries	51
Equitation	97	Motorcycles	49
Family Notices	1	Music & Sound	78
(Anniversaries, Births, Deaths,		Personal	8
Engagements, Funerals, Marriages, etc.)		Pets Corner	95
Farming	93	Photography	80
Farms & Small Holdings	43	Plots & Properties	42
Flats for Sale	35	Poultry & Livestock	99
Flats to Let	34	Repairs & Services	52
Flats Wanted	36	Situations Wanted	31
Florists	2	Specialist Services	26
For Hire	28	Sporting Goods	83
For Men Only	11	Stamps	84
Found	6	Swaps	86
Funeral Furnishers	3	Tuition	17
Furniture	72	Vacancies	30
Gardening	91	Vehicles for Sale	47
Gemstones & Jewelry	74	Vehicles Wanted	48

CLASSIFIED SMALL ADVERTISEMENTS

CHARGES PER INSERTION:

Cash: Per line or part thereof, $1.30.
Charged: Per line or part thereof,
$1.35 (Minimum charge 2 lines.)
A line = 5 words or part thereof.

Figure 6.1. Test material based on an index

On the other hand, task 2 did have some strengths in terms of my overall aims. It focused on the location of specific information, but it did not simply require recognition of information explicitly stated in the text. The readers were required to notice that the alphabetical ordering of the column headings did not correspond to a similar numerical order, that is, Accommodation was not number 1 but number 33. To answer the question correctly, students had to be able to skim through the headings, find the correct one, and compare the number with those in the answers. Alternatively, they could have skimmed through the numbers and, by a process of elimination, identified the correct heading. The use of these strategies can be seen in the following student's explanation of his response to task 2:

> I didn't take (A) because number 8 is for Personal. Then I lost my dog so it's not suitable there. Then number 99, it's Live and Poultry. A dog is not poultry. Then number 6, it's Found. I lost. I didn't found a dog but I lost my dog.

Another student, Evans, was equally successful in finding the correct answer:

> I think the right answer is (C) because looking at the columns, the column 5 is responsible for the lost property. (A) is not for lost property, and (B) doesn't correspond, the same as (D).

Ariel was much more succinct:

> The dog is lost so the heading must be lost.

These three boys are all Shona speakers and they all indicated that they only speak English at school. They are from the same large urban school and are in the top ability group. They were thus expected to be skilled readers and test takers. All these students are clearly doing what they are intended to do: they are getting the right answer and for the right reason. They are able to go through a text, find the relevant piece of information, compare it to the other pieces, reorganise it, and then sift through the distractors in order to select the appropriate answer. Since the tasks encourage the student to use a range of skills, it would seem that they are more effective than is indicated by standard methods of item analysis.

The next task, 3, tested the same type of skills as task 2 and referred to the same text, but according to traditional techniques of item analysis, it was not as effective.

Table 6.4 Distribution of choices for task 3

Task	(A)	(B)	(C)	(D)
3	4	3	0	81

This task would be regarded as weak since the vast majority of students selected the right answer. The distractors were thus ineffective, but it is necessary to examine the larger context of the question before deciding whether to alter it. One way of improving it would be to have greater variety in the numbers of the column headings and, in particular, replace distractor (C) (38) by some other number. There were, however, only four types of column headings using the word 'houses', and so this deletion might cause an imbalance since it would be obviously incorrect if it did not refer to houses.

Yet task 2 did, in fact, make considerable demands on students' abilities to make lexical distinctions. The question referred to the column headings dealing with houses and within these, there were two sets of contrasts: to buy/to sell or to let/to rent. There were additional complications. 'To sell' appeared as 'for sale' in the text, and readers had to distinguish between the use of 'want' as it appeared in the question, 'You want to sell a house', and as it appeared in the column headings in the text, 'Houses Wanted to Buy' and 'Houses Wanted to Rent'. The different uses of 'want', together with the contrast in vocabulary, make the question actually quite complex.

The interviews showed that the students who answered the question correctly, even those who were not generally good test takers, were indeed making these distinctions. For example, Lydia was by no means a top student: she was considered to be in her school's middle ability group, yet she was aware of the differences between buying and selling, of being a prospective customer or buyer, and was able to relate these concepts to the language of the text:

> (D) Houses for Sale. Um... number 37 is Houses to Let. I think this is not true. And then number 40, it's Houses Wanted to Buy. You want to buy a house but you don't want to sell it. You want... you yourself want to ... Then number 31, Houses Wanted to Rent. If you say Houses Wanted to Rent you'd be looking for an accommodation, so I'm selling an accommodation. I'm not looking for. So I think (D) is the appropriate answer.

Even though task 3 was not effective according to traditional techniques of item analysis, it still forced students to use their critical skills, suggesting again that the adequacy of a question needs to be considered in a broader context, in terms of what it reveals about the reader's skills in interpreting a text.

Below is a schedule for the programmes on radio and television.
Use this schedule to answer the questions that follow.

Today's programmes

Subject to alterations without notice

TELEVISION		RADIO TWO	
12 55	All Songs	5 25	Kutangira Zuva Ranhasi
1 00	Randal and Hopkirk	5 30	Kwaedza
1 50	One Day At A Time	6 00	Nhau
2 15	Big Valley	6 10	Izindaba
3 05	Monte Carlo PTL Club	6 20	Kwadza
3 35	News	7 00	Nhau
3 50	Taika Nemagariro Evanhu	7 05	Izindaba
4 40	Classical Comedy	7 30	Money and Life
4 50	World of Sport	7 45	Gramma Radio Juke Box
5 50	Road to Wembley	8 00	Ngatidzejorerayi
6 50	Gimme a Break	8 30	Weekend Bata Movement
7 15	The Nation	9 00	Nhau
7 45	News and Weather	9 05	Izindaba
8 20	Consumer Report	9 10	Windmill Round-up
8 25	Dallas	9 15	Kuenga Mhurf Kwakanaka
9 25	The A Team	9 30	Dzechimurenga
10 15	Golden Years	9 45	Tuffy Teeth Club
11 05	News and Epilogue	10 00	Religious Music
		10 15	ZMC Record Club
RADIO ONE		11 00	Nhau
6 00	News	11 05	Izindaba
6 10	Good Morning	11 15	TM Footballer of the Week
7 00	News	11 30	Ezakulell
7 10	Songs for Faith	11 45	The Jarzin Man
7 30	Sunday Morning Service	12 00	Reggae
8 00	News	1 00	Nhau
8 10	Press Review	1 10	Izindaba
8 20	Morning Melody	1 25	Dzinofarirwa Nemhuri
9 00	Gardening in Zimbabwe	1 45	Radio Doctor
9 15	Waltz Time	2 00	Szinofarirwa Nemhuri
10 00	Sunday Kaleidoscope	2 30	Ndangariro
11 00	News	3 00	Sugar Sunday Soccer
11 05	Blue Print Africa	5 00	Disco
11 20	Sunday Potpourri	6 00	Nhau
11 50	Our Natural Resources	6 05	Izindaba
12 00	Comedy Half-Hour	6 10	Mamiriro Ekunze
12 30	Lyons Maid Hits of the Past	6 15	Dzandakusarudziral
12 45	Kine Movie Go-Round	7 00	Nhau
1 05	Agritax Farm Diary	7 10	Izindaba
1 15	News and Weather	7 20	Dzakapomhedzwa
1 27	The World This Week	7 45	News
2 00	It's In The Air	8 00	Tener Kehungwaru
3 00	Sunday Sport	8 15	Ngatibuyisaneni
5 00	Melody Hour	8 45	Madirativhange
6 00	News and Weather	9 45	Zvopasi Rine
6 11	Shades of Evening	10 00	News
6 30	Sunday Evening Service	10 10	Izindaba
7 00	Dinner Music	10 15	Mazwi Erupenise
7 45	News and Weather	10 20	Close Down
8 00	Haunted		
8 30	Sunday Concert		
10 00	News Round-up		
10 05	Help Me Make It Through the Night		
11 00	Music ex-Radio 3		

Figure 6.2 Test material based on a schedule

The skills of skimming and scanning were also measured in Test B in a set of tasks based on a programme guide for television and radio. Since the tasks in this test did not use the multiple-choice format, the students had to write the answers in the spaces provided. The text on which their responses were to be based is shown in Figure 6.2.

9. Every Sunday evening at 5 p.m. there is a programme called Disco. Where would you find it?

10. Every evening around 11 p.m. there is a news programme. Where would you find it?

In tasks 9 and 10, the students had to locate a particular programme within the guide. Most of them had no difficulty with the tasks. Again in a norm-referenced test such tasks would have to be deleted as they do not sufficiently discriminate between the students. Information from the student interviews, however, demonstrated that the tasks did encourage the students to use a number of reading skills. Consider, for example, how Tawanda, a student from the top ability group, explains his answer to task 9:

I looked for 5 o'clock on all the programmes, the programme allocations, and I found that at 5 o'clock on Radio 2, at 5 o'clock was the only time there was a programme called disco.

He was equally successful with task 10 which also focused on students' ability to compare and select pieces of information.

[Task 10] says um ... around 11 o'clock, 11 pm And I looked at all the um ... the radio programmes and I found that at 11 pm ... 11 pm, Radio 2 was closed down, and on Radio 1 there was music ex-Radio 3. So obviously it has to be television, so I picked up television as the answer.

Blessing, though not as clear in her explanation, did use skills of comparison and selection to arrive at the correct answer:

[For task 9] I look at the, I think it's the, it's on Radio 2. You look at the, at the time first, then you see the programmes.
[For task 10] And on television 1 there's music. Then you, if you compare that you see that on, on television ...

Both these students are clearly doing what they are intended to do: they are getting the right answer for the right reason. They are able to go through a text, find the relevant piece of information, compare it to other pieces, reorganise it, and sift the information in order to select the appropriate answer.

Let us consider another question from Test A, based on an article from the local newspaper about mbanje (i.e. marijuana), presented in Figure 6.3.

SECTION 2 – READING

Here are some articles from *The Sunday Mail*. Read them carefully and then answer all the questions. Circle the letter next to the correct answer.

Read the article below, 'Mbanje Smoking Boys Expelled', and then answer the questions.

MBANJE SMOKING BOYS EXPELLED

Sunday Mail Reporter

SCHOOL authorities at Makumbe Secondary School in Domboshawa are worried at the increasing incidence of dagga smoking among the pupils, and have launched a massive publicity campaign to combat the problem.

Headmaster Cde David Pasipanodya told The Sunday Mail last week that five boys had already been expelled this year. Two more were expelled last year.

"It's frightening", he said. Citing a recent case, he said on June 28 a boy came to his home almost hysterical. He pleaded with the headmaster to help him "because if you don't, I'm going to go mad very soon". Cde Pasipanodya said he asked the boy why he thought he was going mad, to which he replied that he had just taken mbanje and was not sure whether his mind was still stable or not.

Some pupils had been arrested on several occasions when police found them in possession of dagga.

Sometimes school authorities also caught boys smoking mbanje. "When we discover they had smoked for the first time, we call in their parents and talk to them in their presence. They give a promise that they won't get involved again and agree that if they do, they will be expelled. We then assume that they have reformed."

This had not seemed a deterrent, however, and the school was working closely with the police in Borrowdale. Not much had happened to improve the situation so far.

Figure 6.3 Test material based on a newspaper article

1. Which of the following best describes the main subject of this article?
(A) Drug problems at Makumbe Secondary School.
(B) School authorities at Makumbe Secondary School.
(C) A boy who went mad.
(D) Conversations between teachers and parents.

In this task, students were tested for their ability to distinguish the overall idea of the passage from supporting details. Task 1 differed from the others in Test A, since it was the only one explicitly testing this skill. The distribution of choices in Table 6.5 shows that the majority of students had no difficulty in selecting the correct answer.

Table 6.5 Distribution of choices for task 1

Task	(A)	(B)	(C)	(D)	0*
1	77	8	3	0	1

*Indicates the number of students who did not respond to the task.

Since one of the distractors was not selected by the students and the overall distribution of responses is weak, this task would have to be altered to fit in with traditional testing criteria. But a detailed analysis of the task, using data from student interviews, revealed that it was, in many ways, an effective one.

The task format was similar to that of the reading passages in the students' textbooks since there was a long passage followed by a question. The content was, however, more controversial than anything likely to be found in their books and would probably be more interesting. It was an article about a genuine problem in schools and not something specially written for school children such as the usual simplified narratives to be found in local textbooks. The students had to read a fairly lengthy passage but as they only had to understand the overall idea, they did not have to read it in detail and understand every word. Most students selected the correct answer and were probably helped by the relationship between 'mbanje' in the title of the article and the word 'drug' in (A).

In one of the interviews, a student named Farai seemed to have selected the right answer for the wrong reasons. When asked how he had selected the correct answer, he said he had done so because the information in the other distractors was either not present in the text or incorrect. He claimed that the article had not described a boy who had gone mad nor a conversation between the teachers and parents about the problems at the school. It seems unlikely, though, that Farai had actually misread the text since he did very well overall and was in the top ability group. It is more likely that, in answering this question, he took note of the title and of the fact that option (A) related closely to it – a strategy which is entirely appropriate and especially useful when reading newspapers.

In general, most of the students interviewed seem to have read the passage fairly carefully and used a number of skills in answering the question. Consider, for example, a student named Priscilla who was in the top ability group in her school. This school has a wide range of facilities, including a well-stocked library, and the students are encouraged to read regularly. Priscilla's command of English was excellent, and among all the students tested, she was one of the most able, as indicated by her performance on her class tests as well as on Test A. Here is how Priscilla explained her choice of the appropriate answer to the above question:

> The other titles like 'School Authorities', that's just mentioned almost at the end. And 'A Boy who went Mad' was just an example of the story and 'Conversations between Teachers and Parents' was just a point of the drug problems at Makumbe Secondary School and how they helped by bringing in the parents.

Priscilla's answer demonstrates that she has a clear understanding of the organisation of the passage. She is able to distinguish supporting details from the overall idea and can describe their function. For instance, distractor (C) serves to exemplify the overall theme, and distractor (D) is a consequence of the problem at the school. One of the skills of a successful reader is to be able to distinguish between different rhetorical patterns so as to be able to identify the main points of the text. In view of Priscilla's background, one can expect that she would have this skill and thus be able to arrive at the correct answer.

Other students, not just ones in the top ability group, were able to do this task as well. Consider, for example, the case of Lydia, whose school, though large and well established, does not have the resources and range of facilities that Priscilla's has. The students at Lydia's school are all non-native speakers of English and are all from the surrounding high-density area. Like most of the students in her school, Lydia is a Shona speaker but says she uses English in class and to speak with friends in the playground. Though Lydia is in the middle ability group, she showed the same skills as Priscilla in answering question 1 and was able to demonstrate that she had understood the rhetorical organisation of the passage to determine the correct answer:

> I chose (A) because it's drug problems at Makumbe Secondary School. These certain boys are smoking mbanje so it's the drug, it's the drug problems which are faced by the principals of the Makumbe Secondary School. I think (C) is an example of what was going on at the school. Ah...Conversations between teachers and parents. I think this was from the drug problems. If there was not drug problems there may not going to be conversations between this problem. School Authorities at Makumbe School – I think they're the principals at the schools. They checked not to ... to have their children smoking mbanje, the pupils at their school. They had not allow it, so it's... No, the main subject is the drug problem.

Both these students used their understanding of the rhetorical organisation of the passage to determine the correct answer.

The form below is used for depositing money into a Post Office savings account. A student, Tsitsi Mholope, plans to put $20.65, in cash, into her account. The information Tsitsi needs to use to fill out the form is given below in Question 8 (letters a. to j.). Write each letter in the place on the form where the information should go.

P.O.S.B. DEPOSIT FORM

Name of   Mr.
depositor   Mrs.
and   Miss..
Address

143 S.B. 7

CLASS 3

....

....

Account number

Identification particulars.....................................
(where applicable)

Amount $ c
in
figures

Amount of.................................
deposit
in words   ....dollars

OFFICIAL USE

Date-stamp and details

....cents

of which $..is by cheque
          (details of deposit to be listed overleaf)

Paid in by:

Resultant balance

Signature..

Date..

Symbol code

Figure 6.4 Test material based on a deposit form

In Test B, there was an example of dissonance between the wording of a question and the readers' real-world knowledge. There were a number of tasks based on completing a post office savings bank form, shown in Figure 6.4.

Students were required to put letters representing different kinds of information in the appropriate spaces on the form. Many students, especially the weaker ones, did not understand that they had to transform the information. They treated the form as they would in real life and so wrote the actual information on the form. They read the form correctly and put the information in the appropriate places, but they had not interpreted the instructions accurately. I had not anticipated this problem, and should have realised that using authentic texts, especially ones with which students may be familiar, can prove to be a distraction because students' real-world knowledge may override their attention to the details of the test. The purpose of testing should be to enable students to demonstrate their knowledge rather than to mislead them with poor tasks and thereby penalise them. As indicated in the following extract from an interview, this set of tasks, far from helping the weaker students, proved to be a trap:

> I just, I just first of all read the, the receipt so I saw that the date should be the what, it is written the date. So I wrote 27th September on, on where it is written the date. And twenty and it said the amount deposited in words. So I wrote twenty there.

On the other hand, Tawanda's reply shows that some students did answer correctly:

> Um, I first look at at um the, this form. And um, as there are unfilled places, I just, I just picked out which one was most likely to be in that place. So that way... the date. Um, the only date here is 27 September. So obviously that the answer. Here it said write the letter so, so I put the letter in there.

Unlike Blessing, Tawanda is in the top ability group in his school and did very well in the overall test. His replies in the interview showed that he is very test-wise, that is, he reads instructions carefully, is aware of the different 'tricks' test makers can play with tasks, and uses a process of elimination to select the correct answer. If this set of tasks were to be used again, the instructions would have to relate more closely to real-life use and the students would enter the information on the form as they would do normally. If the form was already partially completed, it would give the students an example of what the task intended. By including additional information from which the students had to select appropriate details, a set of tasks based on completing a form could measure skills such as reorganising information, skimming, scanning, and making inferences.

Conclusions

This pilot study has powerfully demonstrated the difficulties in testing communicative competence. First, in a country like Zimbabwe, social attitudes prevent test makers from developing exams that are radically different from those that have been so powerful in the past. Any new reading test must follow the traditional configuration of texts and tasks and it must be administered in the same testing situation where students work alone and are thus inhibited from using many of the normal strategies for dealing with text through talk. Even my tests, though they conformed to tradition in these respects, occasioned some resistance: one of the students I interviewed, for instance, said he did not like the new test because it did not resemble the existing ZJC. He wanted to retain the traditional reading comprehension passages since they were more like the reading done in school and in the O-Level exam.

Second, the development of a communicative test is severely inhibited by practical and economic constraints. In Zimbabwe listening and speaking cannot be tested at all at this level, while reading and writing can only be tested through a brief exam administered at one sitting. Furthermore, the tasks have to be easily marked, and there is strong pressure to use the multiple-choice format since it is considered to produce tests that are easy to prepare, economical to administer, and statistically sound. All these factors increase the artificiality of the testing situation.

Even the decision to use materials that represented what students would regularly encounter outside school – and that they would certainly need to be able to deal with – backfired in some respects. It was difficult to produce tasks on such materials that discriminated clearly between the students: in the case of tasks in the multiple-choice format the distractors tended to be too obviously wrong, and even with open-ended questions the inclusion of normally occurring textual cues – such as the title of the 'Mbanje' article – made it possible sometimes to perform the task without reading the text properly. Moreover, the use of test-like tasks with an authentic post office form proved to be a trap for some students and penalised them unduly.

The overall effect of trying to develop traditional kinds of items on communicatively oriented texts was to produce tests that were apparently too easy. Test A was of little use in discriminating between the students because too many scored high marks, though Test B fared better in this regard. A major reason for the difference in the performance of the two tests was that Test B included items on six texts whereas Test A was based on only four; so one obvious conclusion is that if the purpose of the exam is to rank students, a wider range of items is required. A second difference was that Test B had open-ended questions so that the students had to produce the answers, albeit short ones, themselves. Given the difficulty in producing strong distractors from the kinds of texts used, it would seem that the short-answer format is more satisfactory, even if the results cannot so easily be analysed statistically. But lengthening the test and using the short-answer format would not solve the problem entirely, since even with Test B the results were not distributed in a normal curve: there were still too many students in the top range of scores.

Another and perhaps significant point to note here is that most of the students who took the pilot tests came from urban areas, and even the rural school where I administered it was not particularly remote since it is only about 80 kilometres from Harare. In the areas where these students lived the types of texts that I used on the tests were readily available; they were thus quite familiar to students even though they had not been used in class. In this particular study, the students at the rural school consistently outperformed the others. This superiority was not surprising since the school is a well known boarding school that attracts able students. In the more remote rural areas, however, newspapers and other print materials are harder to come by, making it much more important that they be brought into the classroom and the skills of using them be explicitly taught if students are to be certified as minimally competent to participate in modern political and economic life. Thus over the entire student population the new exam might be found to discriminate more effectively, with rural students doing less well; but in the long run it might help close the gap between urban and rural areas because it would encourage teachers to bring written materials from the urban domain into their rural classrooms, and thus it could help form a rural reading public.

If we shift our point of view, moreover, the results of the pilot tests may not seem so undesirable after all. Whatever the purpose of the other exams in the system, the ZJC is no longer used – at least, not officially – to determine who may go on to further education. It does, on the other hand, continue to dominate the first two years of secondary school. Thus, the first priority in a new exam is that it should promote the kind of teaching that is appropriate in Zimbabwe's present situation. Hence the importance of using authentic materials and of asking students, as nearly as possible, to do with them what they might do in an actual communicative situation. In addition, where students produced the correct answer, the interview data indicated that in the majority of cases they were doing so for the right reasons: the answer did, indeed, seem to indicate communicative competence on the point in question. Seen in this light, the fact that most students did well on the test should be seen as encouraging rather than otherwise.

Most of the students interviewed did, in fact, take this view. They said that they liked the test and thought it better than the existing ZJC because it meant that more students would pass. Only one student objected, on precisely those grounds, because he said there would not be enough places in school; predictably enough, he was a bright student who could be expected to do well in the existing system. Such an élitist attitude is, however, not an appropriate guide to policy in a country that is attempting to make education universal and relevant to the needs of the whole population. Of that population, only a minority will move on to higher academic studies, but the majority does need basic literacy in English in order to participate in the modern economy and to be fully integrated into the social and political structure of a developing nation. The pilot tests did, in fact, prove capable of certifying such literacy, and if most students can pass them, so much the better. The high failure rate on the traditional exams creates a serious morale problem in a country that needs to encourage, indeed, mobilise its human resources.

But changing the exam is only part of the process. At present, teachers are on the sideline and are only involved in testing when they register as individual markers. For better integration of testing and the curriculum, a much closer relationship is needed between teachers and test makers. Workshops for improving teaching methods could also include a component on testing. Teachers could be encouraged to suggest test materials, and since they regularly write their own classroom tests, they could use such materials to develop ideas they would like to see included in the national exams. Developing the professional skills of teachers and involving them more closely in the testing procedure could diminish the mystique of testing, and bring the test more closely in touch with the realities of the classroom.

Students should be involved too. In the present study all the apparatus of statistical analysis proved of little use in determining whether the items were indeed working as they were intended to do, whereas the interviews with students proved valuable. Since the Ministry of Education intends to develop an item bank, this kind of qualitative information about how individual items function is essential. One of the programmes I used for statistical analysis, the Rasch programme (Wright and Stone 1979) could be used as a first step to getting this information. Since it does supply an analysis of student performance, one could select from the outliers, that is, those who have performed most differently, and use interviews to find out why these students are distinct. In this way, we would be integrating quantitative and qualitative approaches to evaluate tests, allowing one to help the other – and we would be keeping in touch with the population that the tests are meant to serve, as people rather than as statistics.

Finally, we need to consider the parents. Largely uneducated themselves, they have high expectations of education for their children, and have grown up to believe that certificates, in particular, will guarantee good jobs and therefore prosperity. But as the former Minister of Education, Comrade Mutumbuka, has said

The issue is that we should distinguish between the certificate somebody gets and what they acquire so that they can become useful citizens in society. The problem is that there is far too much concentration on certification.... I have told [headmasters] about the importance of changing the attitudes of parents; the importance of demonstrating to the parents what education, particularly mass-based education which we believe is the basic right of every child, is about.... We have ... to convince the parents that academic education is not the solution to their child or to the needs of the country.... (Mbeki 1985, p.3)

Given the widespread respect for the exam system, it is evident that Zimbabwe will not do away with it. Yet the change of attitudes that Comrade Mutumbuka has called for can be encouraged by changing the content of the exams: those that deal with language, in particular, should reflect more closely the communicative practices of the society, and they should be more in line with what the students who are now taking them can be realistically expected to achieve.

Acknowledgement

I would like to thank all those in Zimbabwe who have kindly assisted me in my task.

7 English for academic purposes in Brazil: the use of summary tasks

Andrew Cohen

Introduction

Summarising tasks on reading comprehension tests have a natural appeal in this era of communicative language testing, given that they attempt to simulate real-world tasks in which non-native readers have to read and write a summary of the main ideas of a text. In order to summarise successfully, respondents need both reading and writing skills. First, they must select and utilise effectively those reading strategies appropriate for summarising the source text – identifying topical information, distinguishing superordinate from subordinate material, and identifying redundant as well as trivial information. They must then perform the appropriate writing tasks to produce a coherent text summary – selecting topical information or generating it if none appears explicitly in the text, deleting trivial and redundant material, substituting superordinate terms for lists of terms or sequences of events, and finally, reformulating the content so that it sounds coherent and reads smoothly (Basham and Rounds 1986; Brown, *et al.* 1981; Brown and Day 1983; Chou Hare and Borchardt 1984; Davies and Whitney 1984; Kintsch and Van Dijk 1978).

The problem with using summaries as a means for assessing comprehension of foreign-language texts is that the statistical results from summarising tasks are not always consistent with results from other types of tests such as multiple-choice, short-answer, and cloze. Shohamy, for example, set out to compare tests of summarising English-foreign-language (EFL) texts to tests with a multiple-choice and an open-ended response format – with responses either in native language or foreign language, depending on the test version. She found the results from the summarising data so inconsistent with the results on the other sub-tests that she eliminated the findings from the published study (1984; personal communication).

Also when a task of summarising is included in a test, the testing situation itself imposes constraints on the respondent that would not be found in the real world; so the respondents are more likely to read unnaturally and to write summaries that are quite different from what they would normally do. For one thing, respondents on a test are usually required to furnish a *reader-based summary* rather than the *writer-based summary* that they would most likely prepare in the real world – as when, for example, they make notes on a reading assignment. A reader-based summary calls for considerable discipline in that it must usually satisfy requirements as to length, format, and style, whereas a writer-based one is a personal text for one's own reference and may be somewhat unsystematic, perhaps nothing more than a listing of the main points (Hidi and Anderson 1986).

Even when preparing reader-based summaries, respondents may use different criteria from those used by raters in evaluating them. For example, there are undoubtedly differences of perception regarding what a 'main idea' consists of and the appropriate way to write it up. There may also be differing views as to the acceptability of introducing commentary into the summary. Recent research by Basham (1987) with Alaskan native students showed that these respondents used their own world view as a filter in the summaries they wrote, personalising them. If such differences are not eliminated through prior training and/or through careful instructions on the test, there could be a misfit between the way the summary task is executed and the criteria used by the raters to evaluate it.

Along with possible cultural differences, there are other potential causes of discrepancy between the way respondents are 'supposed' to prepare summaries and the way they actually do it. For example, a study of Hebrew-speaking university students writing EFL summaries found that while the notes they took on the text were of a word-level, 'bottom-up' nature, their summaries were found to be conducted on a top-down basis – that is, they were based on general knowledge. The conclusion drawn by the researchers was that the reading was fragmented rather than reflecting ongoing interaction with the text that would combine top-down and bottom-up analysis (Kozminsky and Graetz 1986). Likewise, a recent survey of Brazilian studies of reading processes (Cohen 1987a) indicated that the respondents involved were often not executing summarising tasks in a way consistent with the model of what summarising should entail, as presented above. A study by Holmes (1986), for example, found that six Brazilian graduate students did little monitoring of their summaries of English texts. They read in a linear and compartmentalised manner, rather than globally so as to extract the main ideas.

What appeared to be lacking in the research literature was an in-depth, case-study investigation of how a summarising task actually works as a testing format, with respect not only to the strategies used by the respondents but also to those used by the raters of the summaries. Since such research would depend on verbal report techniques, it would have to take into account the possible reactive effects of a situation in which respondents are not just completing a test (which in itself may be unnatural) but are also asked to report what they are doing while they are doing it. Furthermore, when a testing situation is used for collection of verbal report data about test-taking processes, it ceases to be an authentic testing situation as the results cannot be used in grading the students. Despite the pitfalls involved in such research, there is a growing literature which would suggest that such intervention may have only negligible effects on the quality of the data, depending on the nature of the tasks (see, for example, Ericsson and Simon 1984).

A basic curiosity concerning what makes summarisation tasks unreliable, plus a certain faith in the value of verbal reports in providing data on cognitive strategies, motivated me to undertake a small-scale study. I was interested in investigating how respondents of different levels of proficiency interacted with source texts in order to produce summary texts of their own; and I wanted to document how raters then responded to these summaries. Specifically, my research questions were as follows:

1. What are the strategies that respondents use in summarising tasks on a sample test of reading comprehension?
2. To what extent does summarising ability differ according to level of proficiency?
3. What are the raters' assessments of the results and what are the strategies that raters use in assessing such tasks?

Methodology

Subjects

The respondents for the study were five native Portuguese speakers who had all recently completed a course at the Pontificia Universidade Católica de Sao Paulo, Brazil (PUC-SP) in English for Academic Purposes (EAP). The course emphasised reading strategies, so they had all received training in how to summarise and were expected to employ the strategies they had been taught. It was also felt that because of the prior training they would not feel uncomfortable if asked to describe the strategies they used. Two of the respondents were of high, two of medium, and one of low proficiency, as determined by their former teacher on the basis of their course grades and general class performance. The high students were Monica (age 26), a graduate student in Humanities, and Roberta (age 45), a graduate student in Social Science. The medium-proficiency students were Maura (age 30), a graduate student in Social Science, and Daniel (age 29), a graduate student in

Humanities. The low-proficiency student, Ana (age 23), had completed an undergraduate degree in Social Science.

Two of the EAP course instructors who regularly rated the EAP exams of summarising skill at the PUC participated in the study as raters. The raters were native English speakers from Great Britain, Rater 1 having lived in Brazil for seven years, and Rater 2 for 11 years. They were both fluent speakers of Portuguese.

Instrumentation

Reading comprehension test. A sample test for assessing EFL proficiency, included in a PUC–SP Resource Package on Language Testing (Silva dos Santos *et al.* 1987) was used as the testing instrument. The test consisted of two parts, the first comprising three short texts in English of 400, 300, and 160 words respectively, the second comprising a longer text of 850 words. For Part I, respondents were asked to choose two out of the three texts and 'indicate the topic treated by each one, in Portuguese'; they were also asked to indicate any difficulties they had in performing the task. For Part II, they were asked to 'indicate the topic of the text' again and, as an exercise in more detailed comprehension, to 'note the main ideas from each section', a section being defined as 'the text relating to each question asked in the article'. The respondents were also asked to state their own opinion of the text and describe any difficulties they encountered in doing the tasks. To ensure that those taking the test would understand what was required, all the instructions were given in Portuguese, the number of points allocated to each item in the test was indicated, a sample passage with answers was provided in Part I, and the first section of the long passage in Part II was described as an example of the more detailed response expected at this point.

Test takers' verbal report protocols. Respondents were requested to provide self-observational and self-revelational data in their native language during the taking of the test; *self-observation* here refers to the inspection of specific test-taking behaviour, while *self-revelation* consists rather of 'think-aloud' stream-of-consciousness disclosure of thought processes (for a fuller discussion of this distinction, see Cohen 1987a). A Brazilian research assistant took notes while they did this, and if a respondent did not readily furnish the information, she intervened with questions such as, 'Why are you looking in the dictionary?' or 'What do you think this word means?'. The research assistant also wrote down any and all observable strategies that the respondents used in completing the test.

Test takers' questionnaire. A questionnaire (in Portuguese) was designed to obtain information from the test takers about whether the EAP course had assisted them in writing the summaries, the extent to which they read in English each week, their reaction to taking a test with this format, their reaction to interventions by a research assistant regarding their test-taking strategies, and whether difficulties in performance on the summary tasks were due to reading problems or writing problems. With regard to the last item – summarisation as both reading and writing – the concern was with the respondents' own perceptions as to where the bulk of their efforts were focused.

Raters' verbal report protocols. The raters were also asked to provide self-observational and self-revelational data in their native language (English) while assessing the tests. They were to indicate (1) the way they determined what the various texts were about, (2) the steps they were taking in their ratings, and (3) their assessment of the respondents' understanding of these texts. The research assistant also wrote down any and all observable strategies that the raters used in completing the rating task.

Raters' questionnaire. The raters' questionnaire requested that raters compare this sample test to previous tests of summarising used by their staff, point out ways in which it may have been innovative, indicate if anything was difficult to score, and comment about the test's format, the selected texts, and the scoring procedures.

Data collection

The data were collected in June 1987, in locales convenient for the respondents (two chose to do it in their offices on campus, one in a classroom, one in the library, and one, Ana, in her own home). Monica's and Daniel's sessions lasted an hour and a half, Roberta's and Maura's two hours (Maura's being divided, for practical reasons, into two sessions of an hour each), and Ana's three hours. While the respondents were taking the tests and providing verbal report data, the research assistant took extensive notes. The data were not tape-recorded so as to avoid a possible source of tension or distraction. Upon completion of the test, the respondents were asked to complete the test takers' questionnaire.

Each rater marked three tests, such that each marked the test of a high- and a medium-proficiency respondent and both marked the low respondent's test (i.e. Rater 1: Monica/high, Maura/medium, Ana/low; Rater 2: Roberta/high, Daniel/medium, Ana/low). They did the rating, provided the verbal report protocols, and filled out the raters' questionnaire in their office on campus. These sessions were tape-recorded, with one of the raters preferring to answer the questionnaire orally. Rater 1's session took one hour, while Rater 2's session lasted for two hours.

Data analysis

In order to describe the summarising strategies of the respondents, the notes from the verbal report protocols were analysed for instances of strategy use, strategies being defined here as consciously selected processes, a sub-set of the total set of cognitive processes involved in reading the source text and in writing the summary text. The summaries themselves were also scrutinised for evidence of unreported strategies.

In analysing the strategies used in producing the summaries, the taxonomy developed by Sarig (1987) was used. This taxonomy is based on an analysis of more than 140 strategies identified in a study of ten high-school students reading native and foreign-language texts both for the main ideas and for the gist. The taxonomy establishes a hierarchy of strategies according to their purposes, from basic processing through clarifying meaning and establishing coherence in the text to conscious decision-making as to which strategy to use. The strategies are identified as follows:

1. Those used for *technical facilitation*, whether of reading or writing. They include marking the text, skipping parts of it when writing the summary, keeping the summary deliberately vague, or including a great deal of detail.
2. Those used for *clarification and simplification*, such as using a dictionary, translating, and interpreting idioms literally.
3. Those used for *coherence detection and production*, including use of the title, sub-titles and illustrations as guides, paying special attention to pronouns and conjunctions, and filling out the information given in the text from world knowledge.
4. Those used for *metacognitive monitoring*, as in planning, directing, and assessing the metacognitive moves involved in the task at hand.

The use of a particular strategy by a given respondent was assessed as either facilitating the summarising task – that is, contributing positively to reading the source text or to writing the summary – or as being detrimental. The decision as to whether a strategy was labelled 'facilitating' or 'detrimental' was based both on the judgements of the raters and also on the researcher's appraisal of the accuracy of the summary. It is important to note that summarising strategies are not inherently good or bad: they may promote or detract from successful writing of a summary, depending on the characteristics of the given text, the given reader, and the context in which the test is being conducted. Sarig (1987) has demonstrated this point in her large-scale research on first- and foreign-language reading strategies.

Once the data had been analysed according to Sarig's taxonomy they were then reanalysed to see if patterns emerged according to the proficiency level of the respondents. Finally, the strategies used by the raters were determined from their verbal reports and observation of their rating procedures.

The texts and the summaries

The texts used in the test are all reproduced here in full. The first, Text A, is the example that was provided, the summary that follows it being intended to serve as a model for the test takers; it is reproduced here to show what kind of summary was expected. Texts B, C, and D are the short ones that the respondents summarised, each respondent choosing two out of the three. Each text is followed here by the respondents' summaries. Text E is the longer text to which all were required to respond, and on which there was also a task eliciting detail. Since my focus here is on the summaries, the more detailed task is not given here, but the summaries are given in full. All the summaries have been translated from the original Portuguese.

Text A

Computing pyramids

C LEVER COMPUTER WORK by French researchers looks like bringing Egyptology to the masses. At the moment only Oxford University and the French Institute of Oriental Archaeology in Cairo are able to print hieroglyphic texts. The variations in size and direction of the 7000 signs commonly found in hieroglyphics means that it takes something like a week to set up eight to 10 lines of text. This means around 108 years to publish the hieroglyphics contained in nine Egyptian pyramids.

Now a Frenchman, Michael Hainsworth, has devised a system to turn each hieroglyph into digital signals. This is done by making a video picture of the hieroglyph and storing it in a microcomputer. The character can be digitised in five to 10 minutes when displayed on the screen. It can then be manipulated or printed on a standard plotter connected to a central computer.

The original idea was for the micro to analyse and search through the text. Printing was only a secondary application. But given the huge cost of printing with conventional methods (about £80 per 300-page book in a 300-book run), the new system may have a commercial future. Instead of the 108 years needed to print the hieroglyphs in the nine pyramids, the new method will take 10 years.

Figure 7.1 Text A (from *New Scientist*, 16 February 1984)

Model summary:

The text deals with a computerized system developed by a Frenchman for printing texts in hieroglyphics. This system, developed so as to transform hieroglyphics into digital signals, will probably have many commercial applications in the future since it represents considerable savings in time and money in relation to conventional printing methods.

Text B

The exclusive people

FROM OUR TOKYO CORRESPONDENT

Japanese society does not think of itself as practising racialism. But it is very exclusive. The most conspicuous victims of this exclusivism are the 650,000 Koreans who live in Japan. They, or their parents, were brought to Japan as forced labourers before 1945. The fact that many speak perfect Japanese and are indistinguishable from their neighbours does not save them from discrimination. The ministry of education recently forbade the employment as a teacher of a Korean resident, saying that only Japanese nationals can be teachers.

In 1945 Russia's recapture of the southern part of Sakhalin Island trapped many thousands of Japanese and Koreans there. The Japanese were soon repatriated but the Koreans, who had been sent there to work for Japan, were not. In 1952 these people were stripped of the Japanese nationality to which they had previously been entitled. Some who had Japanese wives were allowed to leave; others' efforts to get out have been blocked by both Russia and Japan. South Korea cannot negotiate on their behalf as it has no diplomatic relations with Russia. Japan's foreign ministry has expressed sympathy, but nothing has been done.

Japanese exclusivism also hurts those Japanese – more than a million of them –

who are still classed as *burakumin*, untouchables descended from the old *eta* class, which was given dirty jobs like tanning and butchery in feudal times. *Burakumin* complain that they still suffer from discrimination in employment and marriage, and certainly many still live in slums.

In race, Japan, China and Korea are all fairly homogeneous countries where few foreigners live. In an opinion poll taken last autumn South Koreans rated Japan as the country which, after Russia, they most disliked, although less so than a few years ago. The Japanese return the compliment. A journalist with much experience of eastern Asia, the late Richard Hughes, once summed it all up admirably, as follows: "Greater rage has no man than a Japanese mistaken for a Chinese. Save perhaps a Chinese mistaken for a Japanese. Or maybe a Korean mistaken for either".

Figure 7.2 Text B (from *The Economist*, March 1985)

Monica's summary:

> Whereas the Japanese are not considered racists, they are racist to the extent that 650 000 Koreans live there and are treated like foreigners. They do not have the same rights as the Japanese except for those who marry Japanese. And among the Japanese there is racism at the expense of the socially less advantaged. When speaking of race, Japanese, Chinese, and Korean are seen by others as homogeneous, but the Japanese see themselves as superior to the other races just as South Koreans regard the Japanese as just slightly less antipathetic than the Russians.

Roberta's summary:

> The text speaks about the relations between the Japanese and the other peoples (races) who came to Japan on account of the war and were incorporated into the population – relations which turned into a form of racism in behaviour patterns among Koreans, Japanese, and Chinese.

Maura's summary:

> The author talks about racism in Japan. With a series of practical examples taken from everyday life, he tries to demonstrate that in actuality the image that the Japanese do not practise discrimination is false. He selects as the most victimised the Koreans, since, according to him, the position of the ministry of education is just to educate the Japanese.

Daniel's summary:

> The text says that Japanese society is, to a certain extent, closed and discriminatory. One of its major problems is their similarity in physical appearance to the Koreans and Chinese. The discrimination manifests itself in relation to employment, marriage and social conditions.

Text C

Pocket video cameras

THE JAPANESE company JVC stole the Berlin radio show last month with the unveiling of VHS Videomovie, a combined video camera and recorder that is no larger than an ordinary video camera.

It is smaller than Betamovie, Sony's rival system, and replays its own tapes, which Betamovie cannot.

But JVC was cagey about how the combined camera and recorder (or camcorder) worked. Now a British patent, application 2113893, reveals that JVC has the technology to make camcorders even smaller than the Videomovie.

The Videomovie shown at Berlin uses four heads, spaced equidistant around the drum, instead of two, and the drum is two thirds the standard size. The new patent reveals that JVC can retain compatibility with a drum half the normal size.

Both Betamovie and Videomovie wrap the tape further round the drum than the 180 degrees on a standard machine. For further miniaturisation JVC will wrap the tape almost completely round the drum leaving just a 30 degree "dead area".

The JVC patent has just two video heads, spaced apart by an angle slightly larger than 30 degrees so that one head is always in contact with the tape. The drum rotates at the normal European speed of 1500 revs/min, instead of the double speed used by Sony's Betamovie.

The JVC patent paves the way for truly pocket camcorders in the future, recording tapes which can be played back on today's domestic VHS machines.

Figure 7.3 Text C (from *New Scientist*, 27 October 1983)

Roberta's summary:

> The article discusses a new model of video camera/recorder called a 'camcorder', put out by a Japanese firm. The advantages of the new invention are presented: long-distance reach, types of controls, and technical details of the functioning of the apparatus – with the greatest advantage being that it is pocket size.

Maura's summary:

> This is a technical text about an electrical apparatus that combines a video with sound (a recorder), and which was developed by a Japanese company. The text speaks of the advantages of this technology which can develop an even smaller apparatus.

Ana's summary:

> A Japanese company, JVC, stole the idea of a portable radio that would be the inauguration of a VHS Videomovie system which would combine a video machine with a recorder not as large as a regular video machine and smaller than a Betamovie one. But there was a recognition of the patent by the British in favour of JVC. JVC not only thought of the idea of them, but also that of improving them so that they would be half the normal size. This new Japanese patent opened up new avenues for future technology.

Text D

Murder of the Gorilla Scientist: A New Suspect

a very poor photograph of Dian Fossey, showing her long hair, appeared at the beginning of this article

NATIONAL GEOGRAPHIC SOCIETY
Whose machete? Fossey

Last December, in the remote mountains of Rwanda, American naturalist Dian Fossey was murdered in her camp, her head split open by blows from a machete. Suspicion centered on poachers from the local tribes, who hunt the endangered mountain gorillas that Fossey had spent two decades studying and trying to protect. Last week the government inquiry shifted dramatically to Fossey's American colleague, Wayne Richard McGuire.

McGuire, 31, had joined Fossey at her research station several months before her death and had been in the camp when Fossey's body was discovered. Rwandan authorities allege that McGuire's "presumed motive" may have been the theft of Fossey's unrivaled research notes. McGuire left the country in July, and at the weekend his whereabouts were unknown. Associates and friends of both Fossey and McGuire dismissed the allegations as nonsense. Says one American official: "They may be trying to cover up their inability to find the murderer. Or maybe they don't want to find him."

Figure 7.4 Text D (from *Newsweek*, September 1986)

184   *From Testing to Assessment*

Monica's summary:

The article tells about the death, or rather, the assassination of a naturalist, Diano Fossey, whose assassin had still not been found, and describes as well a denial which his friend made in the face of an attempt to accuse him of the murder. Like Fossey, the friend, McGuire, also researched gorillas that lived in the mountains, and was with him before he was found dead in his camp with his head chopped off.

Daniel's summary:

The text says that Fossey (a naturalist) was assassinated and substituted for McGuire who suspected that Fossey's notes were the cause of his death. For this to happen would be an absurdity. An American official believes that these suspicions are due to his inability to find the assassin.

Ana's summary:

In the mountains of Rwanda, there was an assassination of a researcher working in nature, ecology. Suspicion fell on local tribes that were involved in the hunting of gorillas. And gorillas were just what the scientist was trying to protect. The government continued to investigate the matter and came to the conclusion that her death was linked to the robbery of her field notes (according to information from a friend of hers).

Text E, being longer, is presented overleaf and the summaries are provided below:

Monica's summary:

The text deals with a special type of headache: migraine. Furthermore, the text details the cause of migraines, the difference between migraines and common headaches, their symptoms, diagnosis, and possible correlations between migraines and the age, sex, and personality of the individual.

Roberta's summary:

The topic discussed was that of 'treatment of migraines', their symptoms, the difference between them and other types of headaches, their causes, their frequency by age, sex, and type of personality.

Maura's summary:

1 – What migraines are. 2 – What the symptoms are. 3 – Differential diagnosis. 4 – Causes. 5 – How to diagnose and treat them. 6 – Correlation with age, sex, and personality.

Daniel's summary:

The text deals with the symptoms, differences, relationship between pain and [types of] people, diagnoses, the characteristics and treatment of headaches and migraines.

Ana's summary:

The text discusses two types of 'illnesses', headache and migraines, but especially the second. The symptoms of each are presented, their causes, the medical treatment for each, not to mention how they differ, and finally mention is made of the age and sex of those who tend to be afflicted by migraines.

Text E

managing
migraines

BY DONALD J. DALESSIO, M.D.

Q *What is a migraine headache?*

A A migraine is a physiological reaction to sensory or emotional stimuli that causes blood vessels to swell, putting painful pressure on tissues around the brain and on head and neck muscles. It may also be preceded or accompanied by the distortion of some of the brain's neural functions, causing vision and speech problems. When this occurs, it's referred to as an "aura."

Migraines can occur on succeeding days or can be separated by years, and each episode can last from less than an hour to several days. They can vary in severity too; in extreme cases the individual may be incapacitated during the attack and must retire to a dark, quiet room to sleep.

Q *What are the symptoms?*

A The symptoms can differ from migraine to migraine and from person to person. The pain, which may be accompanied by throbbing, is often limited to one side of the head. The patient may also experience general malaise, nausea, vomiting and sensitivity to light and sound.

Another symptom is the aura. When this occurs, the individual "sees" blinking lights, jagged lines and other illusions that may temporarily impair vision. Other aspects of an aura may include numbing of the face, mouth or hands and confused speech. An aura may occur before a migraine, but not necessarily each time one is experienced. An aura may also occur alone and is then called a "migraine equivalent."

Q *How is a migraine different from other headaches?*

A In most headaches, tension causes muscular contractions and pain, while in migraines blood-vessel dilation is the root of the pain. And, in tension headaches, discomfort is often felt in a "hatband" around the head, accompanied by a stiff neck. Tension and migraine headaches can merge, however, and either one can trigger the other.

"Cluster" headaches (commonest in men who smoke) are often confused with migraines, as they too involve severe, one-sided pain. These headaches strike in groups, sometimes more than once a day; a series can last up to six to eight weeks, after which the headaches may disappear for a year or longer. But clusters are not accompanied by the neural complications – the visual or speech problems – typical of migraines.

Q *What causes migraines?*

A For predisposed individuals, almost any sensory or emotional stimulus, from noise and humidity to frustration and fatigue is capable of triggering a migraine. Everyone's body reacts to stimuli in its own way; migraine sufferers respond with

Figure 7.5 Text E (from *McCall's*, September 1986)

(Figure 7.5 continued)

an increased blood-flow to the head and subsequent vessel dilation. This type of response may be hereditary.

Some common stimuli that have been associated with migraines are psychological factors, like stress; head injuries or diseases, including brain tumors; biochemical changes, often connected to hormones; and changes in the environment. Some foods – such as aged cheeses, chocolate, chicken liver, vinegar, monosodium glutamate (MSG), cured meats containing nitrites, and alcohol – and medications (birth-control pills, for example) appear to be associated with migraines as well. Research is now under way to determine whether these substances cause the migraine itself or produce allergic reactions that, in turn, bring on migraines.

Q *How are migraines diagnosed and treated?*

A If headache pain recurs and is severe enough that it interferes with daily life, a thorough evaluation is necessary to determine if the migraine is the symptom of a more serious disease.

Diagnosis of migraines is tricky: It's difficult to pinpoint why a person experiences them, because the cause of a migraine may be different each time. The physician must therefore rely on accurate individual reports and medical histories to make a diagnosis.

The first step in treatment is to alleviate symptoms. Two types of medication are used: a pain reliever and a pain preventive. The pain reliever constricts already dilated and painful blood vessels; preventive drugs are taken regularly to prevent the initial dilation of vessels. Preventive medications are intended primarily for chronic migraines.

If migraine bouts can be linked to specific aspects of a person's life, such as professional tension, counseling may be an effective treatment.

A possible next step – retraining the automatic-response system – is perhaps the most difficult treatment. Biofeedback is a tool through which a person can learn to change the kinds of responses the body makes to stressful situations. In turn, the newly learned responses will alter the internal processes that would otherwise produce migraines. The commitment necessary for working with these response systems is considerable, but often worthwhile.

Q *Is there a correlation between migraines and age, sex or personality?*

A A person of any age can get migraines, though the tendency is for them to occur more frequently in youth; by age 50 or so, migraines occur less often.

Until puberty, boys and girls get migraines in equal numbers, but after that females are more susceptible. As adults, twice as many women as men suffer from migraines, and women's migraines are typically more severe – probably because of the hormonal changes that occur with the menstrual cycle. With menopause, the number of migraines is often reduced.

Much has been made of the personalities of migraine sufferers: They are often characterized as compulsive, meticulous people. This kind of generalization is unfounded, as people of all personality-types have migraines. Some individuals, though, may handle stress in a way that predisposes them to the condition.

Donald J. Dalessio, M.D., is chairman of the Department of Medicine at Scripps Clinic and Research Foundation in La Jolla, California, and a clinical professor of neurology at the University of California, San Diego.

Reactions to the test

The respondents' comments

In the section of the test where the respondents were asked to identify their difficulties, they commented most frequently on particular words. For example, in Text C, 'Pocket video cameras', both Roberta and Maura remarked on the technical nature of the vocabulary, Maura mentioning specifically the word 'drum', while Ana said she had problems with 'cagey', 'drum', 'reveals', 'further', and 'truly'. Similarly, in Text E, 'Managing migraines', Monica mentioned 'aura', 'pain', 'disease', 'reliever', 'effective', and 'handle'; Roberta, 'malaise', 'blinking', 'numbing', 'pain', 'root', 'cluster', 'liver', 'tricky', 'worthwhile', and 'youth'; Maura, 'aura', 'numbing', 'pain', 'stiff', 'merge', and 'trigger', Daniel, 'managing', 'migraines' (both in the title), 'headaches', and 'pain'; and Ana also 'managing' and 'migraines' in the title, as well as 'aura', 'numbing', and 'pinpoint'.

Problems were also mentioned with regard to whole phrases or sentences. In Text C, for instance, Maura commented on the technical description in the fourth paragraph, '... wrap the tape further round the drum than the 180 degrees on a standard machine' and '... will wrap the tape almost completely round the drum leaving just a 30 degree "dead area"' and in the fifth, '... always in contact with the tape. The drum rotates at the normal European speed of 1500 revs/min, instead of the double speed used by Sony's Betamovie'. In Text D, Daniel said the expression 'Fossey's unrivalled research notes' was unclear to him, and in Text E, Roberta said that she had to read repeatedly and translate several portions, such as 'Migraines can occur on succeeding days or can be separated by years, and each episode can last from less than an hour to several days'.

Comments on organisation or content were less frequent. Only Maura raised a question concerning rhetorical structure: with regard to Text E, she found the last question and answer ambiguous with reference to age, and wondered whether the only reference to age was in the first paragraph of that section, the second paragraph being about sex. Otherwise, comments above the level of individual sentences were more general statements about whether the text was difficult or not.

The fact that most of the comments were so specific suggests that the respondents were processing the texts in a bottom-up manner. On the other hand, their summaries are global representations of the texts, not simply translations, and even their mistakes indicate in some instances more global strategies for interpretation. These strategies are discussed in terms of Sarig's taxonomy below, but first let us consider the data presented in the respondents' questionnaire.

The respondents' questionnaire

From the questionnaire, it was evident that the respondents saw a close relationship between their EAP course and the summary test. They all said that the course had helped, though it is interesting that they specified different techniques that they had learnt from it. Monica and Daniel both commented that it had taught them how to read globally as well as how to look for English words with Portuguese cognates. Daniel also mentioned that he had learnt how to identify key words in a text. Roberta and Maura, on the other hand, commented on what they had learnt about graphic cues – the importance of format and attention to illustrations. Roberta also mentioned a number of other features of the course: the emphasis that had been placed on technical texts, the identification of different types of text, and the teaching about specific linguistic features such as the nucleus of a phrase and the occurrence of homonyms. As for Ana, she, like Monica and Daniel, said that the course had taught her to look for the general meaning of a text, and that she had learnt to use the dictionary sparingly; like Roberta, she mentioned work that had been done on phrase structure, and one comment that she alone made was that through the course she had learnt to use her background knowledge of the topic in interpreting an English text.

With regard to general reading habits, it seems that only Monica and Daniel read English regularly: Monica said she read English texts every day, while Daniel said that he read them every week, all of this reading, in both cases, being academic. Roberta, who claimed to read English less regularly, also read it only for academic purposes, but both Maura and Ana said that they read it for pleasure – Ana, indeed, said that was the only reason she read it. Neither Maura nor Ana, however, claimed to read English frequently.

The responses to the test were almost entirely positive, with only Daniel expressing some reservation about the artificiality of a situation in which he had to explain what he was doing while he was doing it. But even Daniel, together with Maura and Ana, said that the research assistant's interventions were helpful rather than otherwise, heightening awareness and not interrupting the flow. Roberta and Ana were particularly positive about the exercise, Roberta saying that it had reactivated for her what she had learnt in the course, and Ana claiming that it was useful to read anything in English, even if the topic was not particularly interesting. In characterising the difficulties they encountered in doing the test, Monica, Roberta, and Daniel emphasised reading problems over writing ones, while Maura claimed to have no noticeable problems in either activity.

Strategies used

Technical facilitation strategies

The most obvious technical facilitation strategy, used by all the respondents, was underlining words. The sort of words underlined varied between individuals, and so did the apparent purpose of the activity. Monica, for example, underlined verbs in the shorter Texts B and D (perhaps reflecting that these texts largely constitute descriptions of actions) and noun phrases in Text E, the longer, more scientific and technical text; Roberta, by contrast, underlined words that she thought important to include in her summary and said that she particularly liked to underline discourse markers, such as 'The first step ...' and 'A possible next step ...' in Text E. Maura, like Roberta, underlined words and phrases that she thought might help in writing the summary, particularly main ideas and examples. The strategy did not necessarily work: in Text B, for instance, she underlined 'The ministry of education recently ...' and 'only Japanese nationals can be teachers' but then erroneously wrote in her summary that the ministry of education had decided to provide education only for the Japanese, rather than that it had restricted access to the teaching profession. Daniel also underlined, in Text B, a set of words that he used in his summary – 'employment', 'marriage', and 'slums' – except that he translated 'slums' as 'social conditions'. For him, too, the strategy of underlining was counterproductive since he misconstrued the words to refer to the main topic of the text, namely discrimination against Koreans, when in fact they referred to intragroup discrimination among the Japanese. In Text D, Daniel underlined the phrase that he commented on as causing difficulty, namely, 'unrivaled research notes'. Similarly, Ana underlined words that she did not know, some of them for the purpose of looking them up in the dictionary. Ana also paid particular attention to pronouns, especially in Text E, where she circled two of the four feminine possessive pronouns, 'her'; this may explain why she got the naturalist's sex right whereas the other two respondents who summarised that text did not.

Another common technical facilitation strategy, manifest in the writing rather than in the reading, was to skip material. This strategy was most apparent with Text E, 'Managing migraines', the only compulsory text. Although the article's structure is clearly indicated by the questions that head its six sections, all the respondents except Maura omitted mention of the first section, on 'What is a migraine headache?' However, this omission can be explained by the fact that a model answer for this section had been provided for the more detailed questions on Part II (see p. 178); but Daniel also failed to mention the fourth section, on 'What causes migraines?'. Similarly, in summarising Text B, both Monica and Roberta skipped the point made in the second paragraph about the differential treatment of Korean and Japanese workers trapped on Sakhalin as a result of the war, and Roberta also omitted the discrimination against Japanese 'untouchables' described in the third paragraph.

A similar strategy was to deal with difficult material by describing it only in very general terms – 'lowering the informativity level' as Sarig has put it (personal communication). For example, Daniel wrote in his summary of Text B that Japanese society was closed and discriminatory, but he did not specify who it discriminated against, apparently because he was somewhat confused on the point. In the same way Maura, who found the technical material about the camcorder in Text C difficult, dealt with it by keeping her summary general, vague, and short (35 words). Maura's strategy for summarising Text E, by presenting the points covered as a list, may be interpreted as serving the same purpose, since it meant that she did not have to make explicit the links between the various sections of the text. An alternative, quite different strategy, is to include many details from the text in the hope that some of them will be important ones. Of these respondents, only Ana resorted to this strategy: in summarising Text D, 'Murder of the gorilla scientist', (which she did before tackling Text C) she gave quite a full account of the story, omitting only the two possible motives for the killing and the American government's denial of the local government's claim. In the same way she dealt with the difficult technical details in Text C by mentioning quite a number of them, including subordinate material such as that the patent mentioned had been taken out in Britain. The result is a relatively long summary (80 words) that contrasts quite noticeably with the briefer ones produced by Roberta and Maura.

Clarification and simplification strategies

The clarification and simplification strategy used by most respondents was translation. Roberta used it on all the texts that she summarised, but this did not prevent her from missing some key information, not only the point about the 'untouchables' in Text B, mentioned above, but also the point in Text C that the JVC device described was paving the way for a truly pocket camcorder that would appear in the future. Maura also used translation at some points when reading Text E to check if the meaning was clear: for example, she translated the sentence 'Tension and migraine headaches can merge, however, and either one can trigger the other'. Similarly, Daniel translated parts of Text B to himself, though, as we have seen, this did not apparently help him to achieve a precise understanding of what it was about; and in Text D he mistranslated the phrase 'gorilla scientist' and thought that a gorilla had been murdered. He used the same strategy from time to time when reading through Text E.

A second clarification and simplification strategy, used most of all by Ana, was to refer to the dictionary. She did this with many of the words that she underlined, and then she wrote glosses for these words in Portuguese in the margin: for 'split', 'blows', 'poachers', 'shifted', 'theft', and 'unrivaled' in Text D, and for 'recorder', 'ordinary', and 'reveals' in Text C. On Text E she also turned to the dictionary often, although she wrote down glosses for only four words, 'managing', 'aura', 'root', and 'tricky'. In Ana's use of the dictionary we can see again the attention to detail that distinguishes her from the other respondents and that accounts for her spending so much longer on the test – three hours as opposed to the others' two or less.

Another strategy, one that proved less successful in this study, was to interpret words used in an idiomatic or technical way in their more common or general sense. Ana, for example, interpreted the expression 'stole the show' at the beginning of Text C to mean that someone had literally stolen something – namely, 'the idea of a portable radio'. Similarly, Roberta, when working with the same text, interpreted the technically used word 'equidistant' in terms of the more common word 'distant', thus assuming the text had to do with long-distance videotaping, when it actually dealt with the spacing of video heads around the drum.

Coherence detection and production strategies

All the respondents used their world knowledge to fill out and make connections between the bits of information gleaned from the text. Thus on Text B, Monica used unsuccessfully the coherence production strategy of adding information that was not in the text – namely, that Koreans in Japan are not discriminated against if they marry Japanese (marriage is mentioned in the third paragraph, but only that of Japanese among themselves). On the same text, Maura followed a similar strategy when she allowed her world knowledge about how peoples may be deprived of education to predominate over the information that she had chosen to underline (see p. 190 above). In Ana's summary of Text C, we can see an example of such a coherence production strategy interacting with a clarification and simplification strategy: her error in interpreting 'stole the show' had a spin-off effect on other information in the text – i.e. that the JVC company had obtained an English patent for the camcorder; because she thought that there had been a theft, she assumed that mention of the patent indicated a legal squabble, which was a fabrication of her own. Monica and Daniel again were probably using their world knowledge when they assumed that the scientist in Text D was a man.

The respondents also drew on explicit textual signals for purposes of coherence detection. Daniel claimed, for example, that he paid special attention to pronouns and conjunctions, although this did not prevent him missing the significance of the pronoun *her* in the text about the gorilla scientist. Ana used the same strategy on this text, in combination with the technical facilitation strategy of circling the pronouns; in her case, as we have seen, it was more successful.

Daniel also made use of illustrations, at least with respect to Text B, assuming that the material in illustrations would be linked to a main idea in the text. But this coherence detection strategy worked to his disadvantage. The text included a cartoon of three identical people, all presumably sure of the others' identity as either Korean, Chinese, or Japanese. The text did not state that members of these races look alike to outsiders, but it did say that members of one group do not like to be mistaken for another. Daniel erroneously stated in his summary that the text referred to a major problem of distinguishing the three groups from each other; and the last part of Roberta's summary suggests that she also used this strategy. It is interesting to note, however, that Daniel does not seem to have used the illustration that accompanies Text D, 'Murder of a gorilla scientist' (a photograph of Dian Fossey that shows her long hair) and Monica seems to have ignored this illustration too. Perhaps they both did so because the photograph was not clearly reproduced.

Finally, the respondents made use of titles and subtitles. When working on Text B, for instance, Daniel read it through once and correctly noted how the title, 'The exclusive people', linked racism to the Japanese. The strategy was not always successful, however. In Text C, Roberta made the reasonable assumption that the title, 'Pocket video cameras' referred to the apparatus described in the text. Her summary listed various features of this camcorder, including that it was of pocket size. In actuality, the text noted that the JVC device was paving the way for truly pocket camcorders that would appear in the future. This text-processing error is perhaps an artefact of a summarisation task, where the emphasis is on rapid reading of the main ideas, rather than on meticulous concern for detail. It could also be said that the title was misleading in this case.

The title of Text E, 'Managing migraines', also caused problems, at least to Daniel and Ana, who both complained that they could not understand it (the research assistant actually explained it to Daniel as the word 'migraine' was not in the dictionary they were using). On the other hand, the subtitles were evidently useful to them all, since they all based their summaries on them. It is curious, however, that not only did everyone, except Maura, omit mention of the first section, but they all, except Maura again, changed the order of the sections.

Metacognitive monitoring strategies

From time to time the respondents indicated that they were monitoring their own performance in reading the texts and writing the summaries. For example, Maura, when deciding to do Text C ('Pocket video cameras') noted that her ability to read critically was impaired because of her unfamiliarity with the topic. Similarly, Daniel commented on his difficulty in understanding Text D ('Murder of the gorilla scientist') and therefore read the text three times before writing his summary. He noted that the basic information 'was right there', but that he could not put it together in a meaningful way, and he indicated that he did not like being tested on this text. Ana, too, when dealing with Text E ('Understanding migraines') commented at the outset that she did not even understand the title.

An example of a more explicit metacognitive monitoring strategy was provided by Monica when, with regard to Text B ('The exclusive people') she chose to read the text just once and then write the summary; she had arrived late and felt under pressure to do the task quickly, and so she announced that she would read it through just once. What made it a metacognitive monitoring strategy was the element of conscious planning. In addition Monica was the only respondent to make a metacomment on one of her summaries, once it was written: she expressed concern that the ending of her summary of Text D was weak. Ana also used a metacognitive monitoring strategy when writing her summary for Text E. She decided to see if she could make a global statement first, thus beginning her summary with a generalisation about the article.

Summarising ability and level of proficiency

The surprise of this study was that Ana, the respondent considered the lowest in proficiency based on her grades and teacher's appraisal of general performance in the EAP course, actually received the highest number of points from one of the raters on the three summary tasks. The high-proficiency respondents did, however, consistently outperform those rated as medium in proficiency.

The fact that Ana performed the best, in one rater's judgement, may underscore the lack of reliability and validity that seems to plague such summarising tasks. One would expect the lowest proficiency respondents to be judged the poorest on tests of reading comprehension. Of course, in this case the test was untimed, and Ana took the longest time. It is possible that a weak student, when given enough time, a propensity to use a dictionary judiciously and effectively, and a willingness to apply principles learned in class, will compensate for the weaknesses. It is also possible that she did not do as well as others in the course because, as an undergraduate, she was less experienced; alternatively, the teacher's rating of the students' proficiency may have been based more on reading fluency and accuracy in writing the target language than on summarising ability *per se*. At all events, aside from Ana's major misinterpretation of the idiom 'to steal the show', there would be nothing in her reading and writing behaviour in this study that would single her out as low-proficiency.

Regarding the relationship between specific strategies used and proficiency level, an analysis of the strategies used by the respondents would suggest that, in this case, the most successful strategy user was again Ana. She used at least six strategies to her benefit. With respect to reading the source text, she used effectively technical facilitation strategies (underlining discourse markers and words to look up, and circling pronominal referents), clarification and simplification strategies (using a dictionary), and coherence detection strategies (paying special attention to pronouns and conjunctions). With respect to writing the text summary, she effectively used technical facilitation strategies (providing a detailed answer to include the main ideas) and metacognitive monitoring (giving a generalisation plus the main idea).

Ana's strategy of supplying many details in her (lengthy) summaries with the hope that they would contain the main ideas reflects a shot-gun rather than a lazer-beam approach to the task. As long as raters do not penalise for lengthy summaries, then the strategy can be a facilitating one. Ana's strategy of generalising and then moving to main ideas worked with one rater and not with the other (see below). Her literal interpretion of an idiomatic phrase did not work, perhaps an indication of why she was assessed as low-proficiency – her control of vocabulary and especially of idiomatic uses may have been limited.

As for the high-proficiency respondents, in her reading of the source texts Monica used a technical facilitation strategy (underlining noun phrases and verbs) and a metacognitive monitoring strategy (reading a text only once and summarising directly) as facilitating strategies – though it is not clear how much her extensive underlining of verbs helped. In writing the text summary, a coherence production strategy (using sub-titles as the basis for the summary) also facilitated the task. In her reading, Roberta effectively used a technical facilitation strategy (underlining discourse markers) and a clarification and simplification strategy (translating to check on meaning). In writing her summaries, a technical facilitation strategy (using words that she had underlined) was of benefit.

Monica used unsuccessfully a coherence detection strategy in reading (adding facts through world knowledge, as shown in her summary of Text B) and two technical facilitation strategies in writing (skipping paragraphs because of confusing details, and keeping the summary general). As strategies detrimental to reading, Roberta used a clarification and simplification strategy (using the lay meaning of a common word which had a technical meaning in the text) and a coherence detection strategy (assuming the title constituted the main idea of the text). In her writing, Roberta's technical facilitation strategy (excluding paragraphs from the summary) also proved detrimental.

The medium-proficiency students employed fewer facilitating strategies and more detrimental ones. In her reading, Maura used a clarification and simplification stategy effectively (translating to check for meaning), but used a technical facilitation strategy (underlining main ideas and examples) in a way that did not support her summary. In her writing, she used two detrimental technical facilitation strategies (writing a summary that was too general, vague, and short, and writing a summary in list fashion).

In reading, Daniel used effectively the same clarification and simplification strategy that Maura used (translating to check for meaning), and a coherence detection strategy (assuming the title represents the main idea in the text). He also used two writing strategies with moderate success – a technical facilitation one (keeping the summary short and general, which had the effect of disguising how little he had understood Text B) and a coherence production one (using the sub-titles as a basis for the summary). Four other strategies used by Daniel could be seen as detrimental: in reading, a technical facilitation strategy (underlining difficult phrases) and two coherence detection strategies (assuming an illustration reflects the main idea, and connecting details through world knowledge); and in writing, a technical facilitation strategy (underlining words to use in a summary).

The raters' responses

Both raters were familiar with the texts used in this test since they were drawn from a text file that the raters themselves had put together. They had also reviewed the test before it was included in the Resource Package. Yet neither used the score key provided. In the case of Rater 1, it was because he wanted to rate the test according to what he thought was an appropriate summary for each text since he had not constructed the exam. He commented that it was always difficult for him to mark a test that someone else had prepared. He did not generate an answer key. He just kept the text alongside as he read each respondent's summary. He graded each respondent in turn. Before starting his ratings, he wanted to make sure he had read the instructions correctly, so he read them over several times. He noted the misleading nature of the instructions in that they ask the respondent to indicate the topic treated rather than to summarise giving the main ideas.

Rater 2 also rejected the score key provided, on two grounds. First, he objected to the fact that the model answers in the score key were in paragraph form. He would have preferred a list of main ideas for each text. Second, he would only accept a score key if it had been rigorously developed and tried out by colleagues, as this one had not. He scored by the topic of the summary, not by respondent, so that his rating of one summary should not influence his rating of another by the same person. He first read the summaries of all the respondents summarising the same text, and then scored them. He gave one point for each main idea included and took off one point for each inaccuracy. He pointed out that if there had been a stack of some forty papers, he would have prepared a list of main ideas for each text to ensure reliability in his ratings.

On the short texts, the raters did not indicate in writing or in their verbal protocols how they arrived at their own interpretations of how the texts should be summarised. It was unforeseen in this research that the raters would not use the answer key, so it would have been informative to have had a record of just how the raters arrived at their own set of criteria for determining what should go in their own mental summaries of the texts.

The scores given by the two raters are shown in Table 7.1. As can be seen, there was considerable difference between the two raters in their

Table 7.1 Scores given by each rater

| | Rater 1 | | | | | | Rater 2 | | | | |
	B	C	D	E	Total		B	C	D	E	Total
Monica	4	–	2	18	24	Roberta	4	2	–	18	24
Maura	2	1	–	18	21	Daniel	3	–	2	15	18
Ana	–	4	4	20	28	Ana	–	1	4	15	20

scoring of Ana's work, suggesting that they may not have been rating her – or, by implication, the other respondents – by the same criteria. This was, of course, particularly likely to happen since neither of them used the scoresheet; and it should also be noted that the instructions given in the test were somewhat imprecise, merely requesting respondents to 'indicate the topic treated' and giving no indication of desired length except for the number of lines provided (which the respondents ignored at times by writing beyond the lines). However, there were also a number of instances in which the raters' criteria seemed to coincide.

One issue that evidently had a considerable effect on both raters was handwriting. They both stated that they would have little patience for a paper written illegibly if there were many papers to mark. Even with only three sets of papers, they were influenced by the handwriting: Rater 1's first reaction to Monica's paper was to complain about it, and to Maura's, to express pleasure at being able to read it relatively easily. Similarly, Rater 2 noted that Daniel's poor handwriting made scoring somewhat of a struggle, and his patience was stretched by Ana's because, he said, her handwriting was so poor.

With regard to content, both raters appeared to be looking for a fairly comprehensive coverage of the main ideas in each text, and seemed to be broadly in agreement as to what those main ideas were. This was most evident in their responses to Ana's summary of Text D, 'Murder of the gorilla scientist'. Rater 1 felt that the summary was basically good but lacked the name of the colleague (McGuire) who had allegedly killed the scientist in order to obtain her field notes. Rater 2 also assessed the respondent as having understood a number of central ideas but as having missed the part about McGuire being considered a murder suspect. In this case, not only did both raters grant her four out of five points on her 60-word summary, but they appeared to use the same criteria and assign them the same number of points. Similarly, Rater 1 based his assessment of Monica's summary of Text D largely on the proportion of the main ideas she had managed to include; he judged that she had about half the ideas, and the question was whether he should give her two or three out of five for this (the question was decided on the basis of another criterion, as described below). Rater 1 also noted Maura's lack of desire to go deeply into Text B, on racism. Rater 2 commented on points of content in Roberta's summary of Text B, noting that she had clearly indicated the issue of discrimination and had mentioned the effect of the war in bringing Koreans to Japan. On Daniel's summary of the same text, he felt that Daniel had expressed the main ideas fairly well but had not expressed the legal problem well – that is, that Koreans were not allowed to be teachers and had been stripped of their Japanese nationality. Daniel had done less well, he felt, in understanding the main ideas in Text D (on the gorilla scientist); in fact, his assessment of the situation coincided with Daniel's own, for he suggested that Daniel had understood a lot of details but had not understood the story.

Both raters also noted instances of misinterpretation of particular pieces of information. Rater 1, for example, on reading Maura's summary of Text B, noticed her misinterpretation of what the ministry of education had done and accordingly gave her only two out of five points. He also gave her only one out of five points on her summary of Text C ('Pocket video cameras'), observing that she did not know what 'drum' and 'head' meant in that context, but he added, 'Probably this person could understand more but couldn't express it here, which is a pity'. Rater 2 noticed a similar problem with Roberta's summary of the same text – that she did not seem to understand the information about 'wrapping tapes around drums' – but he did not realise that she had misused the title; he simply checked the pocket-size feature as being part of the summary, rather than taking off for it, and gave her two out of five points for this text. In Ana's case, both raters noted her literal interpretation of 'stole the show' in Text C, but they rated it differently. Rater 1 was generous about it because, as he pointed out in his protocol, he found that sort of error quite common among the EAP students, and he did not deduct any points for it. Rater 2, on the other hand, was less sympathetic; he took note of the negative spin-off effect of the misunderstood idiom (Ana's suggestion that there was a legal squabble over the patent). He commented that she seemed to have started her summary by doing a rough literal translation with limited comprehension and then began to understand the text, resulting in briefer, more coherent sentences. He gave her only one point for this summary, as opposed to Rater 1's four.

There were also considerable differences in how the two raters responded to the respondents' style of presenting the information, with Rater 1 apparently expecting more explicit framing than Rater 2 did.

The point shows most clearly in their rating of Ana's summary of Text E ('Managing migraines'). Rater 1 was pleased that she noted in her summary that the text was about migraines and other headaches. He also expressed pleasure that 'she had the decency to make a little synthetic paragraph rather than just giving the titles of the headings'. He gave her the full 20 points. Rater 2, on the other hand, was not impressed by her opening generalisation and was put off by her jumbled ordering of the items. He gave her the lowest of the scores for this text, only 15 points. The value put by Rater 1 on the production of a coherent summary text can also be seen in his responses to Monica's and Maura's work. On Monica's summary of Text B ('The exclusive people'), he indicated that she had understood the text quite well and had got the main ideas, but she could have summed it up more briefly; he gave her four out of five points on her 80-word summary (although he does not seem to have penalised such wordiness in the case of Ana). On Monica's summary of Text C ('Murder of the gorilla scientist'), he felt that she had included about half the ideas and therefore considered giving her three points; but then he decided to drop the score to two points 'because she did not sum it up'. In Maura's case, he penalised her for only providing a list in her summary of Text E and gave her only 15 points. His rationale was that whereas listing might be a legitimate reading strategy, for the preparation of a summary she could have added more about the kind of text it was – for example, that it was from a popular magazine and intended as general information for someone with no medical background. It seems likely that his negative assessment of Maura's summary of this text affected his subsequent, and much more favourable, assessment of Ana's.

The data concerning the raters and their ratings demonstrate a situation in which tests of summarising ability may produce unreliable results: when the raters generate their own score keys and do their rating independently of each other. If these two raters had made up the score key together, perhaps the ratings would have been more uniform. Of course, even when a rigorous score key is made up by the raters or one is given them that they have confidence in, there is no assurance that they will adhere to it strictly. Presumably there would be some point at which lack of adherence to the score key would disqualify them from being raters. Part of the purpose of verbal report research is to determine how raters use score keys when assessing summarisation tasks.

Problems with the test

While an assessment of the sample test was not included among the research questions, some discussion of the test itself seems to be warranted. Comments made by the two raters on the Raters' Questionnaire and observations by the investigator and the research assistant all provided feedback concerning the instructions, the texts, the intended collection of ongoing process data during the test-taking, and the scoring.

With respect to the instructions, they are lengthy, and include an example, but, as Rater 1 pointed out, they are 'a bit dense' and do not specifically request summaries of the texts. Rather, they simply request that the respondent 'indicate the topic treated', and they do not say how long the summary should be. The instructions do indicate how many points each summary is worth, but judging from the responses, these points were ignored, as respondents often spent more time and effort on the two tasks worth fewer points (of course, they were not actually being graded on the test, which could help to explain the pattern). There was consensus among the raters and the researchers that the 20 points allotted the third summary was exaggerated, since the task was far easier than were the tasks of summarising the other short texts, in that it simply required the gathering up of subtitles from each of the clearly marked sections.

Another format issue involved the intention of the test designers to have the respondents write their summary of Text E before writing out the more detailed information about the contents of each section of the article. The respondents preferred to handle the details first because it facilitated their writing of the general summary. This approach seems quite logical and provides feedback to test constructors as to test-taking strategies: test takers may not do tasks on a test in the order presented if they perceive that order as counterproductive. This finding is similar to one from previous research on the taking of multiple-choice reading comprehension tests – that better respondents jump to the multiple-choice questions first, read them, and then return to the text to find answers to them, rather than reading the text first as the instructions indicate (Cohen 1984).

Regarding the length of the texts, Rater 1 felt that the short texts were too short, thus encouraging respondents to read them closely and get bogged down in details. For summarising tasks, he would recommend longer texts. With regard to the number of texts, Rater 2 felt that there should be more of a selection. He noted, for example, that Text C was quite technical but thought that this would be acceptable as long as the respondents had enough choice to be able to avoid or select it at will.

The portion of the test intended to be innovative was the inclusion of process data, whereby the respondents indicated after each section the difficulties that they had in doing the tasks, whether with the instructions, the format of the exercise, the topic, vocabulary items, text organisation, or grammar. The example given at the beginning of the test includes comments about the theme of the text, certain confusing sentences, and words that are unknown. Actually, the original intent was to have the respondents indicate how they went about summarising the texts, but this notion did not get operationalised as such. The respondents ended up doing little more than listing a few vocabulary words that gave them difficulties. They did not seem to have a ready metalanguage for describing the strategies they were using. Perhaps in future work it would be possible to provide a checklist of summarising strategies for well-trained respondents to refer to after each section.

Conclusions

This study has underscored the problem outlined at the beginning of this chapter, that of reliability. First, a low-proficiency respondent performed unexpectedly well – although, as has been pointed out, there may be other explanations for this besides the unreliability of the test. Second, there were marked differences between the raters on how they assessed this one respondent. Third, the raters seem to have differed somewhat in their basic criteria: while they apparently agreed on what material should be included, one emphasised more than did the other the production of a coherent, readable text.

However, there are a number of ways in which the problem of reliability can be dealt with. A score key is clearly needed for each text, one that lists the main ideas and connecting schemata, and it must be such that the raters are willing to use it. This means that it must be rigorously developed and tested among colleagues; and there must be some means of checking that raters are actually using it. It might help, too, to establish procedures to be used for the rating, for example, whether raters are to read all respondents' summaries of one text before moving on to the summaries of the next one, or whether they are to rate each respondent's paper in its entirety. The former approach would most likely be more reliable.

Another way to make the test more reliable would be to make the instructions more explicit than those given in the test used for this study. The instructions might state how long the summary should be, whether points are to be deducted for the inclusion of non-essential information, whether the summary is to be considered a first draft or a finished piece, and whether it should be a listing of the main points or a smoothly integrated paragraph. Given the raters' complaints about handwriting in this study, it might be particularly appropriate to advise test takers to copy out their responses neatly once they are complete.

Such written guides as score keys and instructions are probably, however, inadequate for ensuring reliable ratings, especially when test takers respond in very diverse ways. It is important, therefore, that raters receive some kind of training, perhaps by discussing sample responses in relation to the score keys, considering what to do about unexpected misinterpretations (such as idioms like 'stealing the show'), and coming to some consensus regarding the number of words to be used in the summaries and whether and how heavily to penalise poor handwriting. It is also important that students receive training in writing summaries. One finding of this study was that the respondents paid more attention to the reading than to the writing, producing texts 'on-line', often at the expense of legibility and sometimes, as in the case of Ana's summary of Text C, of coherence. If students are to be seriously assessed on such summaries they must obviously learn to produce a more reader-based response, which means not only writing it neatly but also seeing that it is coherent and reads smoothly; and, as with all writing, students can only learn to do this by receiving ample feedback on their work on similar tasks.

The fact that a test of this sort requires such training for students can be seen as detracting from the authenticity of the tasks, given that many real-world summaries are more likely to be writer-based. On the other hand, the respondents' remarks on this study suggest that having to express their understanding of a text in writing does have a beneficial effect on their reading, in that it makes them more aware of where they have difficulties. Also, explicit training towards the writing would help address the major problem observed in this study, namely, that while the respondents had little difficulty in identifying and selecting the topical information, they found it much harder to distinguish between superordinate and trivial or redundant material. They did not have a good sense of balance with respect to how much to delete, making their summaries either too vague and general or too detailed. Teaching that addresses this problem would obviously be of benefit to them in their academic work.

This study has demonstrated another advantage of this kind of testing: the tasks elicited a wide range of reading strategies, as respondents grappled with low-level linguistic problems in order to arrive at global interpretations of the texts – and in doing so they were, by their own account, reactivating what they had learnt in their EAP course. For example, they did not simply underline words they did not know: they paid attention to cohesive signals and to graphic cues such as titles, sub-titles, and illustrations. The use of these strategies was not uniformly successful, but even the mistakes gave useful information about the respondents' capabilities. Moreover, the respondents then had to draw on more productive strategies in order to write their own summaries, such as making generalisations and drawing on their world knowledge to connect the details with each other; again, these strategies were not always successful, but they did require the respondents to be fully engaged with the texts. Thus, well-constructed summary tests may promote a richer, more interactive approach to reading than do comprehension tests that focus more on details.

Finally, given the problems with this kind of test, it is evidently important that more research be done on how people write summaries and how raters respond to them. With regard to the production of summaries, we need to know more about the strategies used: respondents might, for example, be asked to fill out a checklist of possibilities when they have completed each summary task. It would also be helpful to analyse summaries more closely in relation to the original texts: the model described by Flottum (1987) would be useful for this purpose in that it distinguishes each 'sequence' in the summary (i.e. material round each verbal expression) in terms of how closely it follows the source text and how much new material it includes. With regard to the raters, more data on how they score summaries is needed, whether it is collected through verbal report sessions, questionnaires, or other means; studies examining the effects on rater reliability of score keys and explicit instructions would be particularly helpful. Another issue to explore, in the case of cross-language summaries, is whether or not the rater is a native speaker of the language in which the summary is written. For example, to what extent might raters who are non-native users of the language of the summaries focus on the reading comprehension side rather than on the writing because they do not consider themselves able to judge the merits of a summary written in what is to them a second language? Would the focus of native-language readers be different?

Answers to all these questions would not only be interesting: they would help towards making the use of such tests, where tests must be used, a truly practicable alternative. This study has shown that both the taking and the rating of summary tests are complex processes eliciting a wide range of strategies and varying a good deal among individuals: we need to know more about these processes from both the respondents' and the raters' points of view, and we need to work on developing tests that can be scored more reliably while retaining the authenticity of this one. For the complexity of the processes involved in summarising and the consequent difficulty in assessing them should not be taken as a reason for rejecting this form of test. A test is important, not only because it identifies individuals as more or less proficient but also because it has a significant influence on what teachers think they should teach and what students think they should learn; and the evidence shows quite clearly that the respondents in this case found the tasks to be instructive in themselves and a good reflection of the work they had done in their EAP course.

Acknowledgements

I would like to thank Gissi Sarig, Kate Parry, Gabi Kasper, Marsha Bensoussan, Elana Shohamy, and Anne Mauranen for their helpful feedback on this chapter. I would also like to thank Carla Reichmann for her assistance in the collection of the data.

8   An adult learner in Canada: watching assessment take place

Patrick Cummins and Stan Jones

Introduction

An adult literacy programme, by definition, serves learners who have been failed by the formal education system: either they have bypassed it altogether, or, more commonly among those brought up in North America, they have been through school but have not acquired the skills that it is supposed to teach. The reasons for their failure in school are many and various, and so are its effects: while for some individuals illiteracy is associated with serious emotional and social problems, for others it is an inconvenience, albeit a serious one, which they seek to minimise through a range of more or less effective strategies. For an adult literacy programme, it is important to know what kinds of problems prospective students bring with them so that they can be assigned to suitable tutors or placed in appropriate classes; it is also important to know the range of strategies learners use to cope with their problems, for these strategies represent strengths on which they and their tutors or teachers can build.

The standardised tests that are so widely used in North America give no such information. Often they give no more than a ranking, one that for adult learners is invariably depressing, for it places them at the bottom of a scale that was originally designed for children. The tests that purport to diagnose specific difficulties are arguably worse, for in representing literacy as a collection of discrete skills, they can be seriously misleading (Hill and Parry 1989). The inadequacy of such tests has been widely recognised in the field of adult basic education, and programmes are increasingly looking for ways to substitute for or supplement them. In this chapter we shall describe one such attempt, where a more pragmatically based test is administered in the context of an intake interview; the interviewer is thus able to use oral interaction to track how the learner deals with specific tasks on the test as well as other activities in which he engages. As a result of such interaction, the interviewer is able to produce much richer documentation of the learner's capabilities and needs.

Our focus is on a single interviewer, Ellie – an experienced, insightful intake counsellor with an adult literacy programme in a large urban Canadian school board. Our interest in studying her work comes from our conviction that too much energy is expended on trying to design psychometrically better tests in adult literacy, and not enough in finding out what qualitative information is useful and how it can be best obtained. At the same time we believe, as does Ellie, that a systematic approach to assessment is necessary – that whoever conducts an assessment must have a clear idea of what information is being sought and why, and must have an efficient method of recording the information. We also share with Ellie the belief that the assessment should benefit learners directly and should focus on helping them recognise what they are able to do and what they need to learn. Only if both are clear to learners can they make informed choices. Here we present a detailed report on a single intake interview conducted by Ellie, including both her and our reflections on the process.

Background

If you live in Ottawa, Canada, and you are an adult who wants to learn to read and write or do basic maths better, you may well find yourself talking to someone in the Ottawa Board of Education (OBE), the largest of seven boards in the area. Once you get onto the ABE/ESL offices in the Department of Continuing Education, they are going to tell you, first, they do have the sort of programme you are looking for; and, second, 'You have to see Ellie'.

Ellie is the intake coordinator for Adult Basic Education. If she is there, she will talk to you right away and set up an appointment. If she is not there, the receptionist will take your telephone number, and Ellie will get back to you. Ellie's job is to assess and register adult literacy students for the OBE in order to help students choose the appropriate programme, and also to provide information that teachers can use to develop curricula with individual needs in mind.

You are lucky if you are going to talk with Ellie. She is a warm person who respects and cares about the people she sees, and she has years of experience, from which she has learned and is still learning. She does not simply take and record information; she brings out information in ways that help prospective students learn about themselves. She helps them begin to develop educational expectations and objectives that are within their grasp, and to think about practical ways of achieving those objectives. She employs a variety of tools in the process and uses them in different ways to develop a complex body of information about the needs and abilities of individual students. People who are interviewed by Ellie gain something even if they never enter a programme.

During several discussions, Ellie described the process she sees herself involved in; later she allowed us to observe an actual intake interview. We shall discuss that interview in light of Ellie's description and some of our own observations.

The interview

Opening conversation

David's appointment was at 9:00 a.m. Ellie was there early, well dressed, as always, out of respect for her client. David, accompanied by his wife, arrived on time at the counter in the ABE/ESL office and Ellie met them there. She could have stayed working in her own closed-off office until they arrived, as there were a receptionist and other clerical people in the main office at the time, but Ellie prefers to greet new students personally and to make them feel welcome. She led David and his wife into her office and they sat down to talk, Ellie and David at a table along one wall of the office, his wife in a chair near the table. The arrangement was collegial rather than hierarchical and immediately gave the impression that this was to be a joint investigation.

Neither party was coming on this interview cold. As often happens, Ellie had gained a fair amount of information about the registrant before the interview began: the OBE personnel department had contacted her about him, and so had David's wife, who, it appears, was better educated than he and often mediated for him with bureaucracy. From these conversations, Ellie knew that David had worked for a cleaning company for seven years and had recently been laid off because of the recession. He had put in an application with the OBE to work as a cleaner and had been called in for an interview (he took the form away with him and brought it back later, perfectly filled out – an instance of the ways in which his wife was able to help him). He would have been hired by the Board except the personnel officer gave him a short note to read, 'Broken window – 3rd floor', and he could not tell her what the note said. At that point, the personnel officer suggested he contact Continuing Education, learn to read a bit, then come back. David's wife had phoned and arranged this appointment with Ellie.

The interview began with Ellie explaining what they were going to do. They would talk a bit about David's long-term goals and how he liked to go about learning. They would fill in some forms. David would try a short test, but Ellie emphasised that it would not really be a test – more a way of finding out what sorts of things he could already do and how he did them. They would look into what David wanted to do with reading and writing; and they would discuss options – what sort of programme seemed most suitable. Ellie clearly had a definite plan in mind, although as the interview progressed, she did not follow it exactly; she naturally adapted and modified the procedure in response to David's reactions.

They then talked a little about family matters. David and his wife had been married recently and they were expecting their first baby in five or six months. Ellie's interest in people is genuine, and her manner is encouraging; anyone who talks to her for a few minutes feels comfortable and does not feel threatened. David was relaxed in her company, though his wife, off at the side, still seemed nervous that he might say the wrong thing. She did not say anything, but she listened intently. Later she moved further off to the side and eventually got up and left the office, apparently satisfied that things were going well.

Form filling

Ellie needed a certain amount of practical information about David, to be recorded on an intake form entitled *Learner Information*. She gave him the first sheet of this form, which has sections for such things as name, address, educational background, employment, goals, and how the student found out about the programme. She pointed to the first part of the form and told him she would like him to fill in what he could. David took it and wrote his last name and first name in the appropriate boxes in flowing script; but when he came to the part about his address he signalled his own view of his limitations by saying, 'Now I'm in problems'. Ellie quietly took the form back and inquired orally about address, birth date, and telephone number. She wrote these down and filled in other information as it became available during the interview.

Ellie had told us earlier that she learns a lot from this activity, that filling in the form constitutes part of the assessment; she observes how easily students can do it and notes such details as spelling and style of script (printing or cursive). Many adult learners, like David, can write their names without difficulty but are then unable to write their address. Often such students will deal with the problem by taking a card from a wallet to copy the information, and then Ellie notes the fact and observes how easily the copying is done. On this occasion, David had not immediately produced something to copy, so, in order not to embarass him, Ellie filled in the information herself. She also made notes, and later wrote on the confidential Assessment Results page of the intake form, 'Needs help writing address'.

Ellie asked David about his previous school experience and he named the 'basic level' high school he had gone to. He said he thought he had accumulated the required number of credits but, for reasons he did not understand, he never received a diploma. He recalled that he did well in maths when he was in school but he only got by in English with help from his friends, who, as he put it, enabled him to get '50s, 52s' (50% is the passing score). The thing he said he liked least about school was 'standing outside in bad weather'.

There is substantial information here that could bear on David's attitude about going back to school. Feeling that he been unfairly denied his high-school diploma, having been pushed along in English without appreciable learning taking place, and remembering being made to stand outside in bad weather for no apparent reason, he might be expected to be cautious in any new dealings with school. But while Ellie did document David's success with maths, his receiving 27.5 credits without being given a diploma, and his comment about bad weather, she offered no interpretation and she did not mention his report of marginal grades in English.

Moving on to the section on goals, Ellie asked David what he wanted to read. David replied, 'Just enough to get by.' She suggested that he might want to be able to read labels and write things at work. David agreed, and Ellie wrote under 'Educational goals': 'Writing. Read labels.' She did not, however, pursue the topic further at this point – there was no discussion, for example, of what products David had used in his cleaning work, information which would have helped establish which particular labels he might have to read.

Ellie then moved on to the section about 'sponsoring agencies', for which she needed the name and phone number of his representative with the Unemployment Insurance Corporation. David found a card in his wallet, took it out and looked at it, apparently trying to find what she wanted to know. His wife got up from her seat, took the card from David, and handed it to Ellie. Ellie wrote down the information, discussed with David what she needed the information for, and handed the card back to him.

Here, again, was an incident that showed something of David's abilities and strategies with regard to written material. First, he knew which card contained the information needed, and though he was not able to extract the information, he was prepared to try. Second, his wife's action illustrates her mediating role; his relationship with her was clearly an important factor enabling David to deal with information encoded in text. Ellie did not, however, note down these points, nor, indeed, is there any obvious place on the form where they could be written; the only evidence of this interaction would be the form itself with its different handwritings.

With the *Learner Information* form finished, Ellie produced another form headed *Informal Interview*, which she had photocopied from a book called *Litstart*, a book of assessment and teaching strategies for literacy workers. The form had seven questions, of which Ellie asked only three:

1. What are your hobbies or special interests?
2. What are you good at?
3. What do you want to learn how to read?

As to 'hobbies and interests' Ellie learned that David liked watching sports, 'all sports', and playing basketball in pick-up games. She already knew that he was 'good at' maths, and she asked if he did maths at home. He said that he did, so she then asked if he wanted to learn how to read 'bills and things', and he agreed.

With questions like these, Ellie developed some sense of David's social world during the course of this interview, but her documentation of this world on the form itself is skimpy. She wrote down 'Sports (all) – Basketball' for the 'hobbies and interests' question, but not that he liked to *play* basketball and only to *watch* other sports. She wrote 'Maths' for 'What are you good at?', and 'Bills, cheques' as something he would 'want to learn how to read', though she would find out later from the test that he could already read bills and cheques.

This section of the interview ended with Ellie's asking, 'Is there anything else that's important?' David's answer demonstrated his own very practical approach to literacy: 'Get a job after this.' Ellie recorded this practical aim, by writing in the box for 'reason for returning to school', 'Read and write for a job', but she did not add any further details on what David needed to read and write.

Writing

At this point during intake interviews, Ellie usually asks registrants to 'write something'. She provides a guidance sheet that focuses their attention on educational experience and their hopes for the future, but they may, if they prefer, write on some other topic of their own choosing. She tells registrants to write whatever they want and not to worry about grammar or spelling. Nevertheless, grammar and spelling are clearly a concern for her, and probably so for the registrants too, since she says that one of the main uses of the guidance sheet is that it contains words like 'school' to which writers can refer if they do not know how to spell them. Also, although registrants often write illuminating comments about their social lives or the problems they experienced with the school system, Ellie says the most important information she gets from the sample is 'mechanical errors, structural errors'.

When it appears that registrants will not be able to write on their own, she asks them to say two or three sentences which she writes down (in print rather than cursive script) and gives to them to copy. This exercise shows her how well registrants can reproduce what they see and how they form letters. In David's case, Ellie deemed even this activity too difficult; it would only cause discomfort and, in any event, she felt she had learned as much as she was going to learn about his writing from his attempt to fill in the form. She did not ask him to write anything.

By now, Ellie had obtained the standard information that organisations usually require: last name, first name, birth date, birthplace, marital status, gender, telephone number, and first language. She also knew something about David's schooling. Regarding employment, she knew that he was a steady, responsible worker, temporarily unemployed, who could have a good job if he developed a minimal and specific reading ability. She had developed a fairly clear picture of who David was and how he fitted into his community: that he was married, did his share in the house, including the family accounts, and had a baby on the way who would increase his need for financial stability. From watching his attempt to deal with the intake form, she also knew that David experienced severe difficulty with reading and writing. This seems like a substantial body of information, and yet there was the test. What more could Ellie want to know?

Using the test

Ellie had enough information at this point to choose a test which she felt would be appropriate, the options being the Canadian Adult Achievement Test (CAAT), Level A or Level B, or the Ontario Test of Adult Functional Literacy (OTAFL), Level 1. CAAT is a norm-referenced standardised test that uses simulations of real-life texts based on adult themes; it is similar to the Test of Adult Basic Education (see Chapter 5). OTAFL is a criterion-referenced test with items developed from authentic samples of such text as is commonly encountered in everyday life – labels, tickets, advertisements, and the like.

Ellie had told us she chooses the test which will give the registrant the greatest sense of accomplishment, her purpose being, as she says, 'to make them feel good'. She finds the Level B CAAT generally useful, especially for people with technical high-school diplomas (it is intended, according to the CAAT Norms Booklet, 'for adults who have had five to eight years of schooling'). If she has any reason to doubt whether the individual she is assessing can achieve some success on Level B, she will use the easier Level A, designed 'for adults who have had one to four years of formal education'. The test at either level consists mainly of multiple-choice tasks, although there is also a spelling dictation at Level A.

People who would be frustrated by CAAT Level A are given OTAFL instead. Nearly everyone who comes in can achieve some success with OTAFL Level 1 since the items approximate everyday tasks which even the most basic reader has found strategies to deal with. However, when choosing which test to administer, Ellie allows for life experience as well as decoding abilities. Since CAAT, more than OTAFL, resembles the tests students frequently find themselves doing in school, Ellie may offer CAAT Level A to young poor readers who have spent most of their lives in school. She says that even though it presents more complex vocabulary and grammatical structures, CAAT may be easier for them than OTAFL since the latter draws more on adult life experience.

Though both CAAT and OTAFL are clearly labelled as tests, Ellie says it is important that registrants should not feel they are being tested. She tells them that the test, in this context, is not something they can pass or fail, and she does everything she can to signal that she is looking for what they can do rather than for what they cannot. She does, however, make her own record of their performance on a sheet headed *Assessment Results*.

In David's case, Ellie chose OTAFL Level 1 and supplemented it with a phonics check at the beginning and two reading-aloud passages at the end.

Phonics check. For the phonics check, Ellie showed David a sheet with large-font lower-case letters arranged in columns in no special order plus a final column of digraphs (*ch*, *sh*, *ph*, *qu*, and *th*). Ellie pointed to the letter *m* on the sheet and explained, 'I want you to give me the name of the letter and the sound it makes.' She illustrated what she wanted, '*M* - mmm', then asked him, 'Can you think of a word that starts with *m* ?' David offered, 'Milk'. Ellie praised his success and went on to other letters on the page. 'What is this letter?' David answered, '*B*'. Ellie asked, 'Can you think of a word that starts with *b*?' David answered, 'Ball'. David could not say what *e*, *f*, *o*, or *u* sounded like, nor could he start words with them. The letter *c* caused him to hesitate because he knew it could be pronounced two ways; he finally suggested both /k/ and /s/, but could not give any word beginning with the letter. He identified the small *l* as an *i*, but otherwise made no mistakes with the consonants.

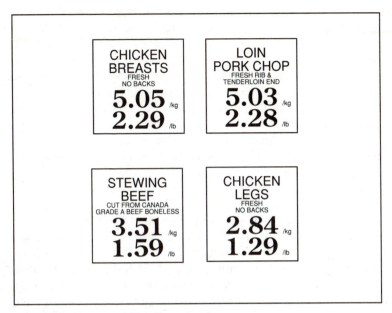

Figure 8.1. Test material based on advertisements

Ellie wrote on the *Assessment Results* sheet, 'Understands sounds of letters. Some difficulty with vowels', but she did not specify which letters had caused difficulty, nor did she suggest any reason for the problem.

OTAFL. Ellie brought out a copy of OTAFL Level 1 and laid it out on the table in front of David. The test booklet gives at the beginning three example items to show people who are taking the test on their own how to respond; in each of these a text and accompanying tasks are set out on one page and then are shown on the next with the answers correctly filled in. In her discussion with David, Ellie used these examples as regular items, without referring to the answers given. The first, reproduced in Figure 8.1, showed four samples from a grocery store flyer, each advertising a cut of meat and giving the unit price per pound and per kilo. Ellie read the question from the test booklet, 'Which is the cheapest meat?' David pencilled a check mark in the box beneath 'chicken legs' and said, 'That'. Not content with simply knowing that David had got the correct answer, Ellie asked him, 'How did you know that?' David did not have to think in order to reply. 'Chicken legs is cheap. I buy the meat.'

This was the first of a number of instances where David used real-world experience in responding to the test. But his answer to Ellie's question does not really tell us how he was applying that knowledge: he may have recognised the phrase 'chicken legs' and then used what he knew of prices to deduce that this must be the cheapest meat; or he may have read the figures, chosen the lowest, and then used his knowledge as confirmation. Ellie did not, however, pursue the point further, but wrote in the corner of this sheet, 'Picks out meat. Good with numbers.' She seemed to be acknowledging David's explanation but was also bringing in information from earlier in the interview, David's own assertions about his maths ability.

The second item, again from the set of three examples, shows a ticket for an Ottawa hockey game containing information in both French and English; it is reproduced in Figure 8.2.

Ellie read the question, 'What date is the ticket for?' and David chose the correct date from the three offered. Ellie cautioned him not simply to guess and asked the next question, 'What time does the game begin?' David answered correctly, 'Two o'clock' and ticked the appropriate space. The third question asks the test taker to 'List your section, row and seat number' on blanks that are labelled 'Section', 'Row', and 'Seat'. The ticket gives this information in the same order, but shows the headings for the numbers in capital letters and abbreviates one of them: 'SEC.', 'ROW', and 'SEAT'; then the numbers are given at the other end of the ticket under the French headings, 'SEC.', 'RANGEE', and 'SIEGE'. Thus, to answer correctly, the test taker must do more than merely match up identical symbols. David wrote down the correct numbers, but he reversed those for section and seat. Ellie asked, 'How did you know this was seat 19?' (it is seat 12 on the ticket). 'What makes you think of that?' David replied, 'Because I used to go there.' Again, his response does not answer Ellie's question, but it does suggest that David dealt with the problems of interpreting written information by referring to the

Figure 8.2 Test material based on a ticket

practical situation in which the information is used rather than by symbol-matching or phonic decoding; and we have no doubt that when he does go to a hockey game, he has no more difficulty than more fluent readers do in finding his seat.

In spite of her question about David's strategy and his potentially useful response, Ellie made no written comment. Nor did she note the reversal of numbers, even though it could have been evidence of perceptual difficulties.

Ellie omitted the third example and proceeded to the main part of the test. It gives tasks on 11 different texts:

(1) three grocery coupons
(2) a notice listing business hours
(3) labels from three over-the-counter medicines
(4) a prescription label
(5) five ads from the side of a restaurant placemat
(6) a specimen cheque
(7) a gas bill
(8) a chart listing emergency phone numbers
(9) a map
(10) a Jell-o package
(11) a chart of textile label symbols

David had no difficulty with the tasks on texts (1), (2), (4), (5), (6), (7), (8), and (11), and the fact that he could handle these so easily (especially the grocery coupons, the cheque, and the bill) confirms his own assertion that he could read sufficiently to handle household accounts. He was not, however, so successful with the tasks on texts (3), (9), and (10).

Text (3) shows photocopies of labels from Dimetapp, advertised as an 'elixir' for 'sinus, congestion, colds, [and] hay fever', Tylenol, described as 'Acetaminophen tablets for relief of pain and fever', and Sucrets, labelled as 'sore throat lozenges' or 'pastilles pour la gorge'. It is reproduced in Figure 8.3.

Ellie asked David to 'put a check in the box under the one you would buy if you had a fever'. David incorrectly ticked off Dimetapp. Ellie asked him what made him decide on this one; he replied, 'Colds and hay fever' and circled 'colds and hay fever' on the sheet. From this response to Ellie's question we can see that David had done more than match the word 'fever' in the question and on the label. He had decoded the whole phrase. This reading had, however, led him to the wrong choice of drugs, most likely because his own vocabulary regarding health-related matters did not suggest a distinction between fever and hay fever; or another, perhaps additional explanation may be that the word 'fever' on

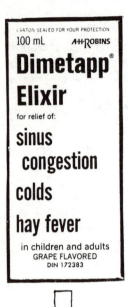

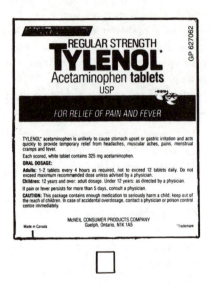

Figure 8.3 Test material based on medicine labels

the Tylenol label was presented less prominently and only after the presumably unreadable word 'Acetaminophen'. Whatever the reason, David's incorrect response, while indicating ignorance of medical terms, does point to a certain decoding ability.

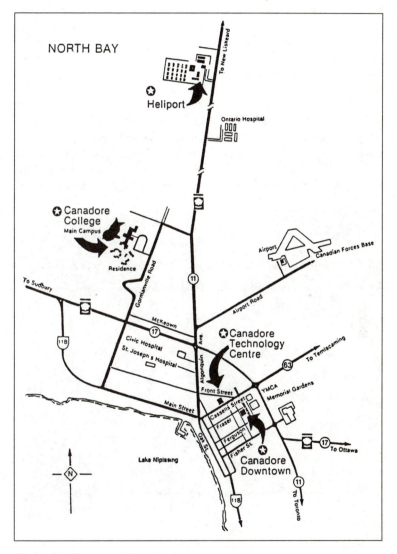

Figure 8.4 Test material based on a map

Text (9) is an attenuated map of North Bay, Ontario, shown in Figure 8.4. Ellie asked a question about the kind of knowledge David was bringing to the text. 'Have you ever been to North Bay?' David replied that he had, but not recently and not often. Ellie then read the first question from the test, 'Find the Civic Hospital located near Algonquin Avenue. Circle the hospital on the map.' David spent some time poring over the map, found *Ontario* Hospital (also near Algonquin Avenue but not *Civic* Hospital) and circled it. Ellie asked him how he knew this was the answer, and David told her, 'It says "hospital".' For this item, David demonstrated some map reading ability but made a wrong choice. Of course, the score on the test shows only the mistake and not the ability he displayed in making it, and though Ellie deliberately asked a question to bring out more information, she did not note it anywhere in writing.

Ellie read the second question given on the map: 'Look at the arrows at the ends of the highways. Which route would you take to get to Ottawa?' David said correctly, 'Seventeen' and wrote the number in the blank. Asked how he knew, David replied, 'I know the highways.' As with the chicken legs, David used his real-world knowledge as part of his strategy for interpreting text and probably could have answered this

Figure 8.5 Test material based on a food label

question just as easily without the map.

Text (10), shown in Figure 8.5, is a photocopy of a Jell-o (instant pudding) package opened so that both the front and the instructions on the side are visible. Ellie read the first question given on this text: 'How much milk do you need to make the pudding?' David searched the page and found a quantity on what would have been the front of the package. He suggested this as a tentative answer, 'Half a cup'; he did not, however, mark it in the test booklet but continued to search until he came up with the correct answer, 'Two cups', written on what would have been the side of the package. It seems probable that the two-dimensional presentation of what would normally be a box-shaped layout contributed to his first error: if he had been handed a Jell-o package instead of the flat photocopy, it would have been clear that the instructions were on the side, and that the writing on the front was not instructions. The shape of the original artefact provides, in this case, an important clue.

Ellie continued to the second question, 'Okay ... and how long should you beat the pudding?' David searched the instructions as if hoping that the correct answer would jump out at him; it did not, and he became obviously uncomfortable. Ellie intervened by suggesting a strategy; she pointed to the sentence containing the information he needed and offered, – Let's read this together.' David began reading slowly, word by word. 'Beat slowly with egg beater or (prompt from Ellie for 'electric') electric mixer at low speed (prompt from Ellie for 'until') well (prompt for 'blended') – about two minutes. Pour into (prompt for 'dessert') dishes and let stand (prompt for 'until set') – five minutes.' On completing the reading, David commented, 'I can't read the longer words.' Ellie again asked how long he should beat the pudding and David answered, 'Two minutes' and marked it in the test booklet.

David's analysis of his problem – that he had trouble with the longer words – obviously has some validity. The passage contained only four words with seven or more letters, and Ellie prompted for three of them. His unfamiliarity with cooking terms may, however, have been a contributor as well; 'blended', 'dessert', and 'until set' are cooking terms and cooking is not an activity that David ordinarily engages in.

Other potentially useful information emerged from this item: for example, David's approach to the text was to scan it for words that might relate to the question rather than to read it straight through; nevertheless, when he did read straight through, slow and painful as it was, he was able to pick out and retain the requested information. Neither his scanning strategy nor his performance on the oral reading was, however, recorded.

Reading aloud. Upon completion of these test items, Ellie brought out more pieces of paper she uses to get at information she believes is important. Two were reading passages from *Litstart*. The first passage, illustrated with a collage of car keys, a dashboard, driving gloves, and sun glasses, is about driving. The passage itself is as follows:

Ten Dollars!

Tim has a new car.
It is blue and white.
He drives it to work.
It uses a lot of gas.
Tim buys gas each week.
He needs ten dollars for gas.

Ellie offered David a choice on how to deal with this reading-aloud passage. 'I want you to read this to me, or we'll read it together.' David elected to read it himself. His reading was not fluent – there were hesitations – but he read all the words. Ellie commented on the content of the passage, not the quality of the reading: 'Ten dollars! Wouldn't that be neat?' She did not write anything down at this stage.

The second passage, accompanied by a picture of a wind surfer is as follows:

At the Beach

What do you do in the summer?
I like to go to the beach and enjoy the sun.
Last summer I learned how to wind surf.
I spent many days on the water,
    surfing with my friends.
That is how I got so badly sunburned.
This year I will be more careful.

Ellie introduced the topic of the passage and what she might have expected to be difficult vocabulary. 'It's about wind-surfing. Do you wind-surf?' David answered, 'No'. People do wind-surf on the Ottawa River during the summer, but Ellie had already enquired about David's sports activities and knew that the only one he participated in was basketball. Her question, 'Do you wind-surf?' was perhaps less a request for information than an indication of embarrassment about using material that was outside David's experience.

This reading was more of a struggle for David than the previous one. He needed prompting for quite a number of words, including 'surfing', 'badly', and 'will'. Ellie did not, however, make any comment on these problems, but focused again on the content of the passage. She asked, 'What happened to this fellow?' to which David replied that he had got himself sunburned. Ellie said she goes to the cottage in the summer but stays out of the sun and doesn't get sunburned. David said he had had a couple of sunburns, but not often. Ellie then brought this section of the interview to a close with a comment that could be taken either as a judgement on the reading or simply a polite transition, 'Super, well done.'

Ellie's focus on content is interesting, given the banal nature of the passages and the record that she eventually made of this exercise. From what she said later, it was clear that she was not comfortable with the material and would prefer to have a selection of passages out on the table, some written by students and some from books or magazines, so that registrants could choose what interested them rather than having something imposed on them. What prevented her from doing this was a persistent belief that she needed passages that would indicate the reader's 'level', so she was delaying introducing new ones until she could get a readability analysis done on them. *Litstart*, on the other hand, does purport to identify levels, as is indicated by the book's instructions to the teacher: beneath the passage about driving are the words, 'If your student had difficulty with the passage, the student is at the beginning level', and beneath the one about wind-surfing, 'If your student had difficulty with the passage, the student is at the beginning to intermediate level.' Ellie was evidently following these instructions, for she later wrote on David's Assessment Results sheet, 'Level I Beginner; Upper Level' – and this was all that she wrote about the reading-aloud exercise.

Recording interests

On finishing the reading aloud, Ellie seems to have thought she had finished and then remembered that there was still one form to be filled. She said, 'Oh, I forgot something' and brought out two checklists, one enumerating language and the other maths interests, which together constitute what is known as the *Interest Inventory*. The language checklist is divided between *Writing* and *Reading* and includes real-world activities such as 'telephone messages', 'forms and applications', 'poems', 'typing', 'telephone book', 'personal letters', and 'using a library' and also some discrete skills such as 'punctuation', 'spelling', and 'grammar'. The maths checklist was divided between practical applications such as 'adding up prices', 'counting change', 'charts and graphs', and 'changing recipes' and operations such as 'adding', 'multiplying', 'fractions', and 'averages'. Ellie generally asks those who are able to check off interests on their own to do so. She advises them to be selective in their choices and, 'not do everything at once'. With David, she kept the checklists in front of her and checked off choices for him. She looked over the list for a moment, then looked up from it and asked, 'What is the most important thing you want to read?'

They had discussed David's interests earlier, and he had been thinking about the question prior to the interview, so answers came easily. 'To get a job. Read the paper. Bills, to write cheques. Want to ... writing my wife's name ... and the kid's.' Ellie ticked off 'forms and applications', 'cheques and bank deposits', 'bills and bank statements', and 'newspaper'. She wrote in blanks on the form, 'my wife's name' and 'my child's name'.

The rest of the skills Ellie checked off on the list were her own suggestions. She asked, 'Can you think about anything? How about signs around the city ... telephone messages?' David agreed and Ellie ticked off 'telephone messages' and 'signs'. 'One more thing. How about reading labels on cleaning materials?' David again agreed. 'And writing things like "broken windows"?' Ellie wrote in 'broken window' under *Writing* and 'labels on cleaning materials' under *Reading*. These ideas were doubtless useful, but they were more in the line of advice than in-vestigation, and David would have acceded to any of Ellie's suggestions.

Ellie says the interest inventory is useful for identifying specific goals as opposed to more global and less immediately attainable ones. 'Short term goals are harder to get. ... A lot of people don't read anything. You dig and dig until you get to the inventory... then, "Oh, yeah!" This appears to help people become more specific or more focused in seeing why they are here.' She thinks the inventory should remain with students' day-to-day work and not go into the teachers' files. 'Both teacher and student forget.' If, in discussing the *Interest Inventory* with a student, she finds only very specific goals, such as 'reading the labels on medicine bottles', she helps him or her to contact an agency which makes individual matches with volunteer tutors; Ellie feels such limited goals may be achieved most efficiently in a one-on-one situation.

Wrap-up discussion

Ellie checked over the forms that had been building up in David's file and made a decision about which location she should assign him to. She chose one that offered relatively structured classes, where students were grouped by level of proficiency and the emphasis was more on teaching and learning than on socialising; whereas for many students, the greatest benefit provided by adult education classes is the opportunity to meet and talk with other people, for David this was not such an important consideration. She checked whether her decision was agreeable to him: 'Do you think this is a good location for you?' David was happy with it: 'One bus.' She wrote out and handed him the times for his classes and he appeared satisfied. She spent about a minute promoting afternoon interest groups – reading, writing, publishing, and others – but David declined to start with any of these, at least for the time being. Ellie wrote out a slip with the time, room number, and teacher's name on it. To end the interview, she stood up and so did David. 'So, we'll start you on March 18th.' She handed him the slip. 'Your teacher's name will be M———. She's French, but she speaks English perfectly.'

Ellie says that students often ask about their test results at the end of the interview, expecting to hear them reported as a grade level. OTAFL is not normed in this way, so she can honestly tell takers of this test that she does not have this information. She does calculate a percentage score and record it on the *Assessment Results* form, which only the teacher sees. She commented: 'I didn't know why I was doing it [recording the score]. Maybe it [the score] helps. ... The real benefit is the help it [the test] gives them, and you get to see them. Strategies give the teachers something to go on.'

For those who do the CAAT, which is a normed test, Ellie records both the raw score and the grade-equivalent with the confidential assessment results; but, though she records the grade-equivalent (largely because teachers say it is important for choosing instructional materials), she does not reveal it to the students and she herself increasingly maintains it is not important. She explained to one student, 'It doesn't mean anything. Can't compare it to an adult. You're not a child. Lots of people do [use a grade level and tell students what it is]. I don't believe in it. You have all kinds of experience that a child doesn't have. The only thing is it might help us choose materials, but that's all ... and maybe for re-test. When you give the re-test it shows how far you've progressed. But it doesn't need to be a grade level. It's just numbers. It could be any numbers.'

The final record

Ellie's observations from the interview were recorded on four sheets of paper:

1. The *Learner Information* sheet. On this was recorded David's name, address, birth date, and telephone number. It also included brief

information about his prior education, work experience, goals, and social agency.

2. The *Informal Interview* sheet. This contained even more abbreviated comments on hobbies and goals.

3. The *Assessment Results* sheet. Despite the pains Ellie had taken to contextualise reading tasks and identify ways David used his knowledge of the world as part of his reading strategies, she recorded only the skills he demonstrated at the local level. Her observations were written down in boxes:

Strategies demonstrated	*Comments*
Matches Initial Consonant	Level I Beginner (Upper level)
Matches Words	Understands sounds of letters,
Can read – Sight words	some difficulty with vowels
No difficulty with Math	Needs help writing Address
Relates to Pictures	No difficulty with Math

The only other notation on this sheet, beyond times and dates, was the test score: Per cent correct (20/24 – 85 per cent).

4. The *Interest Inventory* sheet. On this form Ellie had ticked off, under the heading *Writing:*

    telephone messages
    forms and applications
    cheques and bank deposits
    personal notes and letters.

She had also written in:

    my wife's name
    my child's name
    writing 'broken window'.

Under 'Reading' she had ticked off:

    signs
    bills and bank statements
    personal letters
    newspaper.

And she had written in:

    labels on cleaning materials.

These four sheets constitute the total record emerging from two hours of intensive effort. We cannot avoid asking, 'Was that effort worthwhile?' Yes, we think it was, but there are ways in which it could have been even more so.

Recommendations

One major reason for the final record being so slight was the sheer difficulty of recording all the information that was coming in. Ellie did not use a tape recorder, nor could she, because she did not have the time to listen to the tape later and analyse it; and videotaping each assessment exercise would have been even less practicable. She was thus dependent on handwritten notes, and, as she says, 'You hate to be writing the whole time they're there.' One solution that she suggests is 'a checklist of things I need to [record] – common strategies, skills, abilities. I could just tick them off. At the end of the test or even during the test ... tick them off as they come up.' The idea of a checklist has strong appeal: it would save time; it might encourage more systematic observation; it would provide comparable data which would help in placing students in appropriate classes; it would make it easier to describe to students the successful strategies they are using. But what would go onto the checklist? Ellie's one suggestion was, 'Can match initial consonants', the kind of information about a decontextualised skill that is already getting into the record in one way or another.

One method of developing a checklist might be to observe enough interviews such as this one to allow us to build lists of strategies students use for specific items on the test. For instance, drawing on information from David's interview, we could list two strategies for dealing with the tasks on the North Bay map:

> word recognition ('hospital')
> prior knowledge (knows Route 17 leads to Ottawa)

For the tasks on both the North Bay map and the Jell-o instructions we might add:

> develops too much meaning from individual words ('hospital'; 'half a cup')

For the grocery flyers task we could put a category such as:

> incorporates life experience into reading (refers to buying chicken legs himself)

On the task on over-the-counter medicines we could suggest:

> problems with health-related vocabulary ('hay fever')

Finally, for the tasks based on the hockey ticket we could note:

> reversals (seat and section number)

As other students were observed taking the test, the categories could be further developed until we had for each item a useful typology of strategies used and difficulties encountered. The descriptions built up in this way would be at least as much about students' strengths as about their weaknesses, and the descriptions, in turn, could suggest teaching strategies. In David's case, since he appeared to deal successfully with real-world tasks in the home, a teacher might work at increasing the number of real-world activities involving reading that David participates in; since his difficulty with one item had to do with a lack of information about a health-related matter, she might help him increase his knowledge base in this area – if, indeed, an occasion were to arise in which he needed such information. Noting that whole-word recognition worked relatively well for David, a teacher might work on developing this skill rather than insisting on a phonics-based approach which David found less productive. If reversals were a genuine factor with David, he might make use of a computer program developed to help with this problem.

A checklist developed from close study of what a variety of learners actually do might help to address another problem in Ellie's documentation of what David does – her tendency to record only problems and strategies that have to do with discrete, low-level, skills. Like many workers in ABE, Ellie was trained, as an elementary school teacher, to view reading in terms of a 'bottom-up' model. Her subsequent experience, especially in working with adults, has led her to a broader conception of reading, as her own argument about grade levels shows; but this conception has not been fully articulated, it seems, and when it comes to making the official record, she still depends on the traditional model. The authority of a printed document such as we have outlined above might help professionals in ABE to develop newer and more fluid ways of describing literate behaviour, especially if the checklist were introduced through carefully designed workshops.

Useful though such a checklist would be, it could not address another problem that is apparent from a close look at this intake interview: that is, the way David's interaction with the textual material is constrained by the evidently unequal relationship between him and Ellie. Ellie, as we have seen, did everything she could to make David feel comfortable and to suggest that they were working on a project together – and David clearly saw the endeavour this way and made an effort to pull his weight. Nevertheless, the fact remains that Ellie could read easily while David could not, and she was assessing him and not vice versa. Thus the pattern all too easily developed, as when they were discussing the *Interest Inventory*, of Ellie's making suggestions and David's simply agreeing; despite her attempt to keep the enquiry open-ended, it was nonetheless dominated by her own sense of what someone in his position might need.

Ellie has made suggestions that might reduce this problem. She thinks, for example, that parts of the intake interview might more usefully be done by teachers, especially using the *Interest Inventory* to find out about functional goals. A teacher would still probably be seen by David as someone of superior status, but at least the interaction would be taking place in the relatively neutral space of a classroom, and the presence of other students would make him feel less under individual scrutiny. Better still, as we have found in our own ABE classes, it is often possible for students to work through the *Interest Inventory* sheet by themselves, in groups, with the students who can write most easily keeping the records. Students can also work through test items together, with the teacher looking on but not intervening. In these circumstances, it is much easier for the teacher to make notes, while the students are less conscious of being observed and are therefore less inhibited.

Another of Ellie's suggestions is that the Continuing Education Programme should look more to students' portfolios as a means of documenting achievement and relating it to goals. At a teachers' workshop that she organised, participants discussed how, during an initial interview, a record could be made of what the student hoped to achieve over a given period; then, throughout that period, a collection of documents could be built up that might include:

(1) the record of original goals
(2) samples of writing done by the student
(3) samples of material the student had read
(4) an evaluation by the student of the work done (this could be written down by the teacher or some other scribe, if necessary).

Ellie might then hold a follow-up interview with both teacher and students in which they would discuss this portfolio; the date for this interview would provide a convenient way of delimiting the period under consideration.

Conclusions

The intake interview examined here is clearly not a perfect model of recording student achievement, and we can see many ways in which it could be improved. Nevertheless, we would like to conclude with a comment on its significant merits, even as it stands. First, Ellie shows how simple bureaucratic procedures – collection of personal information such as name and address – can be utilised for assessment purposes so that time spent on such procedures is not, from the instructional point of view, wasted. Second, her method provides for some choice in the tools used for assessment; they can be selected according to the observed capabilities of the individual in question so that the student's time and energy are not wasted on material that is either too easy or too difficult. Third, she is able to get at and record information that no paper-and-pencil test can provide on its own – namely, how students arrive at their responses rather than simply what those responses are – and it is this sort of information that is especially valuable for teachers. Finally, and most important, while collecting information that is needed for the programme, Ellie makes sure that David gets something out of the exercise. As she said to us afterwards, 'He reads a lot more than he thinks he does. As we went through [the interview], I was trying to show him that he could read.' We think that she succeeded in this endeavour, that David left the interview with a clearer, more positive view of his abilities than he had when he went in. An assessment exercise conducted along these lines is thus not only useful for instructors but is an instructional activity in itself, one designed to encourage students like David to make a second attempt at developing the literacy knowledge and skills that they need to participate effectively in the workplace.

Acknowledgement

We are deeply grateful to Ellie Kerruish, ABE intake Coordinator for OBE, whose assistance and cooperation will have been obvious to anyone who read this chapter.

9 Assessing adult literacy in the United Kingdom: the Progress Profile

Deryn Holland and Brian Street

While much of the discussion about assessment in this volume has tended to be critical of present practice and to focus upon the problems of 'testing', we would like to describe some positive innovations in this area and to shift attention from *testing* to *assessment*. We shall describe the development of the *Progress Profile*, intended initially for use in adult literacy programmes in England and Wales. In order to locate this alternative approach within the wider issues raised in this volume, we provide a brief historical background to adult literacy work in Great Britain, with particular attention to the contrasting educational philosophies in Great Britain and North America.

Background

Adult literacy in the 1970s and 1980s

During the last 15 years in the UK adult education programmes have paid particular attention to the question of basic literacy. This concern followed the development of community literacy schemes in the 1960s, which evolved into an action campaign mounted by the British Association of Settlements for a national literacy campaign and agency (Baynham 1993). A nationwide television programme called 'On the Move' in the mid-1970s drew attention to the difficulties many adults faced with reading and writing. The then Labour government responded with funding for an Adult Literacy Resource Agency (ALRA), which attempted to create curricula and teaching aids for local institutes that were helping the adults who sought tuition. At first, these institutes relied on volunteers teaching individual students, often in their own homes, and the funds were devoted to organisation and to development of appropriate materials.

Over the first decade a great deal of experience was built up and some institutes, such as the Friends' Centre in Brighton and the Lee Centre in London, began to develop their own locally produced materials and to acquire distinctive approaches and expertise. Often teachers started as volunteers and then moved into employment in this area, and many of them now have more than a decade of experience. Most came into the field of adult literacy infused with vision and commitment. There is still, in fact, some tension between the volunteer ideal and the trend towards professionalism: the development of a career structure for practitioners may, some fear, lead to a loss of the volunteer's wholehearted commitment to the students.

Many teachers showed enthusiasm for the Freirean model of basic education and the debate still runs in the field as to how far literacy teaching is a political and even revolutionary activity, or is about confidence building rather than just skill learning (cf. Levine 1986; see Kirkwood and Kirkwood 1989 for an application of the Freirean approach in Scotland).

In the mid-1980s there was a move away from individual tuition towards class-based instruction. There were various reasons for this shift, including uncertainty as to what was happening in the paired arrangements, the fear that old-fashioned teaching methods were being employed, and even the suspicion that in many cases a dependency was being created.

Within this context, in an area marginalised from mainstream education, with its own developing culture and expertise and defined in many perceptions by the failure of formal schooling, the issue of assessment was a particularly charged one. The government agency dealing with materials and overall policy – first known as the Adult Literacy Resource Agency (ALRA), then as the Adult Literacy Unit (ALU), and currently as the Adult Literacy and Basic Skills Unit (ALBSU) – was not inclined to press the local agencies who were actually doing the teaching to produce standardised forms of measurement. It was felt that in a personal, one-to-one situation, 'achievement' was best left to the individual students to decide, according to their own aims in coming forward in the first place. The forms of teaching and evaluation available from the elementary schools sector, such as reading schemes or Janet and John books and children's standardised reading tests were found to be inappropriate: the vocabulary, assumptions about maturity, and the level of social experience expected were simply not suitable for adults. As Jones and Charnley put it, 'Imagine a man of 45 announcing to his wife that he had attained the reading age of a child of 8!' (1977, p. 109). They follow this statement with the suggestion that such tests are set more often for the teacher's benefit than for the student's.

In the United States there have been attempts to modify school tests to take account of these differences, as Hill and Parry (1989) have shown in an apt criticism of mechanical adaptations. In the UK, by contrast, the teachers and organisers of literacy education looked in other directions for the means of assessment. Charnley and Jones (1979) emphasised the assessment of social factors, such as success in getting jobs, or of personal development, such as growth in self-confidence. Progress defined in these ways reveals an educational experience that is wider and more significant than the mere remedying of skill deficiencies.

Assessment, like the curriculum, evolved with the individual student or group and related directly to the teaching. Its purpose could be described as educational, the outcomes useful to both student and teacher. Evidence from case studies undertaken by Holland (1988) suggests that assessment of progress in adult literacy in England and Wales has continued to be dominated by informal procedures. Progress has been described by students and teachers mostly in terms of personal and social development. These, then, were the principles out of which the Progress Profile emerged. Although the situation in the UK has changed considerably, a brief account of this earlier phase and its differences from both the US model and current pressures in the UK will help bring out the distinctive nature of the Progress Profile.

Assessment in the UK and USA – some comparisons

In the UK the funding agencies, usually local education authorities, looked to a variety of sources as the means of validating expenditure such as detailed reports on classes, evidence of progression routes, and job acquisition. In the USA, on the other hand, the emphasis has been on standardised multiple-choice tests. At the adult level, some of the differences persist in the contrast between the widespread use of the Test of Adult Basic Education (TABE) in the US and the tradition of learner-centred teaching and assessment described above for adult basic education in the UK.

These differences between approaches to assessment in the UK and the US may be explained in a number of ways. Street has suggested elsewhere that such differences are not simply matters of educational judgement but lie deeper in the respective ideologies of the two countries and in concepts of nationalism (1990). American adult literacy teachers are often surprised to find how casual and unpressured their British counterparts have been about assessment, while British teachers work to different agenda and mean different things when they talk about 'assessment'. One British teacher suggested, for instance, that in the UK people are not surprised to find someone from an impoverished background having reading difficulties; the poverty and deprivation are themselves explanations. Social rather than individual causes are seen as the root of students' problems, and the measurement of progress in literacy programmes has tended to be in terms of social and personal skills rather than purportedly objective ones. In the US, on the other hand, with its greater emphasis on individual achievement as a measure of national achievement, and on everyone, in principle, having access to all levels of the society, the appearance of large numbers of low-literate adults represents a challenge to the basic ideology and to the ideals of the nation state. The fact that many Americans might not be surprised that disproportionately large numbers of black people have difficulties with reading and writing, whether they interpret this as indicative of social deprivation or of racial inferiority, does not undermine the emphasis on individual responsibility that dominates perceptions in the USA. The society as a whole thus pays more attention to data on illiteracy, and the responsible agencies are expected to measure their work in terms of individual achievement and objective standards. In effect, the measurement of literacy is a key component of nationalism (Gellner 1983, p. 28). The recent talk about a crisis in education, falling standards, and mass illiteracy exemplifies this principle (Bloom 1987; Hirsch 1987; Kozol 1985).

In the US, too, it has been argued, there is a closer link between literacy and pedagogy – that is explicit, institutionalised instruction usually within the context of the school. A pedagogised model of literacy (Street and Street 1991) appears to be the only one considered appropriate when adults turn up in search of what is then seen as 'remediation'. In the UK, the response is more in terms of searching for varied ways to deal with social problems, whether at the personal level of confidence building or at the functional level of developing specific tasks. This broader-based social approach to literacy teaching further explains British reluctance to use techniques developed for children for the purpose of assessing adults, the differences between which are well brought out by Rogers (1992).

In the context of small-group teaching and attention to individual needs, it may also be that the UK situation lends itself more to teaching a literate-oral mix rather than literacy-in-itself as though decoding letters were independent of speech: the oral skills necessary for job applications, often in situations mixed with form filling and other literacy processes, are seen by UK teachers as part of the adult student's requirements in a way that may be harder when the teaching has to be geared to standardised literacy tests like the TABE and where the definition of 'need' has already been determined by prior literacy tests and screening. The tendency is for such tests to determine the learning curriculum.

This situation has been described by Law as 'the exam tail wagging the curriculum dog' (1984, p. 62).

We would not wish to overstate the differences between literacy assessment in the United Kingdom and North America and we acknowledge the long and radical tradition in the latter of student-centred approaches, exemplified in recent years by alternative assessment programmes put forward by Susan Lytle (Lytle *et al.* 1988), Michael Holzman (1988), John Willinsky (1990) and others. Nevertheless the differences at official levels are quite marked, and identifying them enables us to bring out the principle that underlies the assessment model we are putting forward here.

Changing attitudes in the UK

The United Kingdom model is changing. New forces are at work and we are now witnessing a radical transformation of the education system. A greater consciousness of national identity in politics may be a key factor in this shift. The shift may have been stimulated by the then Prime Minister, James Callaghan's speech given at Ruskin College, Oxford, in 1976, and the subsequent so-called 'great debate' on education, which led to the development of a National Curriculum in the 1980s. The relationship between education and employment was also made increasingly more explicit by the Conservative government of the 1980s. Evidence of the shift towards an economic ideology of education can be seen in the emphasis on training rather than education and in the funding of programmes such as Employment Training, which directly serve the needs of the labour market. This change has continued into the 1990s, fuelled by the related dynamics of demographic trends and the needs of the economy. The British government is now concerned with assessment in the context of accountability and cost-effectiveness; thus assessment has a more administrative focus than in earlier periods, and the criteria for it are determined by bureaucratic demands rather than educational needs. In such a situation, success in the classroom becomes more important than success outside it, and test scores tend to count more than coping in real life.

The major agents affecting change are the Education Reform Act, 1988, the introduction of National Vocational Qualifications (NVQs), the increasing use of performance indicators, the current development of Training Enterprise Councils (TECs), and the government's proposed new funding arrangements for further education including adult basic education. An Act of Parliament passed in 1992 made it quite clear that the government only wishes to fund courses and training that lead to recognised qualifications, namely NVQs or NVQ-related accreditation. The government's emphasis for the post 16 curriculum is on work-based vocational training.

None of these factors is designed to create broad-based opportunities. Trends are towards a narrowing, employment-related, income-generating curriculum kept in line by the emphasis on cost-effectiveness and efficiency and the assessment methods imposed to determine whether the set targets are being met. An emerging trend is that employers are being given major responsibility for planning, delivering and funding vocational training. Training Enterprise Councils have been instituted by the government as local bodies independent of the education authorities to manage funds for vocational training in their area and are having increasing influence on both training and education, particularly through their financial control. In fact, they have already been referred to as 'alternative local education authorities'. The 1992 Act reveals the government's intention to give the TECs even greater control of funds, i.e. for the Colleges of Further Education through which adult basic education will be funded. Education and training needs are to be determined by the needs of the economy. Literacy needs are to be determined by the employer rather than by the individual.

Official policy is focusing on accreditation as a means of improving standards in all sectors of education and training. Indeed, it is almost equating accreditation with quality. Paradoxically, there is a parallel development which involves students more in their own assessment, in the large course-work component of the newly established General Certificate of Secondary Education (GCSE) in the UK and the incorporation of elements of the Progress Profile into the B.Tech. assessment. We now turn to the specific aspects of these changes that led to the development of the Progress Profile.

The development of the Progress Profile

Background

In 1987 the Adult Literacy and Basic Skills Unit funded a research project at the University of Nottingham on the assessment of student progress in adult literacy, which led to the development and publication of the Progress Profile. This project was not concerned with accreditation, but with developing student-centred assessment that could help students and tutors in planning future work and at the same time enable programmes to evaluate their own effectiveness with regard to student progress. The project was required to develop practical materials supported by theory and research. Any model would need to (1) inform students of their development and enable them to take increased responsibility for their own learning, and (2) contribute to the organisation's procedures for monitoring and evaluating its effectiveness.

As Research Officer, Holland set about examining the concepts contained within the title of the project: 'The Assessment of Student Progress in Adult Literacy.' How was the project to interpret the term literacy? How did students, teachers, and administrators define progress? If the project was to provide the tools for assessing progress in literacy we needed clear understandings of both these concepts. What did we know of adults as learners that should be incorporated into the project? And finally, what was available in the area of assessment that could be developed in ways that would uphold the notions the project adopted about literacy, progress, and adult learners?

The project was conceived as action research, meaning that Holland – an experienced literacy teacher and organiser – would work closely with students, teachers, and literacy organisers in England and Wales to research and develop new models for assessing student progress in literacy. In keeping with this approach, these questions were explored through workshops, case studies, and literature searches. We offer a summary of the understanding developed of literacy and progress and of how the expanding knowledge of adult learners could contribute to the assessment process. This understanding formed the rationale for the subsequent approach to assessment and the development of the Progress Profile.

The concept of literacy

Fingeret (1984, p. 7) comments that 'literacy is a shifting, culturally defined term, impossible to define in isolation from a specific time, place and culture.' Pinning literacy down to standards and levels in order to measure it is a contradiction in terms.

Street (1984) has suggested that approaches to literacy, both by researchers and educationists, have been dominated by what he calls an *autonomous* model of literacy. Within this model it has been assumed that literacy consists of a single, definable set of skills that are culturally neutral and *autonomous* in the sense that they independently generate consequences across a variety of social contexts. Criticising this approach for its ethnocentrism and its failure to recognise the complexity and variety of literacy practices in different contexts, he proposes instead an *ideological* model of literacy. He employs the term *ideological* rather than some more neutral one such as *cultural* or even *pragmatic* as Hill and Parry propose in Chapter 1, in order to signal that literacy practices are always involved in and constitutive of relations of power and inequality. It is not just that differential access to literacy leads to inequality, but that ideas about what constitutes proper literacy are themselves contested and some views are privileged.

In the context of adult literacy learning, the definition of literacy is crucial to the design of programmes, curricula, and assessment. A skills-based, deficit approach, for instance, will generate different teaching practices, relationships and assessment than will an approach based on Freirean assumptions that literacy is about 'reading the world' and challenging dominant power relations (Freire and Macedo 1987). The underlying ideology determines the teaching and learning strategies and, more significantly in this context, the assessment strategy and design. The design of the Progress Profile involves an attempt to operationalise these theoretical perspectives in a specific assessment instrument.

Venezky (1986) suggests one way in which this might be done, by arguing that if literacy is seen as the application of particular skills within a specific social context, then the focus in teaching and assessment should be on how the learner's world can be brought to bear on the literacy task. Charnley and Jones (1979) focus on the notion of student confidence in using literacy skills. Drawing on these sources, Holland describes literacy as consisting essentially of reading, writing, listening and speaking, together with the confidence to use these skills, in the particular cultural context in which an individual may be placed. Literacy for these purposes is multi-faceted, changing, culturally varied and defined differently from one student to another. How to measure progress within this definition of literacy becomes much more complex and challenging than previous 'autonomous' approaches suggest.

The concept of progress

There is little in the literature that explicitly refers to progress. What there is mostly assumes progress to be indicated by test scores and reflects the traditional emphasis on measurable outcomes of knowledge and skills, that is, on product rather than process.

Holland began with a consideration of the Shorter Oxford Dictionary definition of progress as 'forward or onward movement in space; advance, development'. Which aspects of this could be fruitfully applied to the concept of student progress in adult literacy? Was progress to be defined as movement in one direction only? Was movement only to be valued if it was linear – and forever onward and upward? Might not such a definition limit the kind of progress that could be documented and limit the model of literacy that could be assessed? Such a narrow interpretation would fail to encompass the variety of change and movement that students, teachers and organisers describe as progress and that is evidently central to literacy practices in terms of the ideological model (Holland 1989).

In the East End Literacy Scheme in Toronto, Canada, students frequently expressed progress in terms of changes in attitude such as 'feeling better', 'expressed myself better'. They also expressed progress as an ability to do something new or to go somewhere they had not been before (Horsman 1989). Charnley and Jones (1979) suggest that evidence of success is looked for in those changes that students perceive as being positive. They make the interesting observation that, as more time is spent on tuition, so goal orientation shifts from cognitive skills to affective goals having to do with self-concept and self-confidence. These findings are supported by Balliro (1989), who asked teachers in Boston, USA, to identify what 'counted' as progress. Balliro categorised her findings under the headings of affective; social interaction in the classroom; literacy and speaking/listening; metacognitive awareness; and learning strategies. She suggests using these headings as a framework for identifying progress. Within this framework, what people report as progress and what they cite as evidence is mostly in terms of the affective part of the curriculum, an area neglected by traditional tests.

The Nottingham research project took the more liberal view of progress as outlined above, reflecting the definitions given by students and teachers in adult basic education in many contexts. They explained progress as being about positive change as reflected in moving towards identified aims, improved self-confidence and increased self-value. They spoke of progress in terms of students being able to do things they could not do before and daring to try things they had not had the courage to try earlier. Improved skills were offered as indicators of progress, as was the achievement of passing an exam or getting a qualification, but usually all parties, whatever their role in adult literacy, referred to progress in terms of students gaining the confidence to use their new or improved literacy skills in some aspect of their lives away from the classroom. As one student put it: 'I went into the doctor's waiting room the other day and I could read the signs. It made me feel much better. I AM learning!'

Holland (1988) defines progress in terms of movement made by individuals from their own starting points towards their own goals. She sees progress as more than the achievement of the aim or the arrival at the chosen destination. It is about the journey as well as the arrival. The definition adopted in the Progress Profile goes still further. Adult basic education is concerned with enabling people to become more independent. Thus Holland concludes that the best indicators of progress must be couched in terms of 'impact' – how students are using their improved basic skills in their everyday lives outside the classroom or tutorial sessions.

In order to identify progress as movement and change, it is vital that learners know where they started, and while the emphasis is on moving away from the starting point, it is important to recognise the part played by looking back. Schon in his book *The reflective practitioner* (1983) describes learning as 'reflection in action', and he entreats people to be critical and analytical in the process. If this critical reflection is made part of the assessment repertoire, then assessment can become an integral part of learning. Furthermore, the encouragement of reflection at the outset and at periodic intervals thereafter helps both students and teachers to recognise progress that may not be immediately apparent. A significant minority of adult literacy students are in danger of losing such literacy skills as they have acquired, and without help and support they may well drop out of the literate world altogether. For such students simply 'treading water' is an achievement, and an assessment system based on reflection provides a means of recognising this.

A record of progress for adult literacy students, needs, then, to be concerned with both cognitive and affective development, and it should show not only the products but also the processes of learning and their meaning in the students' lives. So the task for the project was to develop an instrument that could capture and document progress thus broadly defined, in ways that would be useful to all concerned – an instrument that would itself be a learning and teaching tool, informing the future work of students, teachers, and the organisation itself.

The Progress Profile

In keeping with the view of literacy and progress discussed above, the Progress Profile has been deliberately designed to be flexible in language and format, while providing a framework for identifying personal aims, for developing these aims into a programme of work, and for monitoring and evaluating the activity that results. These notions and principles are implicit in the physical form of the material: it is in a ring-binder so that the constituent parts can be reorganised, removed, or added to without difficulty. The package includes a set of guidelines for students and a handbook for teachers (which is separately bound); these explain how to use the material, but they are not an integral part of the instrument.

The Progress Profile itself consists of three parts: (1) a set of five questions, the responses to which provide learners with the basis for their programme of work; (2) a set of prompt cards to assist the responses; and (3) a review form that generates a graphic representation of development and progress and provides data for programme evaluation. This material is expected to be used over a period of 40 learning hours, although individual programmes can alter the length of time to suit learners' needs.

The five questions. The five questions that form the basis of the Progress Profile are as follows:

- Where do I want to go?
- What do I need to learn?
- How am I going to get there?
- How far have I got?
- Where to next?

Each question is printed in large type on a separate sheet with subordinate questions or prompts printed in smaller type below, as shown in Figure 9.1. On each sheet there is ample blank space for

---

1 Where do I want to go?

Decide on your general aims with your tutor.

I would like to be able to:

Figure 9.1 Page for general aims in the Progress Profile

students and/or teachers to write their responses; the handbook suggests that wherever possible students should write the responses themselves (except, of course, where teachers' comments are called for), but teachers may act as scribes if this proves more convenient. The important point is that the response to each question should emerge from discussion between student and teacher, and perhaps from broader discussion with others as well.

The first question, 'Where do I want to go?' asks students to identify their aims. These aims are often, to begin with, unrealistic, but through discussion of the question and use of the prompt cards (see below) teachers can help students to identify what they can reasonably expect to achieve in the short term. Then the second question, 'What do I need to learn?' focuses more precisely on the skills involved in achieving those aims, and on how these skills are related to prior learning. The sheet is divided into two sections, in the first of which students are encouraged to 'Break down your aims into smaller parts or elements', while in the second they are asked to say which of the 'elements' they have identified are things that they can already do. These first two questions thus elicit a picture of students' initial needs, and also value their skills and experience by identifying strengths – a necessary starting-point for programme planning, and also an important record for subsequent assessment of progress. The third question, 'How am I going to get there?' then requires students, with the help of their teachers, to formulate a learning programme. A number of prompts are provided to help with this activity: 'I will begin with ....'; 'Later I will work on ...'; 'These activities may be useful'; and then, overleaf, students and teachers are asked to list the resources they will need (both those they can supply themselves and those that their teachers can provide). Students are also asked to specify how they will know they have 'got there'. Significantly, the prompts supplied for the last point express achievement in terms of both ability and affect – 'I will know I've got there when ... [1] I can .... [and, 2] I feel ...' – thus signalling to students and teachers alike the importance, discussed above, of attitudinal changes and confidence-building.

These first three questions are intended to be answered near the beginning of a period of study; but they are not expected to be answered in a single session, and students and teachers are expected to return to them from time to time, adding to the responses as new needs emerge. The fourth question, on the other hand, is meant to be addressed after a lapse of a few sessions, during which work has been done on the various elements and a record kept of it – the package includes a record sheet for the purpose, but students and teachers are encouraged to substitute their own form of record-keeping if they prefer. With their records in hand students can then look over what they have done and answer the question, 'How far have I got?' Again, the wording of the prompts emphasises the importance of affect: 'Write down what you feel more confident about ... and what you are still unsure of'. There is a space also for the teacher 'to write down her thoughts on your progress.' The responses made to this fourth question may well lead back to the first three and to renewed use of the pack of cards; and the fourth question may itself be returned to several times, so that the process is recursive. Finally, the fifth question, to be addressed at the end of the period of work, asks 'Where to next?' and students are instructed to 'List any aims and elements you wish to continue working on'. The question thus sets up a new starting point for students; they are ready to embark on a new set of five questions.

The prompt cards. Responding to these questions, especially the first three, can be difficult for new students, and so a number of prompts were developed to offer ideas about possible aims and to help trigger responses. These prompts are written on cards so that they can be presented in random order, signalling that they in no way represent a syllabus or order of priorities. The cards are of uniform size, but the aims or elements are written on them in various ways – some as lists, some as spider charts, and some as pictures – and on most of them the writing looks like handwriting rather than print (see Figure 9.2).

The aims suggested on the cards also vary a great deal in terms of both generality and assumed kinds of proficiency, ranging from, for example, 'To improve my job prospects' to 'I would like to write a letter to my daughter'; the effect is to emphasise, again, that literacy may have quite different meanings for different students. Finally, a number of blank cards are provided so that students will be encouraged to make their own, or to rewrite the aims suggested in their own words, and the handbook recommends that individual programmes collect the cards written by their own students to form a local 'bank' and thus suggest a still wider range of possibilities.

We emphasise the form of these cards because the responses to them in the piloting phase demonstrated the truth of Street's point that layout and presentation are intrinsic to how people conceptualise literacy and learning. Initially the aims identified by students and teachers were written on a single sheet of paper, but this, it appeared, implied a recommendation that particular skills be taught in a particular order, thus undermining the basic principles of the Progress Profile. Then, when the cards were first introduced, students in one of the pilot studies

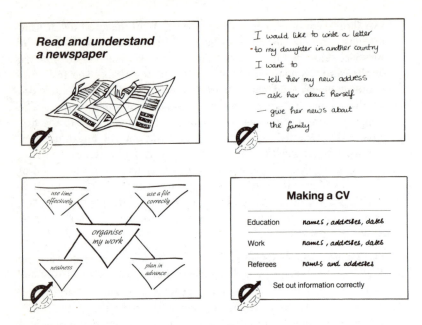

Read and understand a newspaper

I would like to write a letter
• to my daughter in another country
I want to
— tell her my new address
— ask her about herself
— give her news about
  the family

use time effectively
use a file correctly
organise my work
neatness
plan in advance

Making a CV

Education	names, addresses, dates
Work	names, addresses, dates
Referees	names and addresses

Set out information correctly

Figure 9.2 Prompt cards in the Progress Profile

PROGRESS REVIEW   READING . WRITING . LISTENING . SPEAKING . CONFIDENCE

Aims	Elements								
Look at the Elements and shade ▶ in the amount you have achieved									
Look at the Elements and shade ▶ in the amount you have achieved									
Look at the Elements and shade ▶ in the amount you have achieved									
How have you used what you have learned?									

Figure 9.3 Page for progess review in the Progress Profile

experienced difficulty in expressing their own ideas in the format provided; only at that point did it become apparent that the cards all followed the same format, thus suggesting that it was the one prescribed. When a new set was designed with a variety of formats, students felt more at ease: as one of them put it, 'The new ones were much more friendly.'

The Progress Review. The Progress Profile also asks students and teachers at the end of a specified period (we suggest 40 hours, but different programmes may adjust this to their own needs) to fill in a form entitled the *Progress Review*. While the 'five questions' may be thought of as 'formative' assessment, the Progress Review is 'summative', its purpose being to provide graphic representations of the progress of individual students that can be read quickly and collated easily to present a picture of the programme as a whole.

The form is divided into columns and rows, as shown in Figure 9.3. In the first column, students are asked to write the aims that they identified in answering question 1, and in the columns to the right of it they write the elements that they identified in question 2 as constituting each aim. Boxes are provided beneath the space for each element for the students to shade in as they master the element in question. The guidelines interpret the boxes and the shading as shown in Figure 9.4.

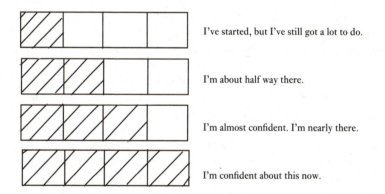

Figure 9.4 Method for displaying progress in the Progress Profile

In discussion with their teachers, students decide how far they think they have progressed in each element of their programme and shade in the boxes accordingly. A final question, but a critical one, is concerned with the impact of their learning on students' daily lives. The space provided at the bottom of the form, beside the question, 'How have you used what you have learned?' encourages students to think about how they have used their new or improved skills outside the classroom.

Thus, when the form has been completed, all of an individual student's initial aims (including those that may have been abandoned later) will be expressed succinctly, together with the particular elements the student planned to work on. The shading beneath the elements will show the extent and areas of achievement, with some rows being shaded altogether and others remaining wholly or partially blank. Thus both student and teacher can see at a glance the areas in which the student is doing well or which need further work. In addition, when the Progress Reviews of a number of students are brought together, administrators and funders can see quickly and easily which areas students are working on (e.g. n per cent are working on spelling, y per cent are working towards the Wordpower Certificate, and z per cent are involved in writing projects) and with what degree of success; such information can then inform decisions about purchasing materials and training teachers: it may suggest, for example, training on the Wordpower Certificate or a workshop on material related to writing projects.

Dissemination

The Progress Profile was developed, from its inception, in close association with adult literacy practitioners: it was formally piloted in four geographical areas of England and Wales, and numerous other programmes tried the materials and offered their comments and suggestions. Through the development and piloting phase it became clear that face-to-face contact with organisers, teachers, and students was necessary for people to grasp the ideas behind the Progress Profile, and that 'hands-on' help was needed if people were to use the material in the flexible way intended. This close involvement with those for whom it was designed can be regarded as the beginning of the dissemination phase. The Adult Literacy and Basic Skills Unit extended the project to enable Holland to conduct 40 one-day training sessions in various parts of England and Wales between October 1989 and April 1990. During these training sessions she worked with some 1300 people in the wide variety of contexts in which basic skills teaching is offered; in prisons, Employment Training schemes, local community organisations, and Church groups. The process gave her a unique overview of and insight into attitudes towards literacy teaching in the UK and the problems of introducing an assessment scheme that does not rely on the autonomous model of literacy.

One of the difficulties that arose most frequently was teachers' resistance to the very idea of assessment. Although the majority of participants on the dissemination days were there voluntarily and could be considered to have some commitment to or at least interest in the idea, it was clear that many organisers and teachers considered any change in their practice with reluctance. Some teachers seemed to equate assessment with criticism: they reacted defensively with remarks like 'Aren't they happy with what I'm doing?' and 'I'm no good with statistics.' Many proffered reasons for not working in the ways advocated by the Progress Profile: 'The students come to be taught, not assessed'; 'It will take too much time'; 'It looks daunting. I'd be put off.' Others claimed that what we were recommending was little different from existing practice: 'Why should we write it down? We do this already.'

Such resistance is predictable when one realises how deeply ingrained in most of us are the traditional notions of assessment. Through our experience of formal schooling, assessment has been associated with examinations and with results expressed in numerical terms, as percentages of a perfect score or as rankings within a class. By such forms of assessment the students who come to adult basic education programmes have, of course, been found wanting, and it is therefore quite understandable that they, and their teachers, should regard such terms as 'measure' and 'count' with deep suspicion when used in relation to literacy. Besides, as participants in the training sessions pointed out, some of the most important changes that can take place through an adult literacy programme – namely, the affective ones such as developing confidence – are not susceptible to traditional modes of measurement. Many therefore saw a conflict between instruction and assessment; as one of them put it: 'Our job is to teach, not to test.'

As people have worked through the Progress Profile, however, it has been found to give structure to the whole learning experience, showing that assessment is integral to learning rather than additional to it. Thus in the training sessions we were able, to some degree, to overcome such resistance. First, we explored the rationale for the material, as described above, so as to give participants a strong grounding for adapting it and using it in ways pertinent to their own contexts. Second, we emphasised the qualitative rather than quantitative nature of the assessment, being careful to use such terms as 'recognising' or 'identifying' progress rather than 'measuring' it. Third, we encouraged participants to 'play' with the material; we wanted them to feel free to rearrange and otherwise modify it so as to make it their own.

This last point proved quite difficult to get across. We found that as the design work progressed and the material looked increasingly professional, many people were reluctant to criticise or alter it to suit themselves: they had been conditioned into believing that printed documents are not to be meddled with, a key factor in the way that literacy is conceptualised. Witness the comment of one group of organisers and teachers who met to explore assessment and used the Progress Profile as a basis for their studies:

> It was really helpful to be told by the author that she was delighted to see how we had altered it to suit our purposes. Somehow we needed to be given permission to 'play with it'. This is an important observation for us to take back to the training sessions we will run to introduce the Progress Profile in our own programmes.

Thus presenting the text in a context of oral interaction has proved an important means of giving its users a sense of ownership. A further means has been provided by computer technology: the Progress Profile is now on disc, enabling people with access to desk top publishing to modify it for their own purposes while maintaining the overall professional look.

An interesting point to note here is that concerns about meddling with the material were expressed more often by teachers than by students. We suggest that this is because adult literacy students have, by definition, had less interaction with the printed word and its conventions and are less constrained by them. The point demonstrates how models of literacy are built up by specific literacy practices: despite their evident sympathy with their students, the teachers' approach seems still to have been based on an autonomous model of literacy formed through their own interactions with print and with traditional modes of assessment. The flexible design of the Progress Profile- is thus an essential factor in promoting a broader model of literacy that is more in keeping with the needs and perceptions of the students.

Another difficulty that emerged in the dissemination sessions was that students and teachers were both uncertain of what could be legitimately included in the record of achievement. It appeared that while they would happily talk about progress and achievement in terms of new things done or increased confidence in using literacy skills in everyday life, they did not consider such indicators significant as part of a formal assessment. An anecdote illustrates this point. At a meeting with students and teachers who had been working with the Progress Profile a teacher commented that a student had read the lesson in church on Easter Sunday. Both student and teacher were proud of this achievement. Holland queried whether it had been recorded on the Progress Review, which asks students how they have used their learning in their everyday lives. 'Can I put that down?' the student asked. Clearly, while recognising the significance of the event, neither teacher nor student had been confident that it could 'count'.

The training sessions were thus of great significance in the establish-ment of the Progress Profile; indeed, they can be considered as part of its development. For the Progress Profile is not a finished document: it is intended to be an interactive tool that will promote literacy by encouraging discussion, reflection, and writing about students' inter-actions with text, and the guidelines entreat its users to adapt it in ways that are helpful to themselves and that can be integrated into their established methods of working. Many users had to be told through oral interaction that we did indeed mean what we said, but having been convinced, they have been developing the material: one programme, for instance, reported that while they had originally designed a single record sheet, individuals and groups had modified it so that they now had numerous versions of the same sheet. In general, once people have become familiar with the concept behind the Progress Profile, they are able to work through it and adapt it to their own purposes, and, having done that, they find that it gives structure to the learning programme and encourages real dialogue with and between students. Thus it serves the main purpose of adult basic education by supporting student-centred learning.

Conclusions

Like any text, the Progress Profile is the product of particular social and historical circumstances. Adult literacy practitioners in the UK have, as we have shown, developed a specific educational philosophy and culture, one with Freirean overtones but also a distinctively British character, as the contrast with adult basic education in the US brought out. This culture has recently come under pressure from government initiatives to tie education, particularly for adults, more closely to economic goals; the pressure, together with a growing professionalism within the field, has created a need for systematic ways of recording achievement that will address demands for public accountability. However, the traditional model, particularly the American one, of measuring progress through periodically administered tests was not acceptable in this environment. It was necessary to develop a different method of assessment, one that was more in accordance with the experience and beliefs of adult literacy teachers and with the expressed needs of the students themselves. The Progress Profile is the result, and, tied as it is to a particular situation, we would not want to present it as a model to be imitated in other educational and geographical contexts. We argue, however, that those in other environments who are looking for alternative methods of assessment should consider carefully the general principles on which it is based, as expressed in the process by which it was developed, the physical form in which it is presented, and the means by which it is being disseminated.

The initial development of the Progress Profile was, as we have pointed out, based on a careful examination of the key concepts of literacy and progress. This examination was conducted through extensive interaction with teachers and students in the field, requiring them to question their assumptions and to articulate their values with regard to literacy. It became apparent that these assumptions and values could best be described in terms of Street's ideological model of literacy, a model that recognises the multiplicity and variety of literacy practices, their dependence on specific social contexts, and their role in expressing and, indeed, constituting relationships of power and authority. It was also evident that some of the most important aspects of acquiring literacy were not by their nature measurable, for literacy has been found to involve much more than a set of mechanical skills – it includes, most importantly, confidence in relating to text, and it is firmly embedded in oral interactions. Such an examination of the fundamental nature of literacy has been and continues to be all too rare in the development of assessment instruments; the new vocational training and testing in the UK, for example, tend to assume a neutral teaching of technical skills measured simply in terms of a final product, and they are disingenuously opaque regarding the underlying educational philosophy or ideology.

The physical form of the Progress Profile is expressive of the assumptions and values outlined above. The designer worked hard to present the materials in a form that would be physically robust enough to withstand handling and to serve as a durable record, while at the same time being evidently flexible and inviting its users to alter it to suit their needs – hence the significance of the ring-binder with loose-leaf sheets, the large amount of blank space on each sheet, and the easily shuffled and variously expressed prompt cards, including blank cards to emphasise the open-endedness of the approach; and we note with pleasure that with the recent production of the Progress Profile on computer disc the text can become even more flexible. We would also like to note the significance of asking students to shade in a row of boxes to indicate achievement rather than tick off items on a list: the idea is powerfully suggested that literacy is incremental and not a simple question of whether one can or cannot read.

Finally, the discussions and workshops through which the Progress Profile has been and continues to be disseminated have raised a number of important issues. First, they have demonstrated how deeply embedded the autonomous model of literacy and the notion of assessment as testing are among even adult literacy teachers – though, not, interestingly enough, so much among their students. Ideas that are so thoroughly internalised are difficult to change, especially when they are unexamined and unarticulated, and we have found that a mere text, even one as carefully designed as the Progress Profile, does not have sufficient impact on its own. The text is not autonomous – it has to be supported by talk. On the other hand, and this is our second observation, once it is presented through oral interaction with its author, its users can perceive themselves as working with it and on it themselves, and so they can develop a sense of ownership – a point that is essential to the enterprise of building up the confidence to use text among people whose experience with it so far has been one of failure. Third, the dissemination process has shown us that work on the Progress Profile is by no means complete: it has to be modified and adapted as the needs of its users change. This finding has, we believe, particularly wide relevance, for as a society changes, so will its literacy practices, and any socially applicable assessment system should be able to reflect that fact.

In sum, the Progress Profile presents a truly alternative approach to assessment, one that enables teachers and students to avoid testing altogether and to make assessment instead an integral part of teaching and learning. It is most obviously useful to the population for which it was designed, but we believe it will be of interest to anyone who is concerned that education should be an inclusive rather than exclusive process.

Note

Although this article is based on the Progress Profile – published by ALBSU – we need to make it clear that the views expressed are those of the authors and not of ALBSU.

PART IV

POLICY IMPLICATIONS

We conclude this volume by examining the assessment of English language skills from a policy perspective. We first discuss external factors that must be considered in any pragmatic approach to assessment: namely, how English is used within the larger society and why the assessment is being carried out.

We begin our policy consideration of alternative testing by delineating a set of pragmatic principles to be used in developing test discourse; these principles are illustrated with the test material presented in Chapters 6 and 7. We then consider different ways in which alternative tests can be constructed for large-scale use, though we end our discussion on a note of caution: no matter how carefully a test is constructed, it remains a limited way of evaluating a non-native learner's pragmatic competence in English.

It is for this reason that we advocate documentation as a basic tool of assessment. Operating from a policy perspective, we first review the different kinds of documentation presented in Chapters 8 and 9. We then consider the form of documentation known as *portfolio assessment*, with particular attention to how it can be used to meet the needs of individual learners as well as those of the larger education system. We suggest practical ways of dealing with these tensions so that the needs of both learner and system can be addressed. In closing, we argue against a dual approach to assessment, one that uses mandated testing to meet system needs and classroom documentation to meet learner needs. We recommend a more unified approach in which various kinds of documentation are increasingly relied on to meet both learner and system needs.

10 Assessing English language and literacy around the world

Clifford Hill and Kate Parry

Introduction

In Chapter 1, we showed how reading tests within both British and American traditions reflect the autonomous model of literacy. As we observed, both kinds of tests rest on certain assumptions about text, the nature of communication between individuals it engenders, and the skills they draw on in such communication. We then laid out a pragmatic model based on an alternative set of assumptions: namely, that all texts are socially constructed, that readers and writers are necessarily involved in social exchange, and that the skills used in this exchange are inherently social. Throughout the preceding section, this model was used to explore various approaches to testing and assessment. At this point, we would like to draw together these explorations and consider them from a policy perspective.

Before embarking on this task, we would like to discuss two considerations that are fundamental in any policy discussion. The first has to do with the role that English plays within a particular society and thus what kinds of knowledge and skills can be legitimately expected of non-native speakers. We thus return to the three basic patterns of English language use that we described as *ancillary*, *official*, and *dominant* in the introduction to this volume. In relating assessment to the larger pattern of English language use, we draw on a principle that is often overlooked: any assessment task is considered authentic not by virtue of its intrinsic properties but by its relation to how language is used. Consider, for example, the task analysed by Cohen in Chapter 7, the one that requires university students in Brazil to summarise in Portuguese what they read in English. In traditional approaches to testing, such a task would be challenged on the grounds of a 'one language only' principle: students are to respond in the same language in which the task is presented. This principle, however, runs counter to a common practice in countries around the world that use English as an ancillary language – students using their own language to make sense out of the English texts they encounter. In effect, authenticity in the Brazilian test is ultimately anchored in the way it mirrors what students actually do in their university courses.

Our second basic policy consideration has to do with the range of functions that assessment itself performs: *how* we go about assessing literacy skills depends crucially on *why* we are doing it. Our reasons for assessing students are manifold and, in many instances, run together in ways that are difficult to separate. Nevertheless, we here establish three major purposes for assessment:

(1) monitoring education systems
(2) evaluating individual students
(3) managing classroom teaching and learning.

Or to adapt the terms used by Hill and Larsen (1992), the first two purposes can be described as *system-oriented*, the third purpose as *learner-oriented*.

The monitoring of education systems has become increasingly prominent as management techniques are transferred from the business world to education. These techniques assume a quantitative model of accountability and so call for efficient forms of testing that can be used to monitor education not only at local levels – the individual school or administrative unit within which it immediately functions – but at higher levels as well – in these days of international competition even national systems of education are monitored. In this volume we have not attended directly to this purpose and so do not address it in any detail here. We would like, however, to make three observations. First, any monitoring of an education system should use methods of random sampling so that only the minimum number of students is tested. In this way, the excessive use of formal testing – and its negative consequences on classroom practice – can be reduced. Second, such testing should reflect the pragmatic principles that we shall shortly delineate as we consider testing as a limited component within a larger approach to assessment. Third, such testing should be supplemented, at least to some degree, by alternative methods of assessment that sample students' work more directly.

It is perhaps the second purpose – evaluating individual students – that most frequently comes to mind when we think of testing and assessment. There are many aspects to such evaluation, and it is useful to further divide it into three categories:

(1) selection
(2) placement
(3) accreditation.

Within this volume, the first two, particularly selection, were dealt with in Chapters 2 and 3 (i.e. the TOEFL and an entrance exam to major Japanese universities); and the third category – accreditation – was dealt with in Chapters 4 and 6 (i.e. the West African School Certificate Exam and the certifying exam that was developed for Zimbabwe, although these exams are also used for the purposes of selection). The major rationale for a test such as the TOEFL is that students from all over the world can be compared according to a single objective measure. There is increasing reason, however, to challenge both the fairness and reliability of such a test. As to its fairness, the increasing use of coaching schools provides an undue advantage to students who can afford the fees. In prosperous Asian countries, such as Japan and Taiwan, students often pay a substantial amount for a course that prepares them to take the TOEFL; and recent studies show that these courses can be extremely effective in raising student scores (Lin 1993).

It is with respect to the third purpose – managing classroom teaching and learning – that we believe a pragmatic approach to assessment can be most fully realised. Those committed to traditional testing have generally conceived its role in the classroom as largely diagnostic: a teacher administers a test to find out which particular skills individual students are lacking, devises instructional strategies to remedy these deficiencies, and then administers another test to find out whether the strategies have been effective. For those who support pragmatic assessment, this test–teach–test approach is misguided on two counts. To begin with, it assumes that student learning can be parcelled out into discrete skills and thus ignores the complex ways in which such skills are integrated. Moreover, the diagnostic tests that claim to measure such skills can be quite misleading. In reviewing the *Test of Adult Basic Education* (TABE), we pointed out how its diagnostic scheme was based on the notion that a discrete skill could be aligned with a particular target response on a given task. But such an alignment oversimplifies what a test taker has to do when working with a multiple-choice format:

> The real demands of a given task are anchored in the total configuration of choices, i.e., the reader has to work through each choice, evaluate what its particular demands are, and then come up with some way of evaluating which choice is, in fact, the most appropriate one. Such a process forces readers to develop an overall tactical approach, no matter how implicit it may remain, for selecting one choice over the others.... (Hill and Parry 1989, p. 31)

As we point out, the diagnostic scheme of the TABE fails to take account of such complexity.

Those who advocate pragmatic assessment take a broader view of managing how students learn. They do not attempt to isolate discrete skills but rather set up extended projects that allow students to draw on such skills in an integrated way. In this way, any concern with skills is in the context of a project where they have functional value. Moreover, the concern is not with external diagnosis but rather with development of the individual student's capacity for self-monitoring. Clearly such capacity is better developed by sustained projects than external exams. In working with students on such projects, the teacher does not function as an external judge of the final product, but rather one who guides them in evaluating their own work as they are in the process of developing it.

A pragmatic approach to assessing English literacy skills

In describing pragmatic assessment of English literacy skills, we make a fundamental distinction between practices that fall within a testing paradigm and those that fall outside it: the former we refer to as alternative testing, the latter as documentation. As Hill and Larsen (1992) observe, four features are crucial to the traditional paradigm of testing:

(1) a single time frame of specified duration
(2) prescribed tasks presented in stable form
(3) individual responses not based on external resources
(4) a pre-established evaluation scheme.

We should point out that an activity, even when these core features are present, should not be considered a test unless it is designated as such. In effect, an activity becomes a test only if it is institutionally constituted as one.

In recent years this paradigm has been challenged by alternative activities that go under the name of a test, but do not incorporate all these features. Consider, for example, an activity known as *collaborative testing:* the very name suggests that the traditional paradigm is being violated since the third condition – an individual response – is not respected. In collaborative testing, various individuals are asked to carry out an activity together. Moreover, they are allowed, indeed, encouraged, to use external resources such as a dictionary. The rationale for such testing is that it reflects more faithfully the way in which work is carried out in the real world.

In describing alternative testing, we shall not attempt to encompass activities that radically extend the traditional paradigm of testing. Rather we shall assume a relatively stable paradigm and examine what kinds of adjustments can be made, if any, that result in tasks with increased pragmatic validity.

Alternative testing

In Chapter 1 we discussed a fundamental difficulty in constructing a reading test. The aim is to present a sample of text so as to obtain a sample of reading, but test makers, in the very act of constructing an instrument, necessarily change text by changing its context: it ceases to be part of a book or a newspaper and becomes part of a test. The result, as we have shown, is an arbitrary collection of materials, the totality of which represents nothing but its own genre – a reading test (Peirce 1992); and as we pointed out, this genre is concerned almost exclusively with the degree to which readers can restrict themselves to surface information in the text.

This problem will not go away as long as a test is conceived of as an arbitrary set of unmotivated texts. It can be mitigated, however, if a fuller context is provided for each sample text within a test. Contributors to this volume show how this contextualising can be achieved at different levels: at a basic level, the Ontario Test of Adult Functional Literacy (OTAFL) used in adult literacy in Ottawa (Chapter 8) uses bank cheques and instructions on medicine bottles; at an intermediate level, the junior secondary exam for Zimbabwe (Chapter 6) incorporates newspaper extracts and bureaucratic forms; and at an advanced level, the Brazilian test package (Chapter 7) uses complete articles from newspapers and magazines, the sources of which are made explicit.

In using such authentic materials, three basic principles are followed. One is that the material should be presented, as far as possible, in facsimile form so that readers have available such cues as type-face and format. These cues can help them to reconstruct the original context and, in the light of their experience of different kinds of text, approach the material in a more realistic fashion. This practice runs directly counter to reproducing all test material in a standard format, a practice presumably designed to neutralise the very features that we here argue should be accessible to readers. The traditional practice is a further embodiment of the autonomous model of literacy, which seeks to obliterate any signals that go beyond what the actual words of a text convey.

Second, the text can be framed by explanatory material that gives readers some purpose – aside from demonstrating their capacity to recycle local detail – for reading it. Given large-scale testing, such framing material can often do no more than ask students to imagine some context for reading a particular bit of text. For example, Allen, in presenting a classified advertisement, asks her readers to imagine that they are searching for a lost dog. As test takers indicated in subsequent interviews, they were easily able to enter into the make-believe.

Third, any internal evidence that a text provides of its provenance and motivation should be taken seriously. We have pointed out elsewhere (Hill and Parry 1989) that the new version of the TABE (1987), despite its claims for greater authenticity, includes tasks that require readers to ignore such evidence. One passage, for example, is a tribute to a talented musician who died at an early age, which ends with the following paragraph:

> Simmons's interests covered the whole realm of music. As a young artist himself, he encouraged the achievement of other young musicians. Continued help for young talent can be a fitting memorial to Calvin Simmons.

One of the tasks requires readers to identify 'the purpose of the passage', and the response designated as correct is 'to tell about a talented young man's remarkable success'. On the basis of the final paragraph, the purpose of the text would be better described as something like 'to raise money for a memorial scholarship fund'. Such a task is by no means accidental, for an autonomously oriented test forces readers to ignore the complex ways in which text embodies its own pragmatic orientation.

Once the question of using authentic text has been resolved, the next question is which texts should be selected for assessing readers. Traditional tests, whether of the American or the British variety, select from a fairly narrow range of texts: school textbooks and magazine articles are the regular fare. This is all well and good insofar as it is appropriate for the population for which the test is intended and the purposes for which they are taking it. Cohen, for example, uses similar material, though in a less fragmented form, since he was dealing with university students who need to handle such prose in their academic courses. For a general certifying test, on the other hand, of the kind that Allen developed for Zimbabwe, a wider range of materials is appropriate. Since the test is intended to certify test takers' ability to function in a society where English is used as an official language, the material should reflect the range of written material that test takers are likely to come across in everyday life. Clearly test makers need to be more aware of what Street (1984) calls 'the social embedding of literacy': they need to be cognizant of which texts are important in a society – and why these texts are important – so that they can make informed decisions about which ones to use for a test designed for a particular population. In order to develop this awareness, they need to incorporate sociolinguistic research into the test-making process itself.

The social uses of text must also be borne in mind as test makers construct tasks. As we pointed out in Chapter 1, the crucial text that test takers deal with is not the passage but the passage and tasks combined; and just as a passage should represent material actually used in the society, so tasks should represent what readers ordinarily do – or should be able to do – with that material. In developing such tasks, we combine a socio-educational model of comprehension (Bloom 1984) and a psycholinguistic one (Van Dijk and Kintsch 1983) in order to identify three levels of response (the psycholinguistic model is presented in Chapter 5 where Hill and Anderson establish the fundamental distinction between *text base* and *situation model*):

(1) literal (apprehending the text base)
(2) inferential (constructing an appropriate situation model from the text base)
(3) experiential (relating that situation model to personal experience).

These three kinds of comprehension call for different processes in reading, which can occur simultaneously and are thus not easily distinguished from each other. Indeed, the three kinds of comprehension – and the processes by which they are achieved – are best understood as a continuum. As Hill and Anderson point out in Chapter 5, literal comprehension shades off into inferential, particularly with respect to the more restricted kinds of inferencing described as *invited*. By the same token, inferential comprehension shades off into experiential, particularly with respect to the more open kinds of inferencing described as *extended*. Nevertheless these three kinds of comprehension do provide a useful framework in which to develop tasks for reading assessment.

We acknowledge that this framework is difficult to apply to system-oriented testing, particularly when it is conducted on a large scale. To begin with, a multiple-choice format is not appropriate for inferential and experiential tasks since it provides the appropriate responses in advance; such tasks, by their very nature, call for constructive responses, so readers should not select from choices already provided. Moreover, it is difficult to develop reliable marking schemes for such tasks, given the extended range of inferential and experiential responses that readers can legitimately make to a given text. This difficulty is particularly pronounced in countries where resources are limited and the teaching force is largely untrained in marking tests. Despite such difficulties, we still recommend that any test bearing the name *reading comprehension* should, in principle, incorporate all three kinds of tasks. Given the powerful influence of testing on what goes on in the classroom, we run the risk of seriously impoverishing pedagogy if we restrict testing to the literal level of comprehension.

We here outline two basic ways in which this broader model can be used to develop a test of reading comprehension. One way is to construct a test with distinct components, each clearly marked as calling for a different kind of response. In reviewing the new version of the TABE, we (Hill and Parry 1988) suggested that its reading-comprehension section could have been more usefully divided into two components, the first calling for literal responses and the second for inferential ones. At that time we did not set up a distinct experiential component since the TABE was not itself structured along such lines; in constructing the inferential component, however, we did include certain tasks that call for an experiential orientation. The first component would include a range of text types to be used at different levels: at the basic level indexes and tables of contents, and at more advanced levels expository material that includes tables and charts as well as bureaucratic documents such as insurance forms and tax returns. The nature of the literal tasks would vary according to the kind of texts used. In responding to indexes and tables of contents, test takers would identify the pages on which a particular topic is covered, or the sequence of topics in the book as a whole. In responding to material with graphic displays, they would pull information out of tables and charts; and in responding to a bureaucratic document, they would simply do what it calls for – write information in various blanks.

The second component would include a range of text types for which inferential – and, in certain cases, experiential – responses would be more appropriate. The new version of the TABE, for example, includes advertising, letters, and poetry, all of which call for different kinds of inferencing. This component should be designed to assess inferences that play a useful role in non-native learners' use of text. In responding to advertising, they could be asked to identify claims that are exaggerated or misleading (thus demonstrating a critical awareness about textual practices that can be personally damaging to them). In responding to a letter, they could be asked to infer the writer's probable motives (thus drawing on the repertoire of interpersonal skills they habitually use to make sense out of oral interaction). In responding to poetry, they could be asked to describe imagery and its relations to underlying themes (thus demonstrating their capacity to use text for self-enrichment).

Constructing a test with distinct components encourages readers to respond strategically to different kinds of textual material. It thus reinforces the crucial point that we established in Chapter 1 – that reading is a form of social interaction that calls for varied responses to text. Such a test also has the potential of providing sharply delineated information about individual readers: for example, the degree to which they can attend only to textual information where it is appropriate to do so or to use that information to make appropriate inferences. If such a test is properly designed, it can provide strategic insights into readers' capacities to vary the inferences they make as they move from one kind of text to another.

Despite these potential benefits, a test with separate components may suggest an oversimplified view of how readers respond to text. As we have pointed out, readers respond holistically, and it can thus be misleading to deal with literal, inferential, and experiential responses separately. An experiential response to a poem, for example, does not – or, at least, should not – bypass the other two kinds of response. There is also the practical problem of actually constructing a test with separate components. It is difficult, for example, to include a sufficient range of text types within each component; beyond the most elementary level, a representative set of complete texts – including sufficient variety of content to allow for differences in background knowledge – may be unduly cumbersome.

In order to avoid these difficulties, we can use an alternative format in which all three kinds of comprehension tasks immediately follow each passage. Even in using this format, we can still present the three kinds of tasks separately, as illustrated by the following material that we developed at a workshop for teachers and test makers at Ahmadu Bello University in Nigeria:

> There is abundant evidence that African infants, in comparison with Euro-American ones, show accelerated development in psychomotor skills (e.g., sitting, crawling, smiling) during the first few years of life. This precocity is undoubtedly related to an enriched psycho-social environment characterised by extended family living, multiple caretakers, and intensive physical manipulation of and personal interaction with the child. A child is carried around on the shoulders or back, is constantly bathed and elaborately massaged while stretching his limbs and facial features, is sung and talked to, is cuddled and caressed and is rarely left to sleep or eat by himself. In addition, breastfeeding is prolonged for at least a year and its frequency is controlled by the child's demands.

LITERAL TASKS

(1) African infants are different from Euro-American ones because they develop psychomotor skill _____
(2) This difference occurs because African children grow up in the following circumstances:
    (a) _____
    (b) _____
    (c) _____

INFERENTIAL TASKS

(1) How do you think the writer views Euro-American child-rearing practices? Briefly provide evidence for your response.
(2) There is often debate about whether differences between races are due to heredity or culture. Which of these two does the writer draw on, or does (s)he draw on both? Explain your answer in a brief sentence or two.

EXPERIENTIAL TASKS

(1) From what you have observed, are the writer's generalisations about African life justified? Write a short paragraph to support your answer.
(2) In your opinion, are African child-rearing practices always beneficial? Write a short paragraph to support your answer.

As can be seen, variation in format is used to signal the different kinds of questions:

(1) literal tasks call for students to complete a sentence by filling in a blank
(2) inferential tasks call for students to answer a wh-question with a short answer
(3) experiential tasks call for students to answer a yes–no question and write a short paragraph to support their answers.

Test makers who produce conventional tests question the use of such variable formatting, for they are especially trained to use a single format to minimise the test taker's confusion. This emphasis on format stability masks, however, a more insidious source of confusion. As Hill and Anderson point out in Chapter 5, test takers are often unsure as to what the point of a task is, even when it is presented in a stable format (i.e. they are not sure whether it calls for a literal response or an inferential one). If the format clearly distinguishes between literal tasks and inferential tasks, test takers are not forced to make artificial decisions about how they should approach each particular task.

In developing this approach to testing reading comprehension in Nigeria, the question naturally arose as to how it might be used in national exams. Our own response was to recommend the following approach to such exams at the secondary and tertiary levels:

1. All three kinds of comprehension tasks should be included but a marking scheme should be used for only the first two (i.e. the literal and the inferential).
2. In applying this marking scheme, test markers can use responses to the evaluation tasks, if necessary, to shed light on student responses to literal and inferential tasks.

Experiential tasks, though admittedly difficult to mark, can have pedagogical as well as practical benefits when they are included in national exams. From a pedagogical perspective, their mere presence reinforces the crucial importance of students actively relating what they read to their own experience. As Allen points out in Chapter 6, national exams, when properly constructed, encourage teaching practices that reinforce appropriately broad models of reading comprehension. The practical benefit of including these tasks has to do with eliciting more extended writing that can be used to interpret the shorter responses to the literal and inferential tasks. Whenever these responses are not clear, the more extended writing can be used as a backup to ensure that individual test takers are evaluated fairly. It has been our experience that a more extended response often provides important clues in understanding the more elliptical forms of response that students make to literal and inferential tasks.

In ending our discussion of alternative testing, we would like to return to the point with which we began: any test is inevitably, to some degree, artificial. No matter how authentic the constituent texts, a test provides a new, highly charged, and thus potentially distorting context for them; and the tasks, however carefully designed, force students to engage in prescribed activities during a prescribed period of time, usually one that is so short that students have little opportunity to engage in critical thinking. Moroever, these tasks, no matter how authentic, inevitably require externalisation, and thus again distortion, of what is often an internal activity. In the final analysis, a test forces students to engage in arbitrary tasks under considerable time pressure. It is for this reason that many educators have replaced testing – or at least supplemented it – with assessment practices that provide students with not only greater freedom to select the work on which they will be assessed but more extended periods of time in which to execute it.

Documentation

As indicated earlier, we use the term *documentation* to describe assessment practices that fall outside a testing paradigm. It is important to stress, at the outset, that these practices have evolved in response to learner needs, and thus stand in sharp relief to testing practices that respond to what the larger educational system demands. In the pages ahead we explore ways in which this tension between learner needs and system needs might be sensibly handled.

Two forms of documentation were presented in Part III of this volume. In Chapter 8, Cummins and Jones describe how an interviewer, using a diverse range of materials (some of which were taken from a test), records basic observations about a student's capacity to read and write. The purpose of the interview was to provide data that could be used for multiple purposes: placing the student in an appropriate programme of study, providing his teacher(s) with useful information, and setting up a baseline against which his development of literacy skills could be documented.

As Cummins and Jones point out, the interviewer's use of this method presents various problems. She elicits a good deal of information about the student, but only a fraction of it actually ends up in his file. Some of this has to do with the intractable problem of conducting an interview and recording information at the same time. Some of it, however, can be traced to the interviewer's lingering commitment to an autonomous model of literacy; she fails to record the student's use of real-world knowledge and focuses instead on low-level problems.

Cummins and Jones suggest various ways of addressing these problems. To begin with, they call for more research into students' problems and strategies in dealing with test material so that a checklist can be drawn up for interviewers to use; a well-constructed checklist can itself be used as a means of teaching interviewers to look for more global approaches to text. Moreover, Cummins and Jones describe how the interviewer's initial record could be supplemented by material collected by the student. Even in its present form, however, the interview served the learner's needs better than a conventional test; he walked out of it with a firm sense of achievement and a clearer picture of what he needed to work on in the adult literacy programme.

The Progress Profile, described by Holland and Street in Chapter 9, represents a second form of record-keeping. In this case the student is more directly involved since the student and teacher work together to record, at the outset, what the student wants to accomplish and, at regular intervals, the progress that has been made in achieving these goals. The records of achievement may vary a good deal in form: in some cases, they may be simply notes written in the spaces supplied on the Progress Profile (e.g. the student read aloud in church); in others, they may be more extended responses to what the student has read (e.g. the student's personal response to a short story), while in yet others they may be samples of the student's own writing produced without reference to any particular text (e.g. a letter that the student has written to a government office). The Progress Profile is obviously difficult to use for system purposes, though it can provide a quick overview of a student's achievement. Still it plays a crucial role in developing a student's capacity not only to set goals but to monitor progress towards achieving them. Moreover, the very activity of creating and maintaining the Profile provides evidence that a student is developing a crucial set of literacy skills. In effect, the activity itself becomes an authentic means of assessing what a student can do.

It is important to note that these methods of assessment make little or no distinction between reading and writing: the record based on an interview includes a writing sample, where appropriate, and the Progress Profile does the same. In view of the position that we adopt in Chapter 1 – that reading and writing are such reciprocal skills that it is counterproductive to separate them – we consider such a lack of distinction to be entirely appropriate. Accordingly, we would like now to discuss a third form of documentation that has been developed, with particular reference to writing assessment in the United States, but which, we claim, is equally appropriate for reading assessment – or, better still, for the assessment of reading and writing together.

The method we refer to is described as *portfolio assessment* in the United States; the *continuous assessment* that is part of the new British General Certificate of Secondary Education is closely akin to it, while the use of *folios* in Australia is essentially the same. In essence, this method places responsibility on students, first, to develop a representative body of work and, then, to select appropriate samples of that work and present them according to certain guidelines. It is common practice, for example, to ask students to write a cover letter in which they evaluate their own work. Within all these countries the method has evolved in response to learner needs, but there are increasing attempts to use it for system purposes. So far these purposes have been primarily concerned with accreditation, either at a particular institution or even at a state level where students from many different institutions are evaluated. For purposes of illustration, we would like to present two situations – one a local institution and the other a state-wide system – where portfolios have been used with a population that includes students for whom English is a second language. Portfolio assessment, as far as we can determine, has not been used for system purposes in countries where English is not the dominant language, although many teachers around the world have begun to experiment with it in their own classrooms.

The first situation to be examined is in New York City, where portfolio assessment has been introduced in a college expository writing programme that one of us coordinates (it serves about 1200 students each term and is staffed by about 30 teachers). The programme is explicitly concerned with writing, but it inevitably includes a good deal of reading, and a portfolio model of assessment was designed to accentuate the reading/writing connection. When the model was first introduced in 1990, it was used in only a few experimental classes by a group of committed teachers. Students were asked to produce at the end of term a portfolio – that is, a simple manila folder – that contained the following items[1]:

(1) a cover letter
(2) a finished (i.e. revised) essay
(3) a second finished essay with drafts attached
(4) a documented research paper
(5) an essay written in class
(6) a final exam.

This list of items was based primarily on the perceived needs of the learners. First among these was some sense of control over what they would be assessed on: the question of whether they would pass or fail the course would be determined not by a single exam, but by various pieces that they themselves selected from what they had done during the term. The second need was for students to receive some form of reward for time and effort spent on revising their work: this reward was provided by the predominance of revised pieces in the portfolio and the inclusion, for one piece, of preliminary drafts so that readers could see the extent of revision. A third need – and particularly important in the context of the present volume – was some means by which learners could show what they had read and how well they had assimilated it: this need was explicitly addressed by a stipulation that one of the two finished essays (items (2) and (3)) should be based on a text; in addition, the documented paper (item (4)) was obviously dependent on reading, while the topics set for the in-class essay and the exam were generally based on prescribed texts as well. Finally, it was felt that learners should be required to reflect on their learning and on their role as readers and writers: an occasion for doing this was provided by the cover letter (item (1) in the portfolio).

When the portfolios were collected at the end of term, they were exchanged so that teachers did not read those of their own students. The portfolios were graded on a scale of A, B, C, and F. At the same time, teachers assigned grades to their own students on the basis of overall course performance. The teacher's grade was then compared with the external evaluator's grade, and if they differed significantly, another reader was brought in to evaluate the portfolio; any portfolio that was graded as a weak C or F was also read again. The portfolios on which there was disagreement became the focus of discussion in which teachers articulated the values they were bringing into play as they assigned grades.

To judge from the students' responses, this method of assessment has been remarkably successful. Nearly all those who have produced portfolios enthusiastically endorse the approach, and the portfolios themselves provide evidence of the substantial amount of work they do. Tutors in the Writing Center remark that students become more self-critical as they select pieces for their portfolios and write their cover letters. Moreover, a comparison of grades given in portfolio and traditional classes indicates that ESL students, in particular, perform better when they are evaluated on the basis of a portfolio rather than a final exam.

Nevertheless, the approach has encountered a number of obstacles. When it was extended to a larger number of classes and a greater variety of teachers, two basic complaints began to surface: first, that the portfolios took too much time to read and, second, that the grading of portfolios by outside readers infringed on a teacher's autonomy. In response to the first complaint, the original list of items has been gradually reduced so that, at the time of writing, it includes only the following:

(1) a cover letter
(2) a finished essay
(3) a documented essay
(4) a final exam.

The second complaint has been partially addressed by adapting the grading scheme. A portfolio is now graded only as pass or fail with failures and borderline passes being read by a second teacher and discussed as necesary. As Elbow and Belanoff (1991) point out, the use of a pass/fail system substantially increases the reliability of portfolio evaluation since it calls for less fine discrimination. They also isolate two other factors that contribute to increased reliability: the use of holistic evaluation based on initial calibration sessions, and the policy that teachers do not evaluate their own students' portfolios.

Despite the increased reliability in evaluating portfolios, this new approach is, in other ways, less satisfactory: it gives students less choice as to what they can put in, since during the semester they write only one documented essay. Moreover, evidence of revision is no longer required (although it is assumed that both items 2 and 3 will be revised); and the explicit connections between reading and writing have been diminished. Nevertheless, the basic principle of documentation, despite the compromises, has been retained.

The second example of a portfolio approach comes from Victoria, Australia, where it has been developed to certify students who are graduating from secondary schools (Keville Bott, personal communication). This approach is in the process of development, but in 1992, students working for the Victorian Certificate of Education were required to do the following to certify their English language competence:

(1) maintain a workbook in which they set goals and use a journal to document their progress towards achieving these goals

(2) investigate a social issue on the basis of three to five media presentations, two of which are written; students then write a 500-word analysis of the issue and another 500-word essay stating their own opinion

(3) produce a folio containing five different kinds of writing – personal or imaginative, informative, instructional, argumentative, and a freely chosen piece of writing (preliminary drafts for two pieces of writing are included)

(4) respond in writing to a selection of four texts from a list of 20 provided by the Certificate headquarters

(5) make four oral presentations during the last year of school (e.g. students could give a talk to the class or lead a class discussion)

(6) plan and implement a communication project involving three or more people (i.e. students present orally what they had planned, consult an expert, carry out the project, and write a report on it).

Teachers, under the guidance of area supervisors, are responsible for certifying that all the work is done. For purposes of accreditation, the work is assessed on a pass/fail basis. In order to select students for university, a subset of the tasks, described as *common assessment tasks*, is used. These tasks include the work on the social issue and a writing folio containing only three items. In addition, students are required to take an external exam based on one of the set texts. All these tasks are scored by a committee of teachers so that students can be ranked for university admission. A moderation system has been developed by the Victorian Certificate of Education headquarters to ensure that teachers' scoring is reliable.

This portfolio model has aroused a good deal of opposition, expressed, in part, in the landslide victory of the Liberal Party in October, 1992, which was pledged to investigate the Victorian Certificate of Education. The opposition did not come from teachers, who generally approved of the system, though they did recommend certain specific changes; the opposition came rather from the general public which expressed two basic concerns: first, the approach does not reflect sufficiently uniform standards, and, second, it encourages students to seek help from others rather than work on their own. These complaints reflect a widespread acceptance of an autonomous orientation to literacy, for they are premised on the assumptions, examined in Chapter 1, that reading and writing are solitary activities and that the ability to engage in them can be assessed by how an isolated student responds to a limited number of texts.

These complaints also reflect the unavoidable tension between the needs of the education system within which assessment is conducted and those of the learners who are to be assessed. As far as the system is concerned, any documentation approach to assessment must be equitable and efficient. With respect to equity, the system demands that work samples clearly belong to the individual student who submits them. Learners, however, need documentation practices that encourage extensive social interaction around what they read and write. With respect to efficiency, the system calls for a parsimonious sampling of student work that can be evaluated with limited expenditures of time and money. Learners, on the other hand, need documentation that encourages them to interact with a wide variety of texts, and such documentation should, as far as possible, reflect the processes of reading and writing rather than simply the products.

This tension between system needs and learner needs can result in a dual approach to assessment. Some form of standardised testing is retained to satisfy the system, but is supplemented by documentation practices that respond to learner needs. Such dualism has proved frustrating to both students and teachers. As for students, they feel overworked since each form of assessment demands a good deal of preparation time. Teachers, too, feel overworked since they must not only prepare students for tests but evaluate lengthy portfolios. Moreover, both students and teachers end up feeling quite cynical – students because they are forced to operate with a double standard and teachers because their own evaluations are marginalised within the larger education system.

It is for such reasons that we are committed to a more unified approach to assessment – one that attempts to deal with both learner needs and system needs. In implementing such an approach, it is useful to distinguish between two kinds of system needs – accreditation and selection. What students are expected to do for accreditation in English language necessarily varies from one situation to another. In Chapter 6, Allen suggests that, in Zimbabwe, students at the junior secondary level should carry out basic activities such as reading newspapers, filling in forms, and following instructions. In Chapter 7, Cohen suggests that, in Brazil, students at the university level should carry out more sophisticated activities such as preparing summaries in Portuguese of academic texts in English. Once a portfolio is designed around appropriate activities, teachers are required only to certify that the activities have been carried out by the individual in question and to evaluate the work as passing or failing. A system of moderation can be put in place to review all students who fail as well as a random sample of those students who pass. Under such a system the method of assessment would feed directly into purposeful classroom activity, and most students would end up with a certificate that documents their capacity to carry out the designated activities. Moreover, each individual would have a representative set of documents that can be consulted if more detailed information on performance is required.

In order to maintain a unified approach to assessment, the documents assembled to certify students can also be used to select them for further educational opportunities – or, for that matter, for employment opportunities. These documents must, however, be used in a different way in order to meet the more rigorous standards that such evaluation demands. As illustrated by the common assessment tasks in Victoria, a subset of the accreditation tasks can be isolated for more careful evaluation. By reducing the number of tasks to be evaluated, one is in a position to carry out more fine-grained evaluation. In addition to reducing the number of tasks, one can reduce the number of students, by introducing, at the accreditation stage, a special category such as *pass with distinction*. Then at the selection stage, one has to evaluate only students who receive such a pass. If this approach is used, any portfolio that is a candidate for distinction would have to be evaluated more carefully at the earlier stage (e.g. through some kind of monitoring system). During the selection stage of evaluation, one can also require, as in Victoria, an examination to supplement the portfolio. In the New York City example, what students write on a final essay exam is included in the portfolio itself.

Such a unified approach to assessment involves substantial resources, especially well-trained personnel to ensure that, once developed, it can be properly maintained. These resources may strain what many countries around the world can afford, and it is for this reason that we have taken care to describe methods of alternative testing that can be used at a national level. We would, however, like to point out that even relatively poor countries already expend massive resources on national examination systems – Zimbabwe, as described by Allen in Chapter 6, is a case in point (see Nyakunu 1986). What is particularly disconcerting is that these expenditures are accompanied by an inordinately high rate of student failure. As Allen points out, the majority of students in Zimbabwe fail the English component of the national exams; and such failure has demoralising effects on the society that go far beyond what is commonly imagined. Poor families make considerable sacrifices to educate their children who are often sent away, after six or more years, without a school certificate – or with one that is of no practical use – because of their failure on the English exam; they are then unable to obtain the kind of work for which they have been educated, even though they may well possess many of the requisite skills.

It is this extraordinary waste of human resources that lends urgency to testing reform in many countries around the world. As those responsible for assessing the English language skills of non-native learners carry out such reform, they need to consider not only alternative forms of testing but the various kinds of documentation practices that we have presented in this volume. We recognise that these practices call for a considerable investment in order to ensure that they are reliably used by teachers and evaluators, but it is our conviction that the educational benefits are so substantial that it justifies the additional investment. In order to participate meaningfully in documentation, non-native learners of English must be prepared to take greater responsibility for evaluating their own knowledge and skills. They must become involved not only in selecting the work by which they are assessed but in making certain that it adequately represents what they are capable of doing. This greater responsibility itself contributes to greater learning, for it encourages students to use English to express their own interests and values in contexts that are appropriate to the societies in which they live.

Acknowledgements

Carole Deletiner, Debra Suarez, and Jane Weiss helped pioneer portfolio assessment at Hunter College, and Ann Raimes kept the system going while Kate Parry was on sabbatical. We thank them as well as other colleagues at Hunter College for their participation in the project. We also thank Keville Bott, who, in the unlikely environment of Nanjing, China, spent time explaining the approach to assessment in Victoria State, Australia.

Note

1. We are here using *portfolio* in its restricted sense to refer to a collection of work samples that are located in a physical folder. Others prefer to use the term to refer to all samples of student work – artefacts and performances as well as documents – and even records about students that are used for purposes of assessment (Wiggins 1991).

Bibliography

Allen, K O'B 1988 *The development of a test of communicative competence for speakers of English as a second language in Zimbabwe*. Unpublished doctoral dissertation, Teachers College, Columbia University, New York

Allen, R L 1972 *English Grammar and English Grammars*. Charles Scribner's Sons, New York

Altman, R 1992 Assessment: Approaching the 20th century. Plenary address, International TESOL Convention, Vancouver, B.C.

Amano, I 1983 *Shiken no shakai shi* [A social history of tests]. University of Tokyo Press

Bahm, A J 1969 *The heart of Confucius: interpretations of genuine living and great wisdom*. Walker and Weatherhill, New York

Bailey, R W and Görlach, M (eds) 1982 *English as a world language*. University of Michigan Press

Bakhtin, M M 1981 In Holquist, M (ed.), *The dialogic imagination*. Emerson, C and Holquist, M (trans.). University of Texas Press

Balliro, L 1989 *Reassessing assessment in adult ESL/Literacy*. Paper presented at TESOL International Conference, San Antonio, Texas, 1989 ERIC document no. (EDRS: 339253).

Barton, D and Ivanic, R (eds) 1991 *Writing in the community*. Sage, London

Basham, C S 1987 *Summary writing as cultural artifact*. Cross-Cultural Communication, University of Alaska

Basham, C S and Rounds, P L 1986 A discourse analysis approach to summary writing. *Papers in Applied Linguistics - Michigan*, 1 (2), 88–104

Baynham, M 1993 Mediators of Literacy and community interpreters. In Street, B (ed.) *Cross-cultural approaches to literacy*. Cambridge University Press

Besnier, N G 1986 *Spoken and written registers in a restricted-literacy setting*. Doctoral dissertation, University of Southern California

Blake, R 1977 *A history of Rhodesia*. Eyre Methuen, London

Bloom, A 1987 *The closing of the American mind*. Simon and Schuster, New York

Bloom, B 1984 *Taxonomy of educational objectives*. Longman, New York

Bransford, J, Franks, J, Vye N and Sherwood, R 1989 New approaches to instruction: Because wisdom can't be told. In Vosniadou, S and Orleny, A (eds) *Similarity and analogical reasoning*, pp. 470-97. Cambridge University Press

Brown, A L, Campione, J C and Day, J D 1981 Learning to learn: on training students to learn from text. *Educational Researcher*, **10**, 14–21

Brown, A L and Day, J D 1983 Macrorules for summarizing texts: the development of expertise. *Journal of Verbal Learning and Verbal Behavior*, **22**, 1–14

Bruce, G 1969 *Secondary school examinations: facts and commentary*. Pergamon Press, Oxford

Canale, M and Swain, M 1980 Theoretical bases of communicative approaches to second language teaching and testing. *Applied Linguistics*, **1** (1), 1-47

Canale, M and Swain, M 1981 A theoretical framework for communicative competence. In Palmer, A S, Groot, P J M, and Trosper, G A (eds) *The construct validation of tests of communicative competence*, pp. 31-6. TESOL, Washington, D.C.

Central Statistical Office 1985 *Quarterly digest of statistics*. Harare, Zimbabwe

Charnley, A H and Jones, H A 1979 *The concept of success in adult literacy*. Adult Literacy Unit, London

Chauncy, H and Dobbin, J E 1969 *Testing: its place in education today*. Harper and Row, New York

Chou Hare, V and Borchardt, K M 1984 Direct instruction of summarization skills. *Reading Research Quarterly*, **20** (1), 62-78

Clanchy, M 1979 *From memory to written record: 1066-1307*. Harvard University Press

Clark, H H and Clark, E V 1977 *Psychology and language: an introduction to psycholinguistics*. Harcourt Brace Jovanovich, New York

Cohen, A D 1984 On taking language tests: what the students report. *Language Testing*, **1** (1), 70-81

Cohen, A D 1987a Research on cognitive processing in reading in Brazil. *DELTA*, **3** (2), 215-35. (Depto. de Linguistica, Pontificia Universidade Católica de São Paulo)

Cohen, A D 1987b Studying language learning strategies: how we get the information. In Wenden, A L and Rubin, J (eds) *Learner strategies in language learning*, pp. 31-40. Prentice-Hall International, Englewood Cliffs, NJ

Cole, M and Scribner, S 1981 *The psychology of literacy*. Harvard University Press

Conklin, H 1949 Bamboo literacy on Mindoro. *Pacific Discovery*, **2**, 4-11

Cripwell, K 1984 Readability of WHO technical documents. Unpublished paper

Cummings, W K 1980 *Education and equality in Japan*. Princeton University Press

Davies, E and Whitney, N 1984 Study skill 11: writing summaries. In *Study skills for reading: students' book*, pp. 56-8. Heinemann, London

Deakins, Alice H 1985 The informal English sentence: changes since 1450. In *Word*, **36** (2), 109-35

de Saussure, F 1966 *Course in general linguistics*. Baskin, W (trans.) McGraw-Hill, New York

Dore, R P 1967 Mobility, equality, and individuation in modern Japan. In Dore, R P (ed.) *Aspects of social change in modern Japan*. Princeton University Press

Educational Testing Service (ETS) 1990 *Bulletin of Information for TOEFL and TSE, 1990-1991*. Author, Princeton, N.J.

Educational Testing Service (ETS) 1991 *Bulletin of Information for TOEFL and TSE, 1991-1992*. Author, Princeton, N.J.

Educational Testing Service (ETS) 1992 *Bulletin of Information for TOEFL/TWE and TSE, 1992-1993*. Author, Princeton, N.J.

Elbow, P and Belanoff, P 1991 State University of New York at Stony Brook portfolio-based evaluation program. In Belanoff, P and Dickson, M (eds) *Portfolios: process and product*. Boynton Cook, Portsmouth, N.H.

Ericsson, K A and Simon, H A 1984 *Protocol analysis: verbal reports as data*. MIT Press

Exam 1984: The National Center for University Entrance Examinations. 1984 Daigaku Ny˝shi Sentå, Tokyo

Fairman, T 1988 Teaching the Englishes. *International Review of Applied Linguistics*, **26**, (2), 115-126

Fillmore, C and Kay, P 1983 *Text-semantic analysis of reading comprehension tests.* University of California Institute of Human Learning, Berkeley

Fingeret, A 1983 Social network: a new perspective on independence and illiterate adults. *Adult Education Quarterly*, **33** (3), 133-4

Fingeret, A 1984 *Adult literacy education, current and future directions.* (ERIC Document Reproduction Service No. ED246308), ERIC, Columbus, OH

Flottum, K 1987 *The formal structure of school summaries.* Dept. of Romance Studies, University of Trondheim, Norway

Foucault, M 1977 What is an author? In Bouchard, D F (ed.), *Language, counter-memory, practice: selected essays and interviews by Michel Foucault.* Bouchard, D F and Simon, S (trans.). Cornell University Press

Freire, P and Macedo, D 1987 *Literacy: reading the word and the world.* Bergin and Garvey, Mass.

Fries, P H 1981 On the status of theme in English: arguments from discourse. *Forum Linguisticum*, **6** (1), 1-38

Geis, M and Zwicky, A 1971 On invited inferences. *Linguistic Inquiry*, **2**, 561-66

Gellner, E 1983 *Nations and nationalism.* Blackwell, Oxford

Goodman, K S 1967 Reading: a psycholinguistic guessing game. *Journal of the Reading Specialist*, **4**, 13-26

Goody, J (ed.) 1968 *Literacy in traditional societies.* Cambridge University Press

Goody, J 1977 *The domestication of the savage mind.* Cambridge University Press

Goody, J 1986 *The logic of writing and the organization of society.* Cambridge University Press

Goody, J and Watt, I 1968 The consequences of literacy. In Goody, J (ed.) *Literacy in traditional societies.* Cambridge University Press

Gould, S J 1981 *The mismeasure of man.* Norton, New York

Graff, H J 1979 *The literacy myth: literacy and social structure in the 19th century city.* Academic Press, New York

Graff, H J 1987 *The legacies of literacy: continuities and contradictions in western culture and society.* Indiana University Press

Greenfield, P 1972 Oral or written language: the consequences for cognitive development in Africa, US and England. In *Language and Speech*, **15**, 169-78

Halliday, M A K and Hasan, R 1976 *Cohesion in English.* Longman, London

Harris, R and Monaco, G 1978 Psychology of pragmatic implication: information processing between the lines. *Journal of Experimental Psychology*, **107**, 1-22

Heath, S B 1983 *Ways with words.* Cambridge University Press

Henning, G 1984 Advantages of latent trait measurement in language testing. *Language Testing*, **1** (2), 123-33

Hidi, S and Anderson, V 1986 Producing written summaries: task demands, cognitive operations, and implications for instruction. *Review of Educational Research*, **56** (4), 473-93

Hildyard, A and Olson, D 1978 *Literacy and the specialisation of language.* Unpublished manuscript, Ontario Institute for Studies in Education

Hill, C 1992 *Testing and assessment: An ecological approach.* Inaugural lecture for the Arthur I Gates Chair in Language and Education, Teachers College, Columbia University

Hill, C and Larsen, E 1983 *What reading tests call for and what children do*. (Final report for NIE Grant G-78-0095) National Institute of Education, Washington, D.C.

Hill, C and Larsen, E 1992 *Assessment in secondary education: a critical review of emerging practices*. National Center for Research in Vocational Education, University of California, Berkeley

Hill, C and Parry, K 1988 *Reading assessment: autonomous and pragmatic models of literacy*. LC Report 88-2. The Literacy Center, Teachers College, Columbia University

Hill, C and Parry, K 1989 Autonomous and pragmatic models of literacy: reading assessment in adult education. In *Linguistics and Education*, 1 (3), 233-83

Hill, C and Parry, K 1992a English language testing. *Nigerian Education Forum*, 2, 1

Hill, C and Parry, K 1992b The test at the gate: models of literacy in reading assessment. *TESOL Quarterly* 26 (3), 433-61

Hill, C, Anderson, L, Ray, S and Watt, Y 1989 *Testing adult literacy: local detail and textual gestalt*. LC Report 89-1, Literacy Center, Teachers College, Columbia University

Hinds, J 1983 Contrastive rhetoric: Japanese and English. *Text*, 3 (2), 183-95

Hirsch, E D 1987 *Cultural literacy: What every American needs to know*. Houghton Mifflin, Boston, MA.

Holland, D S 1988 *Assessment of student progress in adult literacy in England and Wales – an overview 1987-1988*. Unpublished manuscript

Holland, D S 1989 *Assessment of student progress in adult literacy*. Research project sponsored by ALBSU in association with the University of Nottingham

Holmes, J L 1986 Snarks, quarks and cognates: an elusive fundamental particle in reading comprehension. *The ESPecialist*, 15, 13-40 (Centro de Pesquisas, Recursos e Informação em Leitura, Pontifícia Universidade Católica de São Paulo)

Holzman, M 1988 *Evaluation in adult literacy progress*. Unpublished manuscript

Horsman, J 1989 From the learner's voice: women's experience of il/literacy. In Taylor, M and Draper, J (eds.) *Adult literacy perspectives*. Culture Concepts, Inc., Toronto, Ontario

Hu, C T 1984 The historical background: examinations and control in pre-modern China. *Comparative Education*, 20 (1), 7-26

Hymes, D 1964 Introduction: toward ethnographies of communication. *American Anthropologist*, 66 (6), ii, 12-25

Hymes, D 1974 *Foundations in sociolinguistics: an ethnographic approach*. University of Pennsylvania Press

Ingulsrud, J E 1988 *Testing in Japan: a discourse analysis of reading comprehension items*. Unpublished doctoral dissertation, Teachers College, Columbia University

Johnston, P H 1984 Assessment in reading. In Barr, R, Kamil, M L, Mosenthal, P, and Pearson, P D (eds) *Handbook of reading research*. Longman, New York

Jonçich, G 1968 *The sane pragmatist: a biography of Edward L Thorndike*. Wesleyan Press, Middletown, CT.

Jones, H A and Charnley, A H 1977 *Adult literacy – a study of its impact*. National Institute of Adult Education, Leicester

Kintsch, W and Van Dijk, T A 1978 Toward a model of text comprehension and production. *Psychological Review*, **85** (5), 363-94

Kirkwood, G and C 1989 *Living adult education: Freire in Scotland*. Oxford University Press

Klare, G R 1963 *The measurement of readability*. Iowa University Press

Kobayashi, H 1984 *Rhetorical patterns in English and Japanese*. Unpublished doctoral dissertation, Teachers College, Columbia University

Kozminsky, E and Graetz, N 1986 First vs. second language comprehension: some evidence from text summarizing. *Journal of Reading Research*, **9**, 3-21

Kozol, J 1985 *Illiterate America*. Plume, New York

Law, B 1984 *Uses and abuses of profiling: a handbook on reviewing and recording student experience and achievement*. Harper Education, London

Levine, K 1986 *The social context of literacy*. Routledge and Kegan Paul, London

Lin, H-S 1993 *A TOEFL coaching school in Taiwan*. Unpublished doctoral dissertation. Teachers College, Columbia University

Lyons, J 1981 *Language and linguistics: an introduction*. Cambridge University Press

Lytle, S *et al.* 1988 Approaches to the assessment of learning at the Center for Literacy. *Who's learning to read. How do we know?* National Adult Literacy Symposium, Washington, D.C., 8 September

Madsen, H 1983 *Techniques in testing*. Oxford University Press

Mbeki, M 1985 Education system is destined for restructuring. *The Herald*, p 3

Meredith, M 1979 *The past is another country: Rhodesia 1890-1979*. Andre Deutsch, London

Ministry of Education, Science, and Culture 1983 *Course of study for upper secondary schools in Japan*.Tokyo

Miyazaki, I 1976 *China's examination hell*. Yale University Press

Narita, K 1978 *Systems of higher education: Japan*. International Council For Educational Development, New York

Nunnally, J C 1972 *Educational measurement and evaluation* (2nd edn.) McGraw-Hill, New York

Nyakunu, T 1986 Exams cost Zimbabwe millions. *The Sunday Mail*, 17 March: 1, 9

Olson, D R 1977 From utterance to text: the bias of language in speech and writing. *Harvard Educational Review*, **47** (3), 257-81

Olson, D R and Hildyard, A 1980 Literacy and the comprehension of literal meaning. Paper presented at the Conference on the Development and Use of Writing Systems, Bielefeld, Germany

Ong, W J 1982 *Orality and literacy: the technologizing of the word*. Methuen, New York

Parry, J 1989 The Brahmanical tradition and the technology of the intellect. In Schousboe, K and Larsen, M T (eds) *Literacy and society*. Akadamnisk Forlag, Copenhagen

Parry, K 1986 *Readers in context: a study of northern Nigerian students and School Certificate texts*. Unpublished doctoral dissertation, Teachers College, Columbia University

Passin, H 1965 *Society and education in Japan*. Teachers College Press, New York

Peirce, B N 1991 Review of the TOEFL Test of Written English (TWE) scoring guide. *TESOL Quarterly*, **25** (1), 159-63

Peirce, B N 1992 Demystifying the TOEFL reading test. *TESOL Quarterly*, **23** 4, 665-91

Pempel, T J 1978 *Patterns of Japanese policymaking: experiences from higher education.* Westview, Boulder, CO.

Plato 1987 *The Republic.* Lee, D (trans.). Penguin, London

Platt, J, Weber, H and Ho, M L 1984 *The new Englishes.* Routledge and Kegan Paul, London

Reischaur, E O and Fairbank, J K 1960 *East Asia the great tradition: A history of· East Asian civilization.* Tuttle, Tokyo

Resnick, D P 1982 History of educational testing. In Wigdor, A K and Garner, W R (eds) *Ability tests: uses, consequences, and controversies*, Part II. National Academy Press, Washington, D.C.

Richards, J, Platt, J and Weber, H 1985 *Longman dictionary of applied linguistics.* Longman, Harlow

Rogers, A 1992 *Adults learning for development.* Cassell, London

Rohlen, T P 1983 *Japan's high schools.* University of California Press

Saita 1985 *Kyotsu ichiji no eigo* [The English sub-test of the JFSAT]. Obunsha Sato, Tokyo

Sarig, G 1987 High-level reading tasks in the first and in a foreign language: some comparative process data. In Devine, J, Carrell, P L and Eskey, D E (eds) *Research in reading in English as a second language*, pp. 105-20. TESOL, Washington, D.C.

Sato, T 1979 Daigaku niji siken no nokosareta mono [Remaining issues from the Second Stage Exam]. *Seiron*, pp. 204-12

Schon, D A 1983 *The reflective practitioner. How professionals think in action.* Temple Smith, London

Senanu, K E and Vincent, T 1976 *A selection of African poetry.* Longman, Harlow

Shohamy, E 1984 Does the testing method make a difference? The case of reading comprehension. *Language Testing*, **1** (2), 147-70

Showa 61 nendo kyotsu daiichiji gakuryoku shiken no shikenmondai ni kansuru iken - hyoka 1986a [Opinions and evaluations concerning the JFSAT test items]. National Center for University Entrance Examination, Tokyo

Showa 61 nendo kyotsu ichiji shiken mondai shokai 1986b [The exposition of the 1986 JFSAT items]. Seibunsha, Tokyo

Silva dos Santos and Staff of CEPRIL 1987 *Resource package V: Testing.* Centro de Pesquisas, Recursos e Informação em Leitura, R Monte Alegre, 984, 05014 São Paulo, SP

Spaulding, R M 1967 *Imperial Japan's higher civil service examinations.* Princeton University Press

Smith, F 1982 *Understanding reading* (3rd edn.). Holt, Rinehart, and Winston, New York

Street, B 1984 *Literacy in theory and practice.* Cambridge University Press

Street, B 1990 *Literacy, nationalism, and assessment.* LC Report 89-1, Literacy Center, Teachers College, Columbia University

Street, B (ed.) 1993 *Cross-cultural approaches to literacy.* Cambridge University Press

Street, B and J 1991 The schooling of literacy. In Barton, D and Ivanic, R (eds) *Writing in the community.* Sage, London

Taylor, J 1983 *The shadows of the rising sun: a critical view of the Japanese miracle.* Quill, New York

Teng, S Y 1943 Chinese influence on the Western examination system. *Harvard Journal of Asiatic Studies*, 8, 267-312

Test of Adult Basic Education: Examiner's Manual (1976 edition). Monterey, California: CTB/McGraw Hill.

Thorndike, E L 1915 An improved scale for measuring ability in reading. *Teachers College Record*, 16 (November), 31-53 and 445-67

Van Dijk, T A 1977 Semantic micro-structures. In Just, M and Carpenter, P A *Cognitive processes in comprehension*. Lawrence Erlbaum Associates, Hillsdale, N.J.

Van Dijk, T A and Kintsch, W 1983 *Strategies of discourse comprehension*. Academic Press, New York

Venezky, R L 1986 Literacy and the NAEP reading assessment. A background and position paper prepared for NAEP Reading Review Sub-committee, NAEP

Vogel, E F 1979 *Japan as number one: lessons for America*. Harvard University Press

Vygotsky, L 1962 *Thought and language*. MIT Press

Walsh, B W and Betz, N E 1985 *Tests and assessment*. Prentice-Hall, Englewood Cliffs, N.J.

West, M P 1964 (first published 1953) *A general service list of English words, with semantic frequencies and a supplementary word-list for the writing of popular science and technology*. Longman, London

Widdowson, H 1978 *Teaching language as communication*. Oxford University Press

Wiggins, G 1991 Standards, not standardization. *Educational Leadership*, 45 (4), 24-9

Willinsky, J 1990 *The new literacy*. Routledge, London

Wright, B D and Stone, M H 1979 *Best test design*. Mesa Press, Chicago

Yoshiya, M 1983 Youth violence in the schools. *Japan Echo* (September), 3-7.

Index